LEARN WHO THEY ARE . . . AND WHAT THEY DID.
THEN T̶H̶E̶Y̶ ̶S̶L̶E̶E̶P̶ WITHOUT NIGHTMARES.

The most ca̶r̶i̶n̶g̶ . . . spouses, chil̶d̶r̶e̶n̶ . . . kept thirty-fi̶v̶e̶ . . . the bodies of the husbands, lovers, and the son she poisoned. . . .

THE ANGEL OF DEATH

She often strikes in a hospital or nursing home, attacking those too weak or defenseless to stop her from administering an injection the doctor never ordered . . . such as Beverley Allitt, who turned a small town's hospital into a house of horror as children admitted there began to die inexplicably. . . .

THE TEAM KILLER

Working in a team with other women or men, her murders are brutal and sexual in nature . . . such as kinky lesbian lovers Gwen Graham and Catherine Wood, who decided the most erotic act of all was murder . . .

AND NEARLY 100 MORE . . .

MURDER MOST RARE

MURDER MOST RARE

The Female Serial Killer

MICHAEL D. KELLEHER
AND C. L. KELLEHER

A DELL BOOK

Published by
Dell Publishing
a division of
Random House, Inc.

The trademark Dell® is a registered in the U.S. Patent and Trademark
Office.

ISBN: 0-440-23473-5

Reprinted by arrangement with Praeger Publishers

Printed in the United States of America

Published simultaneously in Canada

January 1999

10   9   8   7   6   5   4   3   2

OPM

DEC - - 2005

For Jean and in memory of Nina

CONTENTS

Introduction   *ix*

1.	The Quiet Killers	1
2.	Black Widows	27
3.	Angels of Death	85
4.	Sexual Predators	105
5.	Revenge	121
6.	For Profit or Crime	131
7.	Team Killers	151
8.	The Question of Sanity	233
9.	The Unexplained	251
10.	The Unsolved	273

Appendix 1: Statistical Information   *285*
Appendix 2: Alphabetical Listing of
*   Female Serial Killers*   *287*
Appendix 3: Munchausen Syndrome by Proxy   *289*
Selected Bibliography   *295*
Index   *299*

CONTENTS

INTRODUCTION

In 1991, Jeffrey Dahmer went on trial for multiple counts of homicide. He had callously murdered at least seventeen boys and young men in the four years preceding his capture. Each of Dahmer's victims had been sexually attacked, brutally tortured, and killed. Many of the bodies of his victims had been savagely mutilated and used for his sexual pleasure long after they had succumbed to a horrible death. Dahmer's pathological and unspeakable, self-proclaimed purpose had been to create "sex zombies" who would be forever at his command. Thirty years earlier, between 1962 and 1964, Albert Henry DeSalvo, who came to be known in the press as the Boston Strangler, murdered at last thirteen women who ranged in age from nineteen to eight-five years. Eleven of his victims had been sexually assaulted; most died by strangulation, and their bodies had been desecrated and placed in bizarre positions after they were slain. By his own admission, DeSalvo was a man who knew no limits to his compulsive drive to rape for the two years during which he terrorized the Boston area. The Clown Killer, John Wayne Gacy, murdered thirty-three young males between 1972 and 1978. After luring the victims to his home, Gacy would ply them with alcohol and drugs, and eventually, use handcuffs to subdue them. He would then attack them sexually. Following their torture and death, Gacy would bury the bodies of his victims on his own property. After concealing twenty-nine bodies in the crawl space beneath his home and underneath his cement driveway, Gacy found that he had run out of space. He solved the problem by throwing the bodies of his last four victims into the Des Plaines River.

The list of infamous serial killers who have roamed the United States in the past few decades is frightening. Men with monikers like the Night Stalker, the Trailside Killer, the I-5 Killer, and the Son of Sam have become recognizable to even casual readers of the true crime genre. These men represent the classic serial killer, who has become ironically symbolic of the chaotic and merciless violence that is a dark partner of our modern society. Their crimes are indescribable in their brutality and seemingly senseless in their purpose. Their actions are those of a relentless sexual predator who is driven to mindless and inconceivable horror. In the past few decades, the crimes of these predators have become the focus of a large part of American society, often because they represent the most feared and inscrutable of criminals who can be conjured up in our collective imagination.

Popular literature, the entertainment industry, and the media have combined to perpetuate a prosaic understanding of the serial killer that is both incomplete and misleading. To the casual observer, the serial killer is known only as a male sexual predator who relentlessly stalks his prey in a series of compulsive acts that must inevitably end in murder. Woven into this simplified myth is the image of a Caucasian male, sometimes of high intelligence, usually in his twenties or thirties, whose crimes are driven by bizarre and inexplicable fantasies of sexual domination and vengeance. In this sense, men like Dahmer, Gacy, and DeSalvo fit the stereotype nicely. They are the essence of the public understanding of a serial killer. They are the prototypes—men whose exploits have been repetitively used to formulate the popular image of the serial sexual predator. However, they represent merely a surface understanding of the real nature of serial killing. They tell only a part of the long and complex story that encompasses many different types of perpetrators who are driven to commit this heinous crime.

Serial killers are not a phenomenon unique to the late twentieth century, nor are they exclusive to America. These criminals are not limited to sexual predators. Rather, the crime of serial murder encompasses a broad range of violent activities, from the infamous exploits of the gunslinger of the old West to the unspeakable crimes of the Nazi leadership, who perpetrated the Holocaust earlier in this century, to the contemporary Mafia hit man. The history of most industrialized nations is replete with serial murders committed by terrorists, outlaws, pirates, and even members of royalty, who were each driven to kill in a compulsive fashion. Their motives were sometimes complex and, in other cases, straightforward. These killers included criminals of high intelligence and individuals who suffered from debilitating and uncontrollable psychological disorders. They were often common men who were able to wreak their aggression on others by ruse or manipulation. In some cases, they were brutally direct, while in others, they were patient beyond reason. Regardless of their means or motives and despite their social position or secret compulsions, they were men who senselessly brutalized others in a relentless drive toward the ultimate form of violence. However, despite what we think we know and understand about the serial killer, much remains hidden within the horror of the crime and the secret activities of its perpetrator. Much has also been shunted away from the public eye by cultural bias and myth.

One of the myths that has been perpetuated by the press and popular media is that serial murders are invariably and exclusively committed by men. This myth is particularly rampant in the entertainment industry, which produces a seemingly limitless litany of male serial murderer movies, which vary widely in their adherence to truth and reality. In fact, the genuine history of this crime is replete with dozens of female serial killers who were far more lethal—and often, far more successful in their determination to kill—than their male counterparts. Whereas the male serial killer is most often driven to repetitive acts of sexual homicide, the typical female serial killer is a much more complex criminal, whose motivations are often wide-ranging and anything but simple. In fact, as this book will show, the female serial killer typically remains undetected for a significantly longer period of time than the average male serial murderer. She is a quiet killer, who is often painstakingly methodical and eminently lethal in her actions.

Incredibly, despite her morbid ability to succeed at murder, the female serial killer has been virtually ignored in the press and media. So overlooked is this subtle criminal that it has been frequently written that America has experienced only a single female serial killer in its history—Aileen Wuornos. In fact, nothing could be further from the truth.

Although the incidents of serial murder perpetrated by women are far less frequent than those of her male counterpart, we were able to identify nearly one hundred female serial murderers who claimed their victims since 1900. Well over half these women committed their crimes on American soil. Not only is the number of female serial killers shocking to the casual reader, the motives and methods of this perpetrator are even more incredible than those of the male serial killer. In surveying the case histories of this type of criminal, we were able to identify seven distinct categories of female serial killers, excluding those cases in which the perpetrator was not convincingly identified or the crime was never solved.

Whereas the majority of male serial killers are obvious sexual predators, the woman who murders a number of individuals over time rarely commits a sexual homicide. Her motives are far more diverse and, sometimes, quite subtle. Like her male counterpart, the female serial killer usually plans her crimes with great care and carries them out in a meticulous manner. In fact, as this book will show, she is frequently far more successful at evading capture for a much longer period of time than the average male serial murderer.

Judging by the limited information about female serial murderers that has been made public in this country, the very concept of such a criminal seems to have been turned aside by a strong cultural bias that denies her existence. Whereas the male serial killer has been regularly lionized by his outrageous exploits, the female serial killer is typically ignored, viewed as an anomaly, or given far less serious attention than her crimes warrant. Even when this murderer is an active member of a serial-killing team, she is typically overshadowed in her actions by the male partner with whom she operates. However, when her crimes are carefully examined it becomes immediately obvious that, in both her callousness and her methods, this perpetrator is on a par with any male serial killer. Ironically, counterbalancing her blatant criminal activity is the apparent cultural predisposition to dismiss her genuine criminal potential simply because she is a woman. In view of this social bias, it is no wonder that she is often able to go on killing for many years before she is finally apprehended.

Whereas names such as Dahmer, Gacy, DeSalvo, and Ted Bundy are instantly recognized for their heinous exploits, few Americans have heard of Genene Jones, Bobbie Sue Terrell, or Jane Toppan. However, Jones, Terrell, and Toppan each murdered more than 10 individuals throughout their years of crime, and cumulatively, they may have been responsible for as many as 128 deaths. Clearly, these three women were killers whose stature in crime was equal or beyond that of Dahmer, Gacy, DeSalvo, and Bundy. However, to most Americans, these women bear unfamiliar names and their crimes have been largely ignored or forgotten. As this book will clearly show, even these three murderers were not nearly as lethal as a dozen or more other female serial killers who were active since the turn of the century.

There is no question that the crime of serial murder is unsettling, whether it is committed by a man or a woman. It is arguably the most horrific of violent acts that can be perpetrated against another human being. However, this is not a crime that is solely perpetrated by a male sexual predator. The female serial killer is an equally pernicious threat to our society and she is often a far more compelling and difficult adversary for law enforcement officials. The case histories of these killers clearly demonstrate that the female serial killer has been active in many countries and for many decades; they also show that this perpetrator has staked a morbid and undeniable claim as a criminal of capability equal to that of her more familiar, male counterpart.

The history of the exploits of the female serial killer also brings into sharp focus another aspect of this crime—its perpetrator has always been much more than an anomaly in the science of criminology. She has always been a societal threat that is no less significant than a male serial killer. Although the male serial killer has become the ultimate nemesis of law enforcement and a criminal whose exploits have been grimly transformed into a staple of the press and popular media, the female serial murderer has always been among us. She has already taken her place in the history of criminology, although her impact remains generally unrecognized. It is now time to tear the shroud away from this quiet killer and expose her crimes to the light of understanding.

1

THE QUIET KILLERS

These are the quiet killers. They are every bit as lethal as male
serial murderers, but we are seldom aware one is in our midst
because of the low visibility of their killing.
                                            —Eric W. Hickey
                                     Serial Murderers and Their Victims

The terms *serial murder* and *serial killer* have become deeply
woven into the fabric of the American popular media and
press since they were first introduced more than twenty years
ago. Understandably, these concepts have now been transformed into compelling elements in a mosaic of collective
fear, which constitutes a significant part of the American psy-
che. In particular, over the past two decades, the serial killer
has become a fundamental and easily recognized protagonist
in the most popular products of the American entertainment
industry. Television and the film industry have imbued our
citizens with an irresistible visual and visceral link to the
popularized—and often inaccurate—image of this inscrutable
criminal. The pervasive and relentless reporting of the gruesome exploits of the sexual serial killer has fostered a remarkable national intimacy with this crime and its perpetrator.
In essence, the media-created image of the sexual serial killer
of the late twentieth century has become a symbolic national
nemesis whose violent activities have been lionized in print,
on television, and in the movies to a level that is unprecedented among other categories of crime. Because of this phenomenon, terms such as *serial murder* and *serial killer* have

been endowed with a common understanding that has made them an integral part of our collective cultural awareness. However, this common understanding is fundamentally incomplete and misleading, although its power is undeniable.

In truth, there is little about the crime of serial murder that is simple or easily understood. In fact, it is one of the most perplexing and least understood categories of violent crime to plague our society. The very definition of serial murder remains uncertain and constitutes a point of controversy among the most eminent criminologists and behaviorists in this country. Although the general public embraces a prosaic definition of serial murder that has been inferred by the popular media and the entertainment industry, the definition is grossly inaccurate for at least one fundamental reason—it is unacceptably limiting in its representation of the true breadth and diversity of this crime and its perpetrators. In reality, the perpetrator of serial murder who has been so successfully popularized in the entertainment industry is but one of a rather large number of types of serial killers who have been active for many centuries and in many countries throughout the world.

The covert world of the serial killer is populated with a diverse array of characters who cannot be genuinely represented by the single contemporary legend of the sexual serial predator. Furthermore, the crimes of the serial killer extend far into the history of the United States and other countries. This criminal has been active in virtually all industrial societies for centuries—particularly in areas of dense urbanization. It is a common mistake to overlook entire categories of serial murderers, such as the Nazi perpetrators of the Holocaust in World War II, for reasons that remain inexplicable and invalid.

In the contemporary understanding of the term, serial killing is often considered to be the act of narrowly defined individuals who undertake crimes that are heinous, but also narrowly defined. In fact, serial killers may operate alone or in teams; the killer may join others in a highly organized group whose fundamental purpose is to commit murder or may be a woefully disorganized individual with little or no awareness of his or her actions, who operates alone. The perpetrators may be male or female, and they may be motivated by any number of perplexing reasons that defy common understanding. Serial killers may wreak vengeance on those who are completely unknown, acquaintances, friends, coworkers, men, women, adolescents, family members, or children. Their compulsions to kill are surprisingly diverse and frequently convoluted. Their motivations range across the wide plain of human emotions, from the perverse obsession of a sexual predator, to the desire for profit, an obsession with control and domination, or because of psychological impairments that are little understood and, sometimes, completely unrecognized.

Because the crime of serial murder has received far more popularization than serious research, it is understandable that misunderstanding and myth surround the activities of the perpetrator. We are only now beginning to learn something of the dark motivations that lie behind the gruesome crimes of the serial killer. Furthermore, we have yet to understand enough about this crime to even reach a consensus about how to properly categorize the perpetrator or adequately comprehend his or her actions. In part, this dilemma exists because the crime of serial murder is still a relatively rare event in this country. Even though the exploits of the serial murderer capture the attention of the public in a unique and compelling way, this is not a crime that threatens a significant number of citizens. Relative to other violent felonies, serial murder remains a generally impersonal and nonthreatening type of crime to the majority of Americans. It has become an issue in the consciousness of our citizenry because of the horrifying nature of the crime itself, not because of its personal impact in terms of the number of victims claimed each year. However, in recent decades, this situation has begun changing as the number of active serial killers in America increases.

**Figure 1.1: Average Number of Serial Murders
per Year by Decade[1]**

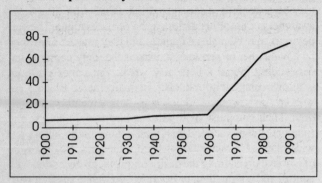

As Figure 1.1 indicates, the crime of serial murder has
been increasing in recent years. In fact, the average number
of serial murders that occur each decade has steadily increased since 1960. However, these statistics may not be as
alarming as they seem on their surface. The crime of serial
murder has only received the abiding attention of researchers,
criminologists, and law enforcement personnel for approximately three decades. Although law enforcement personnel
have long recognized the pattern of related felonies that we
now define as serial murder, this crime has only recently ben-
efited from serious and intensive research. In other words, researchers, criminologists, and law enforcement personnel are
now acutely aware of a category of crime that has finally been
defined and recognized as unique. In addition, law enforcement personnel have recently developed a variety of sophisticated techniques to identify the activities of a serial killer and
somewhat understand his or her motivations, methods of operation, and possible future activities. Because of the rapidly
increasing knowledge of this crime and its perpetrator, it is
likely that criminologists and law enforcement personnel are
now able to recognize and identify serial murders in situations that were overlooked a few decades ago. This increased
sophistication in recognizing and categorizing the crime may,

in part, account for the apparently steady increase in serial murders in recent decades.

However, it is unlikely that improvements in law enforcement strategies or research techniques could solely explain the dramatic increase in serial murders over the past few decades. Thus, it is also necessary to recognize that there are probably more serial killers active in society today than were active in the past. Considering the imperatives that are known to be associated with the commission of this crime, it seems likely that the increasing average number of serial murders each decade is due, in significant measure, to the simple fact that there are more serial killers among us today than in previous decades.

THE CRIME

In order to understand the motivations and nature of the serial killer, it is obvious that we must have some common point of understanding in defining the crime itself. However, this is not a simple matter. A variety of questions naturally arise concerning when to define multiple murders as serial killings. The answers to such questions are numerous and, in the final analysis, completely subjective. For example, how many murders are required to define a crime as the actions of a serial murderer? Must there be a specific minimum period of time between murders to fulfill the criteria? Are the types of murders or method of operation of the murderer important to an accurate definition? Is it significant whether the murderer acted alone or in conjunction with one or more other perpetrators? Each of these questions is valid, and each fosters significant contention among those who seriously study the crimes of the serial killer.

The number of murders traditionally considered necessary to constitute the crime of serial murder ranges from the obvious minimum of two to as high as ten. However, most researchers and criminologists have settled on a minimum of three or four murders to fulfill the definition. A more contentious question involves the minimum period of time required between murders to define the criminal pattern as serial murder. Researchers and criminologists often use a period of thirty days to define a number of murders as serial in nature. Therefore, one common definition of serial murder has become *the act of murdering three or more individuals in a period of thirty days or more*. Using this definition, if a perpetrator murders three or more individuals in less than thirty days, the crime is usually defined as a *murder spree*.

Some researchers point to the perpetrator's method of operation or the qualitative nature of the crime itself as crucial elements in defining an act of serial murder. However, using these constraints tends to classify serial murders in a minimalist fashion by eliminating those perpetrators who slay their victims in diverse and inconsistent ways. In general, the use of the perpetrator's method of operation in defining serial murder is not as widely accepted as the more traditional criteria of a minimum number of victims murdered over a minimum period of time.

Our research into the issue leads to a somewhat broader view of the crime of serial murder. There is no question that the definition of the crime must encompass a minimum number of victims, even in cases where law enforcement officials are fortunate enough to apprehend a perpetrator before he or she reaches that minimum. It is perfectly reasonable to expect that an *intended* serial murderer may injure his or her victims in significant numbers yet fail to murder sufficient numbers to meet the arbitrary minimum of any definition. In this sense, the intent to commit serial murder is a significant element to consider. However, intent is not something that can be easily measured or quantified. For this reason, we agree with the concept that a minimum number of victims must be slain in order to constitute an act of serial murder. We believe that three is a reasonable number of victims to define such a crime.

In considering the minimum period of time that should be

used to define an act of serial murder, we were troubled by the constraints of arbitrarily selecting some number of days, weeks, or months to qualify a crime pattern as serial in nature. Rather, our research indicated that there exists a related and crucial element that was often overlooked in attempting to establish this part of the definition of serial murder. The missing element is the *cooling-off period,* which always constitutes a recognizable component in a genuine pattern of serial murder.

By any reasonable definition, the serial killer attacks his or her victims over some period of time. In other words, serial murder is a series of crimes that take place over time. Whereas the crime of mass murder implies the slaying of a number of victims in a single event, the crime of serial murder is, at its root, a composite of lethal crimes that take place over a protracted period. It is this period of time between murders—the cooling-off period—that truly defines the nature of serial murder.

The cooling-off period is a time of quiescence during which the perpetrator does not engage in lethal activities. Rather, this is a time when he or she will engage in a variety of different activities that are intimately related to an ongoing criminal pattern but do not, in themselves, involve murderous actions. Typically, this cooling-off period involves activities such as fantasizing about a crime that has already been perpetrated or planning for the next violent attack. In effect, this is a time during which the perpetrator considers what he or she has done and will do in the future. It may also be a period during which the perpetrator searches out or stalks his or her next victim. In any event, the cooling-off period is crucial to the activities of the perpetrator and, in our opinion, clearly differentiates the crime of serial murder from other violent felonies.

Therefore, our definition of serial murder incorporates the two crucial elements of number of victims and time in a way that allows for a broader definition of the crime: *the murder of at least three individuals in which each lethal act was separated from the next by a discrete cooling-off period.* In this sense, we have disregarded such elements as the perpetrator's method of operation, the qualitative nature of the crime itself, and the need for any fixed minimum period of time between murders. Rather, the focus of this definition is on the pattern of the criminal activity itself, as it occurs over time. This pattern must clearly demonstrate discrete acts of lethal violence that have been separated by discrete periods of quiescence. To the extent that the perpetrator's activities during the cooling-off periods are known, any indication of fantasy about the crimes committed or any demonstrated efforts to plan a future crime would provide compelling evidence to further support the conclusion that this was truly a crime of serial murder.

THE CRIMINAL

Although the majority of serial killers are male, the history of this crime abounds with a number of female perpetrators who have engaged in a wide variety of heinous murders. In fact, as this book will show, female serial murderers are often highly successful in their crimes and present a challenge to law enforcement personnel that frequently surpasses that of the typical male serial killer. In general, it is difficult for law enforcement personnel to solve most cases of serial murder. By its nature, this crime is complex, covert, and often well planned. The majority of serial killers take pride in their ability to avoid apprehension and make every possible effort to continue their murderous ways for as long as possible. As indicated in Figure 1.2, the average serial killer (of either sex) is typically able to extend his or her period of lethal activity to over four years before he or she is apprehended or the crimes are brought to a halt by some other means. This is also the median period of lethal activity for the male serial killer who acts alone. Because the number of male serial murderers far

Figure 1.2: Median Length of Killing Period in Years[2]

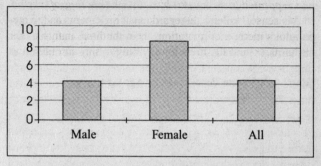

surpasses the number of female, the median killing period for *all* serial murderers closely approximates that for males.

However, female serial killers are able to carry out their crimes for a median duration of over eight years before the killing is stopped—double that of the male serial killer. For a variety of reasons, the female serial murderer is much more successful at avoiding apprehension than her male counterpart. Her choice of weapons, generally careful selection of victims, and methodical planning of the crime, combined with a strong social bias that denies the likelihood of a female serial killer, make this criminal significantly more successful than the male serial murderer. As the case histories in this book will show, the female serial killer who does not operate as part of a killing team is typically very careful in planning and carrying out her crimes; also, she is often eminently successful at avoiding apprehension for a surprisingly long period of time.

Female serial killers are rarely involved in sexual homicides—the overwhelming motivation for most male serial killers. The motivations inherent in serial murder committed by women are usually much different than for men and, for this reason, their crimes tend to exhibit a different victim typology. In general, male serial killers range widely in their choice of victims. Because male serial murderers far outnumber their female counterparts, statistics relating to the victims of all serial killers indicate that adults of either sex are at approximately equal risk for attack (see Figure 1.3).

Male serial killers, acting as sexual predators, tend to target adult female victims; however, in the final analysis, this perpetrator is usually more than willing to slay an individual

Figure 1.3: Victim Percentage by Age Grouping[3]

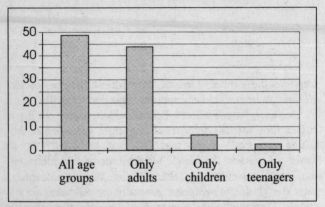

of either sex (see Figure 1.4). On the other hand, female serial murderers are more likely to select their victims for reasons that do not involve the sex of their prey.

The female serial killer who operates alone (as contrasted with the perpetrator who operates as a member of a killing team) exhibits a decided preference for victims who are children, the elderly, a lover, or a spouse. It is rare for a female serial killer to attack an adult stranger—the most likely victim of a male serial killer. When a female serial murderer does attack a person unknown to her, it will almost always be a very young child or an elderly individual; in other words, individuals who are easily dominated and who will be naturally dependent on the murderer.

When a woman carries out her crimes in conjunction with one or more partners, she will sometimes engage in serial killing that is sexual in nature. Even though she will rarely

commit such crimes alone, the female serial murderer can become a monstrous sexual predator when partnered with one
or more individuals who are themselves active sexual predators. In such a situation, the female perpetrator is considered
a team killer and is most often associated with a male who is

Figure 1.4: Victim Percentage by Sex Grouping[4]

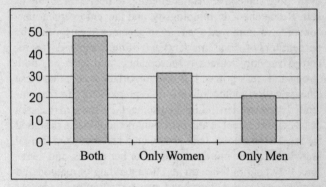

himself a sexual serial killer. On occasion, two or more
women join together to form a killing team; however, their
motives for murder are rarely sexual in nature.

The female serial killer is a complex individual who murders for very specific reasons and usually presents a significant challenge to law enforcement personnel. She is careful,
precise, methodical, and quiet in committing her crimes.
Since she generally murders for reasons very different from
those of her male counterpart, the female serial murderer also
presents significant challenges to those who try to understand
her crimes. Because the male serial killer so dominates the
popular media and most research efforts, it is frequently difficult to even gather basic information about a female perpetrator. Compounding this situation is the obvious social bias
that creates an underreporting of the crimes of the female serial killer, regardless of their brutal or sensational nature.
Nonetheless, it is both possible and practical to carefully

examine her crimes and make an attempt to categorize them. In so doing, we can shed light on the very covert activities of this quiet, but quite lethal, criminal.

CLASSIFYING THE FEMALE SERIAL KILLER

Classifying various types of serial killers is an exercise even more subjective than attempting to define the crime itself. Researchers, criminologists, and law enforcement personnel have employed a variety of schemes to categorize the perpetrators of serial murder. Each of these methods has received varying degrees of acceptance, and each has both strong and weak points. It is also important to note that these categorization methodologies diverge markedly in their intended purpose, depending on whether their use is in research or law enforcement. Categorization methodologies designed for research purposes tend to rely on a historical and factual knowledge of the murderer and his or her crimes, and therefore, they tend to focus on an understanding of method and motivation. On the other hand, categorization methods that prove most useful for law enforcement are designed to develop information about the perpetrator that will aid in his or her capture. The law enforcement–oriented categorization tools must enable the personnel who use them to draw meaningful conclusions from a minimum of established facts.

For example, in their book, *Sexual Homicide: Patterns and Motives,* authors Robert K. Ressler, Ann W. Burgess, and John E. Douglas developed a categorization method for serial killers that utilizes two discrete typologies: *organized* and *disorganized*. The authors postulated that all serial murderers, regardless of their sex, method, or motive, tended to fall into two broad types—a concept that has become widely accepted by law enforcement personnel since it was first presented. According to the authors, the organized serial killer exhibits such qualities as better-than-average intelligence, social competency, a stable employment history, normal sexual functioning, and a capacity to control his or her emotions and reactions during the commission of a crime. The organized serial murderer will commit his or her felonies in such a way as to leave evidence behind that overtly demonstrates a well-planned crime and therefore implies a high capacity for organization inherent in the murderer's personality. On the other hand, the disorganized serial killer demonstrates the opposing characteristics, such as average or below-average intelligence, underdeveloped social skills, an erratic work history, a history of sexual dysfunction, and a crime scene that generally reflects a lack of organization.[5]

In this straightforward and highly effective categorization scheme, serial murderers are judged as one of the two proposed types. This assessment is based primarily on evidence obtained at the crime scene, the method of operation of the perpetrator, and (to the extent that it is known) the perpetrator's background. With the appropriate use of this categorization methodology in conjunction with evidence derived from the scene of the crime, law enforcement personnel can draw certain conclusions about the perpetrator. Armed with this information, they can develop a general profile of the perpetrator that may be used in an effort to narrow the range of suspects in a specific criminal case. This two-part categorization methodology has proved an important addition to the arsenal of law enforcement weapons in that it has enabled investigators to more quickly narrow the range of potential suspects in complex cases of serial murder. However, despite its wide acceptance and practical benefits, this method of categorizing serial murderers cannot be used to effectively study and understand the complex motivations of the perpetrator. As originally conceived and designed, its purpose was that of a powerful law enforcement tool that was more appropriate for solving complex crimes than for undertaking a deep analysis of motivations.

The purpose of this book is to carefully examine the female serial killer from a historical perspective and attempt to come to some understanding of her motives. In this sense, a different method of analytical categorization is needed. Any meaningful examination of motives requires answers to a variety of complex questions. Why do these women resort to such a heinous crime? What compels them to repeat the crime of murder again and again? How do they differ from the typical male serial killer? Why do these perpetrators select certain victims, and how do they do so? What is the pattern of murder that is common to the perpetrator (the course of the crime)? Why do these women present such challenges to law enforcement personnel?

These are among some of the many important questions that surround the covert activities of the female serial murderer. They are questions that must be addressed from a different perspective than that of law enforcement personnel, who are charged with the perpetrator's quick apprehension. This perspective requires a unique way of investigating the crime of serial murder—a method of analyzing the crime and its perpetrator that takes maximum advantage of the facts and time that only become available after the murderer's apprehension.

Female serial murderers fall naturally into two, very broad categories: those who commit their crimes alone and those who act in partnership with one or more other perpetrators. As the case histories in this book will show, female serial killers who operate in a team environment exhibit very different characteristics from the perpetrator who murders alone. In fact, there are few similarities between the perpetrator who acts alone and the criminal who acts in partnership with someone else, particularly if her partner is a male sexual predator. However, this scheme of segregating female serial killers into two general groups is too broad to be of practical use in any effort to intimately analyze motivation. It is clear that the female serial killer who operates with one or more partners must be recognized as a distinct category of criminal, whose motivations are often a composite of her own and those of her criminal partner or partners. However, those fe-

male perpetrators who murder alone must be further ana-
lyzed and categorized if we desire to focus successfully on
motivation. Recognizing this need for more precision, we
have established several categories that account for the rather
wide diversity in the types of female serial murderers that we
encountered in our research (see Table 1.1).

As a starting point, we established the category of Team
Killer to appropriately identify those female serial killers
who operated with at least one other perpetrator and whose
motives for murder were (to some degree) shared. As the case
histories in this book will show, female members of a killing
team undertake their crimes for a limited range of reasons,
and their motives are typically intermingled with those of the
other perpetrators on the team.

Table 1.1: Summary of Classifications

Classification	Definition
Black Widow	A woman who systematically murders multiple spouses, partners, or other family members. She may also claim victims outside of the family. The motives for these murders may be diverse and may encompass other classifications, such as Profit or Crime.
Angel of Death	A woman who systemically murders individuals who are in her care or who rely on her for some form of medical attention or similar support. The motives for these murders may be diverse.
Sexual Predator	A woman who systemically murders others in what are known to be clear acts of sexual homicide. The motive for these murders must be sexual in nature.
Revenge	A woman who systemically murders

	individuals for motives of revenge or jealousy.
Profit or Crime	A woman who systematically murders individuals in the course of other criminal activities (or for profit) but who is not a member of a team of killers and does not meet the criteria for a Black Widow.
Team Killer	In conjunction with at least one other person, a woman who systematically murders others or who participates in the systematic murder of others. The motives for these murders may be diverse, and the woman may not have personally murdered others.
Question of Sanity	A woman who murders in an apparently random manner, usually without a clear and explicable motive, and who is later judged to be legally insane. Alternatively, a woman who murders in a systematic way and is later found to be suffering from a mental disorder that is connected to the crimes. In either event, a psychological disorder must be present and be of such magnitude as to bring the issue of culpability into question.
Unexplained	A woman who systemically murders for reasons that are wholly inexplicable or for a motive that has not been made sufficiently clear for categorization. The perpetrator must not be judged legally insane.
Unsolved	A systematic pattern of murders that may be attributed to a woman (or women) with relative confidence, but which have not been solved.

Although many female serial murderers operate in a team environment, there are several other categories of perpetrator who operate alone and with discrete, singular motives. For example, although it is rare for a female serial murderer to be judged legally insane, it does occasionally occur. Perpetrators who are deemed to be legally insane must be considered apart from those murderers who are clearly not insane if we are to precisely understand the motives of either category. In addition, there are instances of serial murder in which the question of sanity becomes crucial to understanding the crime and its perpetrator, even when no legal definition of sanity has been expressed. For these reasons, we established a category entitled Question of Sanity for those cases in which the issue of the perpetrator's sanity has been legally questioned or is of such obvious importance to the case that it cannot be ignored.

Since most female serial murderers are not judged to be legally insane, and in recognition of the fact that their motivations are generally clear, we have established five additional categories that we believe represent the broad spectrum of this crime when it is committed by a sane individual. These categories include Black Widow, Angel of Death, Sexual Predator, Revenge, and Profit or Crime (see Table 1.1). As different as these categories may seem to be based on their monikers, they share one important characteristic—in each case, they are populated by perpetrators who acted alone in the commission of their crimes. Each of these categories has been designed to emphasize the motivations of the serial murderer and thereby aid in coming to a meaningful understanding of the crime itself. Finally, we constructed two additional categories to emphasize what cannot yet be known about the female serial murder—the Unexplained and the Unsolved. Although troubling, these two categories provide interesting raw material for future research and enhance the possibilities of gaining a better understanding of the crime.

We believe this nine-point categorization method does a

good job of helping to elucidate the complex motives that lie behind the crime of serial murder when perpetrated by a woman. However, this categorization scheme is subjective, and like any other method, it remains open to debate. One could make the argument that these categories attempt to define motivation to a finer degree of precision than is really necessary. For example, we know from our research that most female serial killers classified as Black Widows commit their murders for profit. Therefore, why is a second category, entitled Profit or Crime, necessary? The answer is actually quite simple and, in our opinion, fundamental. Not *all* Black Widows murder for profit, and not all Black Widows murder only family members. There are cases in which women have committed serial murder for reasons that were clearly profit oriented and included victims whose relationship with the murderer extended well beyond even the broadest definition of family. Surely such a perpetrator must be considered different from a Black Widow if we are to emphasize the essence of her motivation and accurately represent the importance of her victims.

When examining the case histories that follow, it must be remembered that we devised this method of categorization to study the motivations of the female serial murderer in an effort to understand both the crime and its perpetrator. However, there can be no question that any similar method, so long as it accurately represented the facts of the case and had the quality of internal consistency, would be equally useful.

PROFILING THE FEMALE SERIAL KILLER

Using the classification system just discussed, we examined nearly one hundred cases of serial murder that were committed by women. Each of these perpetrators committed at least three murders during their criminal career, and at least one murder had to occur since 1900 in order to meet our criteria. Approximately half the cases researched involved crimes committed by an American.

The age at which a female serial killer claimed her first victim ranged from fourteen years (Fugate) to fifty-five years (Becker). In at least two instances, the perpetrator was still

Figure 1.5: Average Age at First Murder

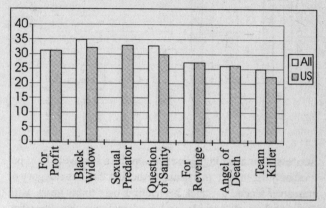

criminally active at the age of sixty-four (Velten and Popova).[1] The average age of female serial murderers when they committed their first murder is shown in Figure 1.5. It is interesting to note that most of the classifications indicate that the typical female serial murderer began killing after the age of twenty-five. Only those perpetrators who were members of a team generally began their lethal careers while under the age of twenty-five years.

As shown in Figure 1.6, the average years of activity for the female serial killer varied considerably depending upon her motive and method. Women who killed for profit (the Black Widow and Profit or Crime classifications) were generally active for a surprisingly long period of time before they were apprehended or the murders ceased for some other reason. In particular, the Black Widow proved to be eminently

---

[1]. See "Appendix 2: Alphabetical Listing of Female Serial Killers."

Figure 1.6: Average Years of Activity

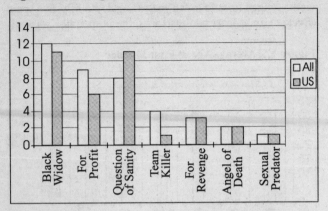

successful at avoiding apprehension for a relatively long period of time. In part, this is due to the fact that this category of murderer tended to attack her victims over many years, with long cooling-off periods, and used methods that were frequently difficult for enforcement personnel to determine. Perpetrators who murdered for profit by attacking individuals outside the family environment generally claimed their victims in the same manner and method as the Black Widow. In fact, as the case histories will show, the two categories of Black Widow and Profit or Crime proved to be closely related.

At the other extreme of criminal career longevity was the classification of Sexual Predator. These perpetrators tended to kill over very short periods of time and often claimed their victims in a haphazard and poorly planned way. However, these incidents were extremely rare among the cases that we researched. Not enough is known about this category of female serial killer to draw any meaningful conclusions about the potential length of her criminal career, simply because the crime is so unusual. When a woman teamed with a man (Team Killer classification) to commit sexual homicide in the United States, the average period of activity was less than two years.

Outside the United States, female members of a killing team
were generally able to avoid apprehension for a longer period
of time. We suspect this may be due, in part, to the advanced
law enforcement capabilities available in this country relative
to other locales in which team killers have been active.

Table 1.2: Monikers for Serial Killers

Male Serial Killers	Female Serial Killers
Nebraska Fiend	Queen Poisoner
The Torture Doctor	Borgia of Somerville
Demon of the Belfry	Sister Amy
The Cannibal	Belle of Indiana
The Moon Mania	Lady Bluebeard
The Gorilla Murderer	Mrs. Bluebeard
Tacoma Ax Killer	Polish Borgia
The Lipstick Murderer	Old Shoebox Annie
The Want Ad Killer	Giggling Grandma
Sex Beast	Borgia of America
The Thrill Killer	Beautiful Blonde Killer
The Measuring Man	Suicide Sal
The Green Man	Lonely Hearts Killer
The Boston Strangler	Grandma
Pied Piper of Tucson	Black Widow
Coed Killer	
Cincinnati Strangler	
The Mad Biter	
Killer Clown	
Freeway Killer	
Skid Row Slasher	
Son of Sam	
.44-Caliber Killer	
Stocking Strangler	
The Ripper	
Trailside Killer	
The I-5 Killer	
Sunday Morning Slasher	
Red Demon	
Night Stalker	

In general, the female serial murderer is most successful when motivated by reasons other than sex and when operating alone. In such a scenario, the perpetrator is usually mature (in her mid-twenties or older) and carefully plans each crime. She is most likely to use a weapon or killing technique that is difficult to discern (such as poison, lethal injections, simulated accidents, or suffocation), and she may exhibit rather long cooling-off periods between attacks. Unlike the male serial killer, who will frequently attack strangers, the female perpetrator who operates alone will usually target victims with whom she has some relationship or who are dependent on her for care. Whereas the male serial murderer may stalk his victims over a diverse geographical area, the female serial killer will usually attack her victims in her home or place of work.

The female serial murderer who operates alone does so in a quiet, planned, and methodical manner. She is often overlooked as a suspect because of her maturity or position of trusted responsibility. Compounding the difficulties faced by law enforcement personnel in apprehending this criminal is the obvious social bias that tends to deny the possibility of such a perpetrator. It is generally difficult for a male-dominated law enforcement system to readily recognize the possibility of a female serial murderer until the evidence of her crimes has become overwhelming. In fact, this form of social bias permeates virtually every aspect of serial murder when it is committed by a woman.

For example, Table 1.2 outlines a few of the monikers used to describe various male and female serial killers over the past several decades. Even a cursory comparison of these monikers demonstrates that the male serial killer is typically described in terms of extreme violence (terms such as "torture," "fiend," "cannibal," and "slasher"), while the descriptions for female serial killers include much milder terms (such as "Borgia," "beautiful," and "grandma"). Media accounts of the crimes of serial killers reinforce this social bias and perpetuate the misconception that female serial murderers are somehow less lethal than their male counterparts. This form of social bias not only inaccurately represents the true nature of the crime and the killer but can lead to false assumptions about the perpetrator and her methods during the field investigation of an unsolved case.

The general social bias that often leads to a longer criminal career for the female serial murderer is particularly apparent in cases that involve a woman who has murdered family members (Black Widow classification) or embarked on a lethal criminal career for profit (Profit or Crime classification). However, when the victims prove to be individuals who are dependent on the perpetrator for care (Angel of Death classification), the evidence of a crime is usually more apparent and the killer is generally apprehended in a much shorter period of time. In part, this is due to the fact that the Angel of Death murderer tends to attack more victims in a shorter period of time and with somewhat less care in planning the crime.

Women who are members of a killing team generally exhibit very different characteristics than the perpetrator who acts alone. Team killers frequently commit sexual homicides if the team is comprised of members of the opposite sex. In these situations, the female partner will usually be younger than the average age of the female serial murderer who operates alone. Because the murders committed by team killers are usually of a sexual nature, the actions of the team tend to be flagrant, sometimes poorly planned, and typically vicious. Probably due to social bias, the female member of a mixed killing team is often perceived as a passive partner in the crime. However, the case histories of these team killers makes it apparent that the female team member is sometimes quite active in repeated acts of sexual homicide. Because the crimes of team killers tend to be flagrant and impulsive, the period of lethal activity of these perpetrators is relatively short compared to murders committed by other types of female serial killers.

In general, female serial murderers can be profiled in two, somewhat discrete categories. The perpetrator who acts alone will often be mature, careful, deliberate, socially adept, and highly organized; she will tend to attack in a secretive manner, using a method that is difficult for law enforcement personnel to quickly identify. On the other hand, the female perpetrator who is a member of a killing team will often prove to be younger, aggressive, vicious in her attack, sometimes disorganized, and usually unable to carefully plan her murders. The perpetrator who acts alone will usually attack her victims in her home, their home, or her place of work, whereas the female member of a killing team will attack her victims in diverse locations as the opportunity for murder presents itself. Female serial killers who operate alone tend to favor weapons or methods such as poison, lethal injection, or suffocation, whereas members of a killing team will often use much more violent means, such as shooting, stabbing, or physical torture.

Regardless of the similarities that may seem apparent among the known incidents of serial murder committed by women, there is no reliable profile of this perpetrator. As the case histories in this book will show, the female serial killer is a complex and diverse criminal who murders for a variety of reasons and in many different ways. Although her presence and impact have long been overlooked by researchers and law enforcement personnel, the female serial murderer is a criminal of surprising complexity and unquestioned lethality.

NOTES

1. David Lester, *Serial Killers: The Insatiable Passion* (Philadelphia: Charles Press, 1995), 29.

2. Ibid., 57.

3. Ibid., 56.

4. Ibid., 56.

5. Robert K. Ressler, Ann W. Burgess, and John E. Douglas, *Sexual Homicide: Patterns and Motives* (New York: Lexington, 1988), 122–123.

2

BLACK WIDOWS

Black Widow: a poisonous spider of the genus Latrodectus,
especially the female, which devours its mate.
Webster's New Universal Unabridged Dictionary

The Black Widow is the archetype of the organized, successful female serial murderer. She typically begins her criminal
career after the age of twenty-five and actively murders victims for a decade or more before she is apprehended or her
killings cease for another reason. Although there is a general
perception that the Black Widow murders only family members, this is usually not the case. Despite the fact that this
category of serial killer will focus her activities on family
members, she will also be willing and capable of attacking
others with whom she has developed a personal relationship.
However, the Black Widow will rarely claim a stranger
among her victims; rather, her criminal activities depend
heavily on a relationship with her victim that provides ample
opportunity for murder. Because of the victim-specific nature
of her crimes, the female serial killer must comply with a rather
strict definition in order to be considered a Black Widow: *a
woman who systematically murders multiple spouses, partners, other family members, or individuals outside of the
family with whom she has developed a personal relationship.*

The Black Widow is typically intelligent, manipulative,
highly organized, and patient; she plans her activities with
great care. Her crimes are usually carried out over a relatively

long period of time, and she is rarely suspected of murder until the victim count has become significant or the number of deaths among her relatives and acquaintances can no longer be considered coincidental. In many cases, the Black Widow begins to murder relatively late in life (often after the age of thirty) and therefore brings a good deal of maturity and patience to the planning and commission of her crimes. She relies on her ability to win the confidence and trust of her victims as a precursor to any attack. For this reason, she is seldom viewed as a suspect, even after she has committed several murders.

The typical American Black Widow claims between six and eight victims during her criminal career (see Figure 2.1). Outside the United States, this number increases to between thirteen and twenty-one. However, such a wide variance is probably misleading, due to (1) sources of information available in the United States about foreign female serial killers

Figure 2.1: Victims of the Black Widow

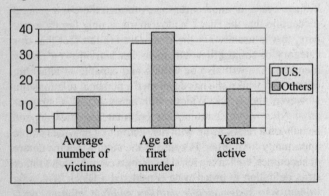

tends to emphasize only the most sensational cases, and (2) it is possible that this country benefits from more sophisticated law enforcement techniques and strategies than many other nations, resulting in an earlier apprehension of the perpetrator. Despite the dearth of data about this criminal, it is reasonable to assume that the average Black Widow will claim between six and thirteen victims during her active period, which generally ranges from ten to fifteen years (see Figure 2.1).

One of the reasons why the Black Widow is so criminally successful is because she generally murders with a great deal of precision while drawing little attention to her lethal activities. As indicated in Figure 2.2, this category of female serial

Figure 2.2: Weapons and Methods of the Black Widow

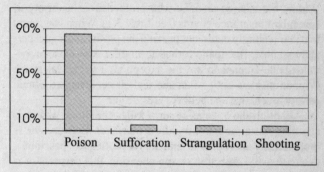

killer overwhelmingly favors poison as a weapon. She is able to attack her unsuspecting victims with a variety of lethal substances because she is trusted by them. Like her namesake, Latrodectus, the Black Widow attacks in a way that is generally unsuspected and at a time when the victim feels secure and unthreatened. She may also show a great deal of patience throughout the attack, frequently poisoning her victims slowly over an extended period of time. As the victims of the Black Widow become increasingly ill, their symptoms are often misdiagnosed and attributed to nonexistent or unrelated disorders. Throughout the killing period, the murderer may play the role of a concerned spouse, parent, or friend while she secretly continues to attack. When her victim finally succumbs, the perpetrator is often viewed with sympathy rather than suspicion. It is only after the number of victims has become too great for coincidence that concerned relatives, friends, or law enforcement officials may begin to view her with suspicion. By this time, the Black Widow will have claimed a significant number of victims.

The overwhelming motive for the Black Widow is profit. She typically murders for the proceeds of life insurance or to otherwise benefit from the assets of her victims. Although it is rare, a Black Widow may occasionally commit other significant criminal acts to further her desire for profit. For example, Judias Anna Lou Buenoano was not only a Black Widow but also an arsonist who profited from a variety of fraudulent insurance claims (see Table 2.1). When she found that arson simply could not provide the profits she so desperately wanted, Buenoano turned to murder. However, perpetrators like Buenoano are the exception. The typical Black Widow murders only when she feels it necessary to obtain cash or assets that she believes are due her.

Although she is a classic serial killer, the Black Widow is anything but a rampant, mindless murderer. Because she is motivated by an insatiable appetite for profit and a passionate desire to avoid detection or apprehension, this perpetrator is the epitome of the careful, quiet female serial killer. When she feels the need for more cash or assets, she will attack again; however, she will not kill in a random way. If the deaths of family members fail to provide sufficient rewards, the Black Widow may begin to target others with whom she has developed a personal relationship and who perceive her as a trusted friend or caretaker.

The Black Widow is generally unconcerned with the age or sex of her victims. Moreover, she will attack members of her own family with no apparent regard for the emotional bonds that would be expected by the relationship. Although the Black Widow can sometimes be indiscriminate in selecting her victims, she frequently favors a trusting spouse, dependent children, or an elderly person for whom she is a caretaker. Since her method of operation is to attack those with whom she has developed a credible relationship, her perceived role of confidante and caretaker often provides the perfect opportunity for murder. Her strategy not only relies on significant trust, but also on regular communication and interaction with her potential victims. She needs to be close to her prey and able to manage their activities and suspicions in concert with her detailed plan of attack. In this regard, the murders committed by the Black Widow are often loathsome in their emotional impact. Because she will deliberately target those who have come to trust her, the crimes of this type of serial murderer violate our basic assumptions about love, loyalty, guardianship, and friendship. By any social standard, the Black Widow is a fearsome criminal because her crimes are those of a person whose heart is deadly cold and whose passion for gain may be insatiable.

Table 2.1: Judias Anna Lou Buenoano

Classification	Black Widow.
Birth Information	Born in Quanah, Texas, as Judias Anna Lou Welty, on April 4, 1943.
Active Period	1971 to 1980. Active from age twenty-eight to age thirty-seven.
Victim Information	Murdered two of her husbands and her son. Attempted to murder a third husband.
Method	Poison.
Motive	Each murder was motivated by the profit from life insurance proceeds. Buenoano also had a history of arson for profit.
Disposition	In 1984 and 1985, Buenoano was tried and convicted on a variety of charges. She was sentenced to death in 1985.

THE PERFECT CRIME?

The life and crimes of Belle Gunness are the stuff of legend for at least two reasons: (1) she was the first American

Black Widow serial killer of the twentieth century, and (2) it is possible that Gunness skillfully escaped apprehension for her many crimes and eventually died a quiet, natural death—a circumstance that is extraordinarily rare in the history of female serial murder in this country. What is known to a certainty is that Gunness was one of the most prolific and successful American female serial killers in the annals of criminology, having never been arrested or charged with any of her dozens of murders (see Table 2.2).

Belle Gunness (commonly known by the surname of her second husband) was born in the small fishing village of Selbu, Norway, as Brynhild Paulsdatter Storset, on November 11, 1859. Throughout her childhood, the Storsets struggled with near-poverty, which persistently plagued the family because of her father's various unsuccessful business ventures. As a teenager, Gunness was unhappy, pudgy, and unattractive, with harsh features and a perpetually sour expression. However, she was naturally bright and manipulative—qualities that Gunness would refine and rely on throughout her later life.

Table 2.2: Belle Gunness

Classification	Black Widow.
Birth Information	Born in 1859, in Norway, as Brynhild Paulsdatter Storset. Immigrated to the United States in 1881 and settled in Chicago. Gunness came to be known as "Lady Bluebeard" because of her notorious crimes.
Active Period	1896 to 1908. Active from age thirty-seven to age forty-nine.
Victim Information	The precise number of victims is unknown; however, estimates range from sixteen to forty-nine. Known victims included two husbands, several children, and a number of workers whom she employed.

Method	Various. The most common method was poisoning.
Motive	Most of the victims were murdered for life insurance proceeds or to rob their assets. The motive for some of the murders remains uncertain.
Disposition	The unidentified, decapitated body of a female was found in 1908 and originally believed to be the remains of Gunness. However, this theory was never proved and various sightings of Gunness continued until 1935.

In 1881, at the age of twenty-one, Gunness left her Norwegian home and immigrated alone to the United States in search of a more rewarding life. After her arrival, she Americanized her name to Bella Storset and would often refer to herself as "Belle" when speaking to her friends. Three years after her immigration, Gunness moved to Chicago to join a growing Norwegian subculture, which offered a more familiar social environment and an opportunity to earn a better income. It was in Chicago, in 1884, that Gunness met another Norwegian immigrant, Mads Sorenson, and fell in love. Within a year, at the age of twenty-five, Gunness married Sorenson and settled into the quiet routine of building a family—an uneventful period in her life that lasted for over a decade.

By 1896, after twelve years of marriage, Gunness had grown tired of her meager existence and bored with her marriage to Sorenson. That year, she and her husband opened a confectioner's shop in Chicago in the hopes of improving their financial situation. However, it proved to be a business that performed poorly from the day it opened, and to Gunness, it was painfully reminiscent of her father's entrepreneurial failures in Norway. A year after it opened, the shop was mysteriously destroyed by a fast-moving fire that Gunness attributed to the explosion of a kerosene lamp; however, investigators were never able to locate any remnants of the kerosene lamp among the wreckage. Despite the suspicious circumstances surrounding the fire, the confectioner's shop had been properly insured and a settlement was soon paid to Gunness and Sorenson. During that same period (just prior to the inexplicable fire), Gunness's oldest child, Caroline, mysteriously died of what medical personnel believed to be acute colitis. The child had no adverse medical history and died quite suddenly, leaving behind an apparently devastated mother. Caroline's life had also been insured, and a settlement was promptly paid after her death. Based on the apparent credibility of her bereaved mother and the supporting opinion of a local doctor, no investigation into the child's death seemed warranted at the time.

Gunness used the proceeds from the two insurance settlements to purchase a new home for her family. However, despite her improved living conditions, the Gunness household continued to experience terrible and inexplicable misfortunes. Two years later, in 1898, the new home burned completely to the ground, providing a more substantial insurance settlement than Gunness had realized from either of her previous disasters. That same year, Gunness's next child, Alex, died of what was (once again) believed to be acute colitis, and she received yet another insurance settlement. As they had done previously, Gunness and Sorenson used the insurance proceeds to purchase a new, even larger home.

Throughout the latter years of their marriage, Mads Sorenson had suffered from an enlarged heart and was often under medical care and unable to work. In 1900, he suddenly died of an undiagnosed ailment that exhibited many of the symptoms of strychnine poisoning. However, given his tenuous medical condition, few questions were asked and no autopsy was performed. Gunness received another insurance settlement, quickly sold her home, and left the Chicago area permanently to purchase a farm. By this time, she had three surviving children in her household: Myrtle, born in 1897; Lucy, born in 1899; and Jennie Olsen, an orphaned girl who had been placed in Gunness's care by a local family. Gunness moved the surviving members of her family to a rural area near La Porte, Indiana, in search of a fresh start and a new business—the Gunness farm.

Two years later, in 1902, Gunness married another Norwegian immigrant, a local rancher named Peter Gunness. The marriage was not a happy one and lasted only eight months; however, Gunness did bear her husband one son, Philip, in 1903. The brief marriage ended that same year when Peter Gunness fell victim to a freak accident—a sausage grinder happened to fall from a shelf and strike him on the head as he was passing underneath. Gunness's husband succumbed to a severe skull fracture without regaining consciousness. Once again, Gunness was widowed, and once again, she received an insurance settlement.

Left with only her young children to help tend the farm, Gunness began to hire casual laborers to assist her with the endless chores. She also began to run advertisements in newspapers that catered especially to the local Norwegian population. Some of these advertisements offered employment at the Gunness farm, while others were designed to draw out prospective suitors for the lonely widow. Her ability to attract men to her farm proved to be nothing short of remarkable, however, and she soon had a constant stream of laborers and would-be partners to keep her company. Unfortunately, many of those who made the journey to the Gunness farm never returned.

In 1906, Gunness's stepdaughter, Jennie Olsen, suddenly disappeared from the household. When neighbors inquired about her whereabouts, Gunness would brag that she had sent Jennie off to a fine finishing school in California. None of those who knew the hard-working, pleasant-speaking Gunness ever thought to question her story about Jennie's mysterious departure from the farm. In the meantime, Gunness continued to cater to her steady flow of male visitors and workers, who by then were disappearing with alarming regularity.

In April 1908, the Gunness farmhouse was completely destroyed by a fire of unexplained origin, which appeared to be arson. When the wreckage had cooled, investigators began to probe the scene in an effort to learn the fate of any victims. Soon after they began, searchers found the remains of three children and an adult female in the basement of the home. The body of the woman was inexplicably headless and investigators could not locate a skull anywhere on the Gunness property. At first, the headless body was assumed to be that of Belle Gunness.

Ray Lamphere, a former handyman who had worked at the Gunness ranch from 1906 to 1908, was arrested and charged with arson and murder shortly after the first bodies were discovered. The following month, on May 5, 1908, investigators began to find the remains of other bodies on the Gunness property. What was left of the bodies indicated that most had been dismembered, wrapped in cloth sacks, and doused with lye. However, it also appeared that some of the remains had been fed to the farm hogs.

Investigators were never able to determine the precise number of bodies that had been scattered about the property; however, it was thought that sixteen individuals were certainly murdered and possibly as many as twelve more. Indeed, many investigators now believe that the actual number of her victims was forty or more. A coroner's report issued in 1908 noted that remains from at least ten male victims and two female victims were positively identified, in addition to those of the Gunness children and an unspecified quantity of human bone fragments. Many of the male remains had been discovered in the hog pen, while the bodies of the female victims had been buried in a garden patch on the property. In addition to her biological children, five of Gunness's victims were eventually identified as Jennie Olsen, two ranch helpers (Eric Gurhold and Olaf Lindblom), and two suitors (John Moo and Ole Budsberg).

Local authorities could not identify the headless corpse

found in the basement; however, the investigation of the farm continued in the hope that more could be learned of Gunness's crimes. On May 19, 1908, Gunness's dental bridge was located among the ruins, which led the corner to revise his final report and declare that Belle Gunness had died in the fire that had destroyed her property. However, the man who was being held on charges of murder in the case, Ray Lamphere, persistently claimed that Gunness was still alive. He told police that Gunness had deliberately set the farmhouse on fire and that he had helped her to escape by driving her to the railway station in Stillwell, Indiana, where she boarded a train for the East Coast. Initially believing his story, law enforcement officials began an intensive search for Gunness and mistakenly arrested a woman who happened to fit her description. However, after the woman filed suit against the police for false imprisonment, they soon agreed that they had misidentified her and reconsidered their investigation. Now dubious about Lamphere's story, the authorities proceeded with their original charges against him and gave up their search for Gunness.

In November 1908, Lamphere went to trial on four counts of murder and one count of arson. At the end of that month, he was convicted on the single charge of arson and found not guilty on the four capital offenses. According to the jury's verdict, there was simply insufficient evidence to believe that Lamphere had committed (or participated in) any of the murders. For the next two years, from his prison cell, Lamphere continuously discussed the Gunness case with all who would listen. His version of events was that Gunness had personally murdered forty-nine individuals and stolen in excess of $100,000 from her victims between 1903 and 1908. Lamphere also claimed that the headless body discovered in the farmhouse basement belonged to an unfortunate victim who had been found in a local saloon and lured to the farm with money. Once there, the woman had been murdered by Gunness and her body had been used to decoy the investigation that would inevitably follow the planned destruction of the farm.

Two years after he was convicted of arson, Lamphere died in prison. However, the legend of Belle Gunness did not die with him, and in fact, it grew stronger with each passing year. Gunness was reportedly seen shortly after the fire, in Indiana, by a railway conductor. She was later seen by another railway worker in Decatur, Illinois. In 1916, Gunness's close friend and neighbor, Almetta Hay, died of natural causes. When neighbors examined her property, a woman's skull was found wedged between two mattresses. Unfortunately, law enforcement officials never pursued this promising lead to the real identity of the headless victim found at the Gunness farm.

Sightings of this notorious Black Widow continued sporadically for nearly thirty years after the alleged death of Belle Gunness. The final report of her location occurred in 1935, in Ohio. However, despite the persistent reports of Gunness's whereabouts, none of the leads were ever pursued by law enforcement personnel and no arrests were made. After 1935, no further reports of Gunness were recorded.

Without question, each sighting of this infamous serial killer added immeasurably to her legend. To this day, it remains uncertain whether Belle Gunness managed to commit the perfect crime and elude apprehension for a lifetime or died in the fire started by her own hand.

THE QUEEN OF POISONERS

Although we are left with only speculation about the fate of Belle Gunness, there is no question that Marie Besnard committed the perfect crime—in fact, thirteen of them. Besnard was born in Loudon, France, in 1896, as Marie Davaillaud. Her childhood was a series of misadventures, despite the fact that she received a strict religious education at a local convent. By the time she was a teenager, Davaillaud was known by acquaintances as a wild girl who knew few limits on her behavior—especially with men.

In 1920, at the age of twenty-three, Davaillaud married an older cousin, Auguste Antigny. For a time, the couple seemed happy together and Marie Antigny settled into a quiet routine of tending to her husband and her home. However, the marriage eventually degenerated into a burden for Marie, whose desires for a more comfortable lifestyle were becoming increasingly apparent. In 1927, Antigny suddenly died, leaving his wife a small inheritance and her much-desired freedom. The official cause of death recorded by local authorities was fluid in the lungs; however, as police would later learn, Auguste Antigny was the first of thirteen victims of a woman who came to be known as the Queen of Poisoners (see Table 2.3).

In 1929, Marie met and married Leon Besnard, thus acquiring the surname by which she would become infamous and a partner in murder who would eventually become one of her victims. Leon Besnard's family was both large and wealthy, providing all the motivation for murder that the Queen of Poisoners would need. Marie Besnard initially set her sights on Leon's two great-aunts, who were each blessed with substantial estates. In 1938 and 1940, both aunts mysteriously died, leaving their wealth to various members of the family including Marie and Leon Besnard. Both women were deemed to have died from lung ailments.

In May 1940, Marie Besnard's father unexpectedly died of what physicians believed to be a cerebral hemorrhage, which further enhanced his daughter's assets. This death was followed a few months later by the demise of Leon Besnard's father, who, the bereaved daughter-in-law claimed, had succumbed to eating poison mushrooms. Despite the growing number of mysterious deaths in the Besnard family, local authorities found no reason to investigate matters and settled for the explanations provided to them by Marie for each of the unexpected deaths.

Table 2.3: Marie Besnard

Classification	Black Widow.
Birth Information	Born in 1896, in Loudon, France, as Marie Davaillaud.
Active Period	1927 to 1949. Active from age thirty-one to age fifty-three.
Victim Information	Murdered at least thirteen individuals for profit. Most of Besnard's victims were relatives.
Method	Poison. Besnard was given the moniker of "Queen of Poisoners" in France.
Motive	All of the murders were motivated by profit.
Disposition	Besnard was first brought to trial in 1952; however, a mistrial was declared. She was tried again in 1954, but the jury failed to reach a verdict. Tried for a third time in 1961, Besnard was acquitted, despite the forensic evidence of arsenic poisoning in thirteen victims and her own earlier confession (which had been recanted). In her homeland, the case of Marie Besnard is considered to be a perfect crime.

Continuing her plot to centralize all the family wealth, Marie Besnard next attacked Leon's mother, in 1941; local authorities decided she had died of pneumonia. Later that year, Leon's sister, Lucie Besnard, allegedly committed suicide by ingesting poison. With Lucie's death, Marie Besnard had managed to murder seven of her relatives and collect an inheritance from each. Now in her mid-forties, Besnard had finally attained the comfortable lifestyle that she had long sought. However, she wanted still more.

Besnard's next victims were an elderly couple for whom

she played the role of a devoted caretaker. Mr. and Mrs. Rivet were both quite fond of Besnard when they came to live in her home and take advantage of her offer to care for them. The Rivets showed their appreciation for the attention that Besnard showered on them by making her the beneficiary of their estate. However, Besnard was not willing to allow nature to take its course. Mr. and Mrs. Rivet died within months of each other, both from an affliction that local physicians assumed to be pneumonia.

Continuing the now-legendary Besnard family curse, the next relatives to die were two cousins, both spinsters who had written Marie and Leon Besnard into their wills. Pauline and Virginie Lalleron each died in the same remarkable way, within a few months of each other—the two women allegedly mistook a bowl of lye for a special dessert that had been prepared by Marie Besnard. Incredible as this story seems in retrospect, it was accepted without investigation by the local authorities. The two unfortunate women became the tenth and eleventh victims to add their assets to those of Marie Besnard.

By 1947, Marie Besnard had fallen out of love with her husband, Leon, and was stricken by an intense infatuation with a German man who had recently emigrated to Loudon. Marie now turned her lethal attention to her husband and began to provide him with a special dessert similar to the one that had claimed the lives of the Lallerons. However, Leon Besnard became suspicious of his wife's attention and mentioned to a close friend that he thought Marie was trying to murder him. Unfortunately, Leon became Marie Besnard's twelfth victim before he was able to tell his story to the local authorities.

Two years later, in 1949, Besnard claimed her last victim when her mother suddenly died. Because of the age of the old woman, no investigation of the death was considered necessary. However, by this time, rumors in the town of Loudon were rampant about the infamous Besnard family curse. Marie Besnard did not take kindly to the cruel gossip that surrounded her and began to make death threats against several of her neighbors. Troubled by her increasingly aggressive behavior and finally suspicious of the Besnard family curse, local authorities launched an investigation into the death of Leon Besnard. On exhuming and examining his body, medical personnel discovered that he had died of arsenic poisoning.

Based on the results of Leon Besnard's autopsy, police ordered the exhumation of all the individuals whose deaths had been connected with Marie Besnard in any way. In all, thirteen bodies were exhumed and examined, resulting in the startling discovery that each had died of arsenic poisoning. It soon became clear to the authorities that the Besnard family curse was not nearly as mysterious as legend would have it. When Besnard was questioned about the murders, she quickly confessed to each and provided authorities with the motive that they had already suspected—profit. However, within a short time Besnard had recanted her entire confession and hired the best defense lawyers that she could find.

In February 1951, Marie Besnard was brought to trial to face thirteen counts of murder. Despite the fact that the prosecution had developed an apparently strong circumstantial case, her cadre of lawyers was ready for the challenge. Besnard's defense team astutely questioned the evidence produced by the thirteen exhumations and convinced the court that new examinations were needed. The reexaminations of the remains clouded the results submitted by the local medical examiners—a tactic that eventually resulted in a mistrial. Not to be defeated easily, the prosecutors reassembled their case and brought Besnard to trial again in March 1954. However, the Besnard family curse seemed now to fall on the prosecutors as the jury failed to reach a verdict.

Seven years later, authorities once again attempted to bring Besnard to justice, a full thirteen years after she had committed her thirteenth murder. In December 1961, Besnard went to trial for a third time, charged once again with the original thirteen murders. However, this trial ended the saga of Marie Besnard permanently when she was acquitted of all charges on December 12, 1961. In an amazing saga of serial murder that had lasted for more than twenty years and included three trials, Marie Besnard rewrote the definition of the perfect crime and eclipsed even the remarkable legend of Belle Gunness.

FOR THE LOVE OF PROFIT

Despite the legendary exploits of serial murderers like Belle Gunness and Marie Besnard, most Black Widows are eventually caught in their own web of aggression and tried for their crimes. Since the overwhelming motivation for the Black Widow is profit, and because her victims of choice are primarily family members, these serial killers exhibit a pattern of criminality that is generally recognizable. However, it is also true that medical personnel are frequently slow to suspect the presence of a Black Widow when confronted with an unusual or inexplicable family death. Rather, in attempting to arrive at a conclusion about the cause of death, physicians usually rely on the information provided by the perpetrator. Adding to the longevity and success of the Black Widow is the failure of law enforcement personnel to investigate many suspicious deaths because they, too, rely on the information provided by the murderer. Finally, there is a general social bias that seems to surround and protect most female serial murderers—a bias that denies the very concept that a woman may be a brutal, repetitive killer.

The Black Widow who murders for profit has been active throughout this century and in many different cultures and nations. Although a few Black Widows, like Gunness and Besnard, have attained legendary status, most perpetrators garner little attention in the media. However, as a class of female serial killer, they are among the most active, tenacious, and prolific of criminals. The female serial killer who murders for profit often targets her husband or children as

primary victims. The reason is usually simple and obvious—
to obtain life insurance proceeds. Incredibly, it is not unusual
for a determined Black Widow to marry several times (and
murder several husbands) in an attempt to satisfy a limitless
desire for profit.

To Marry and Murder

A classic example of a Black Widow, who married and
murdered several husbands, was Amy Gilligan, a serial killer
who was active for over a decade in the early part of the twentieth century (see Table 2.4).

Table 2.4: Amy Gilligan

Classification	Black Widow.
Birth Information	Born in 1869.
Active Period	1901 to 1914. Active from age thirty-two to age forty-five.
Victim Information	Murdered five husbands and several elderly patients in her nursing home.
Method	Poison.
Motive	Each victim was murdered for their assets and the profit from life insurance proceeds.
Disposition	Gilligan was sentenced to life in prison. After incarceration, she was moved to a state asylum, where she died in 1928.

In 1901, at the age of thirty-two, Gilligan opened a private
nursing home for elderly individuals in the town of Windsor,
Connecticut. Her business catered to wealthy senior citizens,
who were often without family members to provide care in
their final years. Between 1901 and 1914, Gilligan convinced
five aging patients to marry her. Unfortunately, all of the mar-
riages proved short-lived. In each case, Gilligan would purchase a substantial life insurance policy for her new husband

and quickly poison him. With each death, Gilligan would receive her late husband's assets as well as the cash settlement from her victim's life insurance policy.

During the same period, Gilligan also persuaded several female patients to name her as a beneficiary in their wills. After the unfortunate women changed their wills to include their loving caretaker, Gilligan poisoned each one. In all, Gilligan managed to insure and then murder nine elderly patients before the relatives of the last victim demanded an autopsy in 1914.

The autopsy on Gilligan's final victim showed clear evidence of poison and prompted authorities to exhume and examine a number of other remains. At the conclusion of the investigation, authorities determined that Gilligan had poisoned nine former patients and received an insurance settlement in each case. The year after her arrest, Amy Gilligan was tried for murder and found guilty. However, she did not spend the rest of her days in prison. After her incarceration, it was determined that Gilligan was probably insane; she was subsequently institutionalized in a state asylum, where she died thirteen years later.

Nearly as prolific as Amy Gilligan in the elimination of her husbands was Lydia Trueblood, who managed to dispatch four spouses between 1915 and 1919, along with her brother-in-law and her own child (see Table 2.5).

A native of Missouri, Trueblood moved to Idaho in 1912, where she married Robert Dooley, a man whom she had known most of her life. Shortly after the marriage, Trueblood convinced her husband and her brother-in-law, Edward, to purchase life insurance policies naming her as a beneficiary. Three years later, in 1915, both men died within months of each other. In both cases, baffled physicians assumed the cause of death to be typhoid fever. Unknown to the attending physicians was the fact that Trueblood subsequently collected a substantial death benefit on both insurance policies.

Dooley had fathered a single child by Trueblood before his death; however, the widow now perceived the child as an

Table 2.5: Lydia Trueblood

Classification	Black Widow.
Birth Information	Born in Missouri.
Active Period	1915 to 1919.
Victim Information	Murdered four husbands, a brother-in-law, and one of her children.
Method	Poison.
Motive	Murdered her husbands for the profit from life insurance proceeds.
Disposition	Trueblood was tried in 1921 and sentenced to life imprisonment. She subsequently died while in custody.

impediment to her freedom. In a brazen act of callousness, she poisoned the child shortly after her husband's death, giving authorities the cause as tainted water from the family well. At the time when they occurred, none of the three deaths in the Dooley family was considered worthy of investigation by local authorities.

Less than two years after her husband's death, Trueblood married William McHaffie, a local man from Twin Falls, Idaho. Shortly after the marriage, she demanded that her new husband purchase a life insurance policy naming her as the beneficiary. However, McHaffie was not fastidious in paying the premiums and allowed the policy to lapse shortly after purchasing it. Whether Trueblood knew about the lapsed policy is uncertain. Nonetheless, in 1918, the year after the couple married, McHaffie suddenly died from what physicians assumed to be influenza. Trueblood collected nothing from her husband's policy; however, she managed to add his remaining assets to her growing estate.

By 1919, Trueblood had moved to Colorado and married her third husband—Harlan Lewis. Once again, Trueblood demanded that her husband purchase a life insurance policy. The couple moved on to Montana to settle down and eventually purchased a life insurance policy for Lewis naming Lydia Trueblood as the beneficiary. One month after the policy went into effect, Lewis died of what was assumed to be ptomaine poisoning.

Not yet finished with her profitable business, Trueblood moved back to Idaho the same year Lewis died. In Pocatello, she met and married her fourth husband, Edward Meyer. The new bride quickly attempted to purchase a life insurance policy for her husband, again naming herself as the beneficiary. However, the life insurance company refused to write the policy. In the fall, Meyer became seriously ill and was hospitalized, and on September 7, 1919, he died while under the care of confused hospital personnel. The attending physicians were suspicious of the cause of Meyer's illness and ordered extensive postmortem medical tests, one of which proved positive for arsenic. Based on the medical findings, Lydia Trueblood was interviewed by police and considered a possible suspect in her husband's death. However, the police were unable to build a convincing case and no charges were filed at the time.

Concerned that law enforcement authorities were hot on her trail, Trueblood moved to California in search of another husband. There, in 1920, she met and married a seaman. Fortunately for her new husband, Trueblood had not found the time to arrange for a life insurance policy before her past caught up with her. Officials in Idaho had been piecing together her activities for over a year and were ready to claim their prize. In 1921, Trueblood was arrested and returned to Idaho to stand trial for the murder of Edward Meyer. That same year, she was found guilty of the charge and sentenced to life in prison, where she subsequently died of natural causes.

The Giggling Grandma

One of the most infamous Black Widows, who specialized in the marriage and murder of her mates, was Nanny Hazel Doss, known in the press as the *Giggling Grandma*. Over a period of several decades, Doss murdered four husbands, three children, two sisters, and her mother—nearly all in the name of profit (see Table 2.6).

Table 2.6: Nanny Hazel Doss

Classification	Black Widow.
Birth Information	Born in 1905.
Active Period	1925 to 1954. Active from age twenty to age forty-nine.
Victim Information	Murdered three children (two of her own and a grandchild), four husbands, two sisters, and her mother.
Method	Poison.
Motive	Murdered for the profit derived from life insurance proceeds and family savings.
Disposition	Doss was found guilty of her crimes in 1955 and sentenced to life in prison. In 1965, she died of leukemia while incarcerated. Doss came to be known as the *Giggling Grandma* because of her nervous habit of giggling when discussing her crimes.

Nanny Doss was born in 1905 and suffered an abusive and wild childhood. At the age of sixteen she married a local man, Charles Braggs, and quickly gave birth to four children. As each child was born, Doss made sure that a life insurance policy was purchased in the child's name, with herself as a beneficiary. By the time Doss was in her twenties, two of her children had mysteriously died in the same year. Both children had been healthy until fed a special meal by their mother, after which they lapsed into convulsions and quickly died.

Suspicious of his wife's behavior and the cause of his children's death, Braggs left Doss and their daughter, Florine, and moved away with their oldest child. With the collapse of her marriage, Doss relocated to Georgia to make a new start with Florine. There she met her second husband, Frank Harrelson, and she soon abandoned Florine to travel with her new love. However, thanks to the intercession of neighbors, Florine Braggs was soon reunited with her father. She eventually married and gave birth to a son in 1945, having little contact with her mother in the intervening years.

Shortly after the birth of her son, Florine decided to visit her mother, who was now living in Alabama. Having left her young son with Doss while she also made a brief visit to her father, Florine was shocked to return home and learn that the infant had mysteriously died while in her mother's care. Local medical personnel attributed the death to natural causes, and no investigation was undertaken. Although Doss would later confess to the murder of her grandson, no motive was ever established for the infant's demise.

A few months after the death of Doss's grandson, Frank Harrelson suddenly died without any indication of prior illness. With his death, Doss collected a life insurance settlement and the remainder of his assets. Pocketing her newly acquired wealth, Doss was able to move out of the area and purchase a small ranch, where she was free to seek new prey.

Doss's third husband, Arlie Lanning, died in 1952 of the same inexplicable disorder as Frank Harrelson. The following year, Doss's mother died in the same manner. Also that year, two of Doss's sisters inexplicably died after receiving a short visit from the Black Widow. In each case, Doss was able to benefit from the proceeds of life insurance or the distribution of her victim's assets. In 1953, Doss married and murdered her fourth husband, Richard Morton. The following year, she met and married Samuel Doss, acquiring the name by which she would become infamous. She murdered Doss, her last victim, only a month after they were married.

The death of Samuel Doss signaled the end of this prolific Black Widow's killing career. His demise aroused sufficient suspicions on the part of medical personnel to require an autopsy. The results of the postmortem revealed that Samuel

Doss had been poisoned with large quantities of arsenic. When the authorities confronted Nanny Doss with the evidence of her guilt, she quickly confessed to a total of ten murders, although she generally denied greed as the motivation for her crimes. In 1955, Doss was sentenced to life imprisonment for her crimes, still claiming that she never intended to profit from any of the murders. Ten years later, she died of leukemia while serving out her sentence.

Messages from the Spirits

Tillie Gbrurek brought a new twist to the business of husband elimination for profit—she specialized in foretelling the deaths of her mates before she carried out her crimes. For a number of years, her predictions made Gbrurek the object of both awe and fear to those who knew her. One wonders how Gbrurek was able to attract five husbands to target as victims given her chilling reputation as a prophetess of doom. Nonetheless, her ability to succeed at this bizarre scheme was well documented. Unlike most Black Widows, Gbrurek's killing career started late in life, at the age of forty-nine. However, she made up for lost time by murdering four husbands and a neighbor within the next seven years (see Table 2.7).

Gbrurek located most of her unfortunate mates through a marriage broker. She was first married in 1885, to John Mitkiewitz, who survived until 1914. In that year, Gbrurek claimed to be the recipient of spiritual visions that predicted the death of those around her. These visions would not only foretell the passing of the unfortunate individual, but also the date of his or her demise. The spiritual messages were particularly potent and accurate when it came to foretelling the demise of Gbrurek's husbands.

In 1914, Gbrurek proclaimed that John Mitkiewitz would die in a matter of weeks. To everyone's amazement, Gbrurek's husband inexplicably died at the appointed time, providing his widow with a life insurance settlement in the process. Once again using a marriage broker, Gbrurek married her second husband, John Ruskowski. Within a few months of the marriage, Gbrurek predicted the death of her new husband, and once again, the message from the spirits was infallible. As in the case of Mitkiewitz, Ruskowski had also purchased life insurance and named his new wife as the beneficiary. Within months of his death, Gbrurek married Joseph Guszkowski. As before, this marriage was a short one and ended just as Gbrurek had predicted—including her receipt of another life insurance settlement.

Table 2.7: Tillie Gbrurek

Classification	Black Widow.
Birth Information	Born in 1865, in Chicago.
Active Period	1914 to 1921. Active from age forty-nine to age fifty-six.
Victim Information	Murdered four of her husbands and a neighbor. Arrested while attempting to murder her fifth husband.
Method	Poison (arsenic).
Motive	Profits from life insurance proceeds and the assets of her victims.
Disposition	Gbrurek was arrested, tried, and sentenced to life imprisonment in 1921.

Almost immediately after Guszkowski's death, Gbrurek married her fourth husband, Frank Kupczyk. This marriage lasted four years before Gbrurek made the dreaded prediction of his death, less than two weeks before the event was to take place. By this time, Gbrurek's reputation had become widespread in the local area, particularly because she had earlier predicted the death of one of her neighbors. Thus, her reputation as a seer became unquestioned when the death of Frank Kupczyk occurred on schedule.

Suspicions about Gbrurek's powers became rampant after

she married Anton Kilmek, her fifth husband, and quickly predicted his demise. Law enforcement authorities decided to investigate this last prediction and the number of mysterious deaths that had befallen Gbrurek's unfortunate husbands. Not completely to their amazement, their investigation found Kilmek on death's door, tended by his loving wife. The police also discovered that Kilmek had been fed arsenic with the meals that his devoted wife had prepared for him. The Black Widow was immediately arrested and later charged with murder after the exhumation of the remains of her earlier victims.

Gbrurek's prosecutors were able to assemble a strong case against the murderer and bring her to trial in late 1921. A jury quickly convicted Gbrurek, and she was sentenced to life in prison without the possibility of parole.

Family and Friends

Louise Vermilyea was another infamous Black Widow who was active in the Chicago area a few years prior to Tillie Gbrurek. However, unlike Gbrurek, Vermilyea's murders went beyond targeting her husbands; they included her children, a stepson, and even four acquaintances (see Table 2.8).

Vermilyea's first husband, Frederick Brinkamp, unexpectedly died in 1893, leaving the widow a substantial life insurance settlement. Brinkamp's death aroused no suspicion at the time, nor did the inexplicable deaths of his two daughters shortly thereafter, despite their young ages (five and eight years old). Apparently ignored was the fact that Vermilyea received additional life insurance settlements from the deaths of her two children. Finally, in 1906, Brinkamp's granddaughter also died suddenly, although it is not known whether her passing added to Vermilyea's coffers.

The seemingly grief-stricken wife, mother, and grandmother eventually recovered her composure and married her second husband, Charles Vermilyea. However, his fate was no better than the Brinkamps'. In 1909, he died of an inexplicable illness, leaving another generous life insurance settlement behind. Still, despite the Black Widow's careful planning, her husband's murder did not go as smoothly as expected. Instead, Vermilyea's death left his son, Charles Vermilyea, Jr., suspicious about his stepmother's behavior, and the two would often argue about a variety of family issues. However, the bickering came to an abrupt end in less than a year when Charles, Jr., was also found dead under mysterious circumstances.

Table 2.8: Louise Vermilyea

Classification	Black Widow.
Birth Information	Born in Chicago.
Active Period	1893 to 1911.
Victim Information	Murdered at least ten individuals, including two husbands, three of her children, a stepson, and four acquaintances.
Method	Poison (arsenic).
Motive	Most of the murders were committed for life insurance proceeds or for the assets of the victims.
Disposition	After authorities began investigating Vermilyea's activities in 1911, she began to self-administer arsenic with her meals. By the end of that year, she had lapsed into a condition of permanent paralysis from the poison.

Vermilyea's next victim was Frank Brinkamp, her son from her first marriage. Brinkamp, too, had developed suspicions about his mother's activities and made the fatal mistake of discussing his concerns with a few close friends. However, he was not able or willing to report his concerns to the police before he fell victim to one of his mother's special meals. Predictably, he had also named his mother as a beneficiary in a substantial life insurance policy.

Now running short on family members, the Black Widow turned her attention to others. Vermilyea's last four victims were individuals to whom she rented rooms or prepared meals in her boardinghouse. Over the next two years (1910–1911), she managed to attack and murder at least four more victims, all with arsenic. These last four murders demonstrated an uncertain motive, since no life insurance settlements were ever at issue. Nonetheless, it is possible that Vermilyea managed to bilk these victims of some of their assets along the way.

Finally arrested in 1911, Louise Vermilyea denied any involvement in murder, for profit or otherwise. However, despite her protestations, prosecutors had built an irrefutable case against the Black Widow, and she was indicted on ten counts of homicide. In a bizarre finale to her twisted life of murder, Vermilyea was never brought to justice for her crimes. Before she could go to trial, she began to self-administer arsenic with her meals. By December 1911, Vermilyea had lapsed into a condition of permanent paralysis from the effects of the poison and plans for her eventual trial had to be abandoned.

Other Black Widows who murdered for profit found no need to extend their crimes beyond their families; they merely eliminated as many family members as necessary to assuage their greed. For example, in 1956, Rhonda Bell Martin confessed to authorities that she had poisoned three of her husbands, her mother, and three of her own children. All the victims had died excruciating deaths except for her fifth husband, who sustained permanent paralysis from the effects of arsenic given to him with his meals (see Table 2.9). Each of the victims had been murdered for the proceeds of their life insurance policies.

Martin was an active serial killer throughout her adult life. However, like many other Black Widows, she was eventually foiled by the results of an autopsy. Arrested and charged with multiple counts of homicide, Rhonda Bell Martin was found guilty and sentenced to death for her lifetime of crime. On October 11, 1957, the sentence was carried out in an Alabama electric chair.

Table 2.9: Rhonda Bell Martin

Classification	Black Widow.
Birth Information	Born in 1907, in Alabama.
Active Period	Throughout her adult life.
Victim Information	Murdered her mother, two husbands, and three children. Martin was believed responsible for the murder of two other (of her own) children; however, these charges could not be substantiated.
Method	Poison (arsenic).
Motive	Each of the victims was murdered for the profit from life insurance proceeds.
Disposition	Martin admitted to some of the murders and was tried for her crimes. She received the death penalty sentence and was executed in the electric chair in 1957.

Unlike Martin, who was an active serial murderer throughout her adult life, Janie Lou Gibbs claimed all five of her victims in a period of two years—an unusually short killing career for a Black Widow (see Table 2.10).

By any standard, Janie Lou Gibbs was an unlikely serial murderer to those who knew her. Living in the small town of Cordele, Georgia, Gibbs was a committed Christian fundamentalist and extremely active in her local church. She had been married to the same man since the age of fifteen, was a grandmother, and appeared to be a devoted and caring mother to her four children.

However, beginning in 1965, Gibbs poisoned her husband and four children by serving them food tainted with arsenic. With each death, the Black Widow became the

Table 2.10: Janie Lou Gibbs

Classification	Black Widow.
Birth Information	Born in 1933, in Georgia.
Active Period	1965 to 1967. Active from age thirty-two to age thirty-four.
Victim Information	Murdered her husband and four of her children.
Method	Poison.
Motive	Murdered her family members for the profit derived from life insurance proceeds.
Disposition	Gibbs was arrested in 1967 and charged with five counts of murder.

beneficiary of a new life insurance settlement, and with each tragedy, she donated a portion of her newly acquired assets to the local church. This serial murderer was eventually discovered when her daughter-in-law demanded that an autopsy be performed on Gibbs's last victim. The discovery of arsenic in the victim's body resulted in an investigation of all the family deaths that had occurred over the preceding two years. When confronted with the overwhelming evidence of her guilt, Gibbs quickly confessed to her crimes.

Beyond America

Throughout this century, Black Widows were also operating outside the United States to accomplish their missions of mayhem and greed at any price. For example, in South Africa, a pleasant, middle-aged woman named Daisy De Melker murdered two of her three husbands and her son in an effort to bolster her assets while gaining freedom from what she viewed as the intolerable constraints of marriage (see Table 2.11).

Daisy De Melker's plan was both familiar and lethal. Using arsenic hidden in the meals she served, this Black Widow dispatched two of her husbands and collected an insurance settlement with the death of each. However, unlike most Black Widows, De Melker had an accomplice—her son. Unfortunately for Daisy, however, Rhodes Cowle could not keep his mother's crimes to himself and instead began discussing the murders with his friends. To seal his fate, young Cowle then attempted to blackmail his mother. De Melker did not take well to this breach of trust and turned her lethal tactics against the youth, using arsenic once again.

Table 2.11: Daisy Louisa Cowle De Melker

Classification	Black Widow.
Birth Information	Born in 1885, in South Africa.
Active Period	1923 to 1932. Active from age thirty-eight to age forty-seven.
Victim Information	Murdered two husbands and her son.
Method	Poison (arsenic).
Motive	De Melker murdered two of her husbands for the proceeds of their life insurance. She murdered her son when he tried to blackmail her for the murder of her husbands.
Disposition	De Melker confessed to her crimes. She was hanged in 1932.

Again unfortunately for De Melker, the unexpected demise of her son prompted a medical investigation that disclosed the cause of his death. On exhuming the bodies of De Melker's other victims, authorities soon learned of the Black Widow's lethal activities and promptly arrested her. As is often the case with Black Widows, Daisy De Melker confessed to her crimes immediately after being arrested. She was found guilty at trial, sentenced to death, and hanged on December 30, 1932.

In the year Daisy De Melker claimed her last victim (1932), Marie Alexander Becker, a native of Belgium, claimed her first. However, Becker extended her lethal ways

well beyond her immediate family, eventually even claiming
victims who were clients of her dress shop (see Table 2.12).

Table 2.12: Marie Alexander Becker

Classification	Black Widow.
Birth Information	Born in 1877, in Belgium.
Active Period	1932 to 1936. Active from age fifty-five to age fifty-nine.
Victim Information	Murdered twelve individuals, including her husband, her lover, and at least ten elderly female customers of her dress shop.
Method	Poison (digitalis).
Motive	Becker's victims were all murdered for profit.
Disposition	Becker was arrested in 1936, found guilty at trial, and sentenced to life in prison. She died while in custody during World War II.

Becker claimed her first victim when she was fifty-five
years old—an unusually late start in life for most Black
Widows. While well into her middle years, Becker fell in love
with a local man and decided to remove the obstacle to her
happiness—her husband—with a fatal dose of digitalis. On
the death of her husband, Becker received a significant insurance settlement and the full attention of her new lover, Lambert Beyer.

Unfortunately, Beyer proved a disappointment to Marie
Becker. In fact, the Black Widow was so unhappy with the
new relationship that she poisoned Beyer rather than marry
him. In order to sustain her newfound lifestyle, Becker then
used the proceeds of her insurance settlement to open a dress
shop in Liege, Belgium. Her shop specialized in clothing for
senior women, and its proprietor was known to take a special
interest in their shopping experience. Over the next four

years, Becker managed to befriend at least ten special customers, whom she bilked of their assets and then murdered with digitalis.

However, Marie Becker could not keep the secret of her successful murders to herself and instead disclosed to a friend how she had dispatched the hapless clients. By October 1936, Becker's secret was known to the police and she was in custody, having confessed to a dozen murders. Exhumations and medical examinations followed, providing gruesome support for the veracity of the Black Widow's confession. Marie Becker was subsequently tried for her crimes, found guilty, and sentenced to life imprisonment.

All the Children

Perhaps the most disturbing crimes ever committed by a Black Widow in search of profit were those of Diana Lumbrera. In an unbelievably cruel reign of serial killing that lasted for over a decade, Lumbrera murdered six of her own children for the proceeds of life insurance policies that had been purchased for each of the unfortunate victims (see Table 2.13).

Table 2.13: Diana Lumbrera

Classification	Black Widow.
Birth Information	Born in 1957, in Texas.
Active Period	1977 to 1990. Active from age twenty to age thirty-three.
Victim Information	Murdered six of her own children.
Method	Strangulation and suffocation.
Motive	Each of the children was murdered for the profit from life insurance proceeds.
Disposition	Lumbrera was arrested in 1990. She was tried in several court jurisdictions for the murders and was eventually sentenced to three life terms in prison.

Diana Lumbrera was born in 1957, in Texas. At the age of seventeen, she married a local man and quickly gave birth to three children: Melissa, in 1975; Joanna, in 1976; and Jose Lionel, in 1977. As each child was born, Lumbrera made certain that a life insurance policy was purchased naming her as the beneficiary. The policies ranged in value from $3,000 to $5,000.

Lumbrera's lethal career began with the murder of Joanna Lumbrera at the age of three months when the distraught mother rushed the baby to a local hospital emergency room. Diana reported that the infant had suddenly gone into convulsions and stopped breathing. Unfortunately for the infant and her yet-unborn siblings, Joanna was already dead when she arrived at the hospital, where attending physicians attributed her demise to an undefined seizure. As anticipated by the Black Widow, the death of her daughter was soon followed by her receipt of a modest life insurance settlement.

Two months after he was born, Jose Lionel Lumbrera was also rushed to the hospital with an identical explanation from his mother. However, unlike with his sister, Jose's life-threatening condition was stabilized, and confused physicians immediately hospitalized him for observation. Three days later, while still hospitalized, the infant suddenly died following a crib-side visit from his mother. Remarkably, physicians once again attributed the death to natural causes, and once again, Lumbrera collected a life insurance settlement.

On October 2, 1978, Lumbrera brought her three-year-old daughter, Melissa, to the same hospital, describing the same inexplicable convulsions and breathing disorder that had claimed the lives of her other children. Sadly, Melissa was already dead when physicians began their examination. Once again, the death was attributed to natural causes and no investigation was considered necessary. For a third time, Lumbrera collected an insurance settlement from the murder of one of her own children.

The year after Melissa's death, Lumbrera divorced her husband and began a long series of affairs with a number of men. For the next decade, the Black Widow changed location several times and gave birth to three more children, each by a different lover. In turn, each child was insured and soon succumbed to the mysterious convulsions and breathing disorder that had devastated the original Lumbrera children. In each instance, Lumbrera received an insurance settlement on the child's death—except for that of the last victim.

Born in 1986, Lumbrera's third son, Jose, became suddenly and inexplicably ill in his fourth year. On May 1, 1990, Lumbrera presented the child at a local hospital with the familiar symptoms. Sadly, he was already dead when he arrived. However, members of the hospital medical staff were suspicious of the circumstances of the boy's death and reported the incident to local authorities.

Prompted by the insistent medical personnel, police investigated Jose's death and that of Lumbrera's other children. Because she had moved from Texas to Kansas, and had murdered in both states, the investigation into this Black Widow's activities was extensive and difficult. However, it soon disclosed the horrifying extent of Lumbrera's crimes of well over a decade.

In July 1990, Diana Lumbrera was indicted in Palmer County, Texas, for the murder of her first three children. This indictment was followed by two additional indictments (from two separate jurisdictions) for the murder of her other children. In September 1990, Lumbrera went to trial on multiple charges of first-degree murder in the slaying of her first three children. The case for the prosecution was so overwhelming that the jury took less than an hour to find her guilty. She was subsequently sentenced to life imprisonment.

Later that same year, Lumbrera again faced trial for murder in a second jurisdiction. Rather than risk the possibility of a death sentence, the Black Widow confessed to the crimes for which she was held and received another sentence of life imprisonment. Several months later, she faced trial for the third indictment of murder and again presented no defense.

In a repetition of the previous court decisions, Lumbrera received her third sentence of life imprisonment, thus finally ending her long and brutal career of serial murder.

Death Row Grandma

Despite her egregious crimes, Diana Lumbrera was able to avoid the death penalty, even after the willful murder of six of her own children for profit. However, the crimes committed by Margie Velma Barfield, a Black Widow who was active a decade before Lumbrera, resulted in her execution for a similar number of slayings. Whereas Lumbrera's motives were clear and obvious, Barfield's have remained the subject of heated speculation and, because of her execution, will never be known to a certainty.

The question of why Barfield, a fifty-two-year-old grandmother of three, suddenly turned to serial murder as she entered middle age is both complex and disturbing. Some believe her motive was greed, while others point to her unmanageable addiction to prescription medications—a reason that Barfield herself claimed to be the impetus for her crimes. However, the true motive for her crimes will forever remain a mystery because this woman—a murderer with a kindly face and welcoming disposition—was executed by lethal injection on November 2, 1984 (see Table 2.14).

Barfield's sorrowful journey to death row began on October 23, 1932, in Cumberland County, North Carolina, where she had been born Margie Velma Bullard. Reared in a large family by strict parents, Barfield later claimed that her father had repeatedly molested her, starting at age thirteen. However, this version of her background was vehemently denied by all seven of her siblings.

At the age of seventeen, Barfield dropped out of high school and eloped with her teenage sweetheart, Thomas Burke. For the next fifteen years, she quietly settled into the role of housewife and mother, bearing her husband two children. However, in 1964, when she was thirty-two, Barfield's marriage began to rapidly disintegrate. Thomas Burke had lost his job, suffered significant injuries in an automobile accident, and started to drink heavily. In desperation, Barfield reluctantly arranged to have her husband committed to the Dorothea Dix Hospital in Raleigh, North Carolina, to cure his addiction to alcohol. With that decision, Barfield's life was abruptly set on a debilitating course of addiction and crime over which she never gained control.

Table 2.14: Margie Velma Barfield

Classification	Black Widow.
Birth Information	Born in 1932, in North Carolina.
Active Period	1969 to 1978. Active from age thirty-seven to age forty-six.
Victim Information	Known to have murdered four individuals (and possibly as many as seven), including a husband, her fiancé, and her mother.
Method	Poison.
Motive	Murdered her victims for the profit from life insurance proceeds or other assets.
Disposition	Barfield confessed her crimes and was later found guilty at trial. She was executed by lethal injection in 1984.

It was during her husband's confinement at the Dorothea Dix Hospital that the frightened, overworked, and lonely Barfield first sought medical help for her growing depression. Barely able to cope with the financial pressures of supporting her family, Barfield hoped for some support to stabilize her deteriorating emotional condition; however, the support she received was nothing more than a drug regimen of prescription tranquilizers, to which she soon became addicted.

When Thomas Burke was finally released from the hospital, he was a sober, but broken, man. He was also angered at what he perceived as an act of betrayal when he discovered that his wife had become hopelessly dependent on the drugs that had been prescribed to combat her depression. Bitterness and intense arguments punctuated the relationship between Burke and his wife, and over the next few years, the marriage became irreparably damaged. Then, in 1969, the first in a series of coincidental tragedies began to invade Velma Barfield's life.

In what was dismissed by authorities as an accident, Thomas Burke was found burned to death in his bed. Whether in reality this was a case of careless smoking or the first of Barfield's many murders still remains uncertain. In any event, the death of Thomas Burke marked a profound change in Velma Barfield and signaled the beginning of a course of lethal behavior that was to continue for years.

In 1971, two years after her first husband's death, the lonely widow met and married Jennings Barfield, acquiring the surname that she would use for the rest of her life. Throughout the short duration of her second marriage, Barfield was severely addicted to a variety of prescription medications and had to be hospitalized for drug overdoses on at least four different occasions. The couple had only been married for six months when Jennings Barfield suddenly and inexplicably died of what physicians assumed to be natural causes, coincidentally leaving the bereaved widow a few dollars, which she desperately needed for her medication.

Shortly after her second husband's demise, Barfield again found herself short of cash and began writing bad checks to cover her growing medical expenses and escalating addictions. However, her activities were quickly reported to the police and she was charged with a misdemeanor offense. Much to her relief, however, Barfield received only a stern reprimand for her actions and was sent home to resume her activities—and her addictions.

In 1974, Velma Barfield's mother, Lillie Bullard, unexpectedly died with no prior history of illness. No autopsy was performed, and the death was attributed to natural causes. However, this event happened to coincide with the forging of Bullard's name on a $1,000 loan application in favor of her daughter, Velma Barfield—a coincidence that obviously escaped the attention of local law enforcement personnel.

In 1976, still suffering from chronic depression and completely reliant on prescriptions that her physicians continued to fill, Barfield accepted a job as live-in maid for the aging Dollie Edwards. It was during her employment with Edwards that Barfield met the woman's nephew, Stuart Taylor, with whom she began a torrid romance that would last for two years. The relationship was convenient for both Barfield and Taylor, as the couple met surreptitiously under the guise of Taylor's regular visits to his aunt. However, Barfield's employment with Edwards proved short-lived when, in February 1977, her employer unexpectedly died. Physicians diagnosed Edwards's death as due to acute gastroenteritis and ordered no autopsy in the case.

Within weeks of Edwards's death, eighty-year-old John Lee and his wife hired Barfield as a live-in caretaker. After a month in her new job, Barfield again found herself short of funds and began forging checks on the Lees' bank account. In April of that year, yet another of the many strange coincidences that persistently followed Velma Barfield occurred. Barfield realized that she could not cover a recent $50 forged check that she had written on the Lees' account for her medications, and shortly thereafter, John Lee suddenly developed a mysterious and severe stomach ailment. Over the next two months, Lee's illness worsened and he lost more than sixty-five pounds. Finally, on June 4, 1977, he died in agony.

Barfield continued her employment in the Lee household, tending to the frail and bereaved widow in her usual efficient manner. However, in October of that year she was offered a job at the nearby Lumberton rest home. Since the new offer included much-needed additional income for Barfield and her family, she resigned her employment with the Widow Lee and moved on.

Still on intimate terms with Stuart Taylor, Barfield transferred her habit of forging checks to his bank account. At first, Taylor was willing to overlook her indiscretions after a brief argument and Barfield's inevitable promise to never cheat him again. However, he eventually grew distrustful of the Black Widow when her promises invariably proved to be false. On January 31, 1978, after a particularly fierce argument with Barfield, Taylor began to feel ill. Intense abdominal pains continued to plague him over the next few days until, on February 4, 1978, Stuart Taylor died of acute gastroenteritis. However, unlike the others, this death would not go unnoticed.

Perhaps it was only a hunch, but Taylor's relatives strongly disagreed with the official cause of his death and demanded that a full autopsy be performed. The results of the postmortem were devastating for both the victim's family and Velma Barfield, for they disclosed that Stuart Taylor had actually died from arsenic poisoning. This turn of events resulted in the quick arrest of Velma Barfield, who was not only a perennially suspicious character to the Taylor family but known by law enforcement personnel to be the last person to be with Taylor before the onset of his inexplicable illness.

Under questioning, Barfield quickly admitted to spiking Taylor's beer with lethal amounts of arsenic and, to the surprise of interrogators, she offered much more. Barfield also confessed to murdering her second husband, Jennings Barfield, in the same manner as Stuart Taylor. Her mother, Lillie Bullard, had received a fatal dose of insecticide to eliminate the possibility of the bank contacting her about the loan papers that Barfield had forged. However, according to Barfield's ongoing confession, John Lee's death had been a mistake—she had only wanted to incapacitate the old man until she could cover the bank deficit, which she was sure would be discovered. The murder of Dollie Edwards (by arsenic poisoning) appeared to have been without motive, since no theft or diversion of her assets could be found. The cause of Thomas Burke's death was never completely determined, although it remains suspicious. Based on her startling confession, Barfield was bound over for trial on multiple charges of murder.

At her trial, Barfield claimed that all the deaths were actually bungled attempts to incapacitate her victims while she covered the various thefts that had financed her uncontrollable drug addiction. However, the jury was not sympathetic to her defense. After less than an hour of deliberation, Barfield was convicted of first-degree murder and sentenced to death.

While awaiting her execution at the Women's Prison in Raleigh, Barfield came to be widely known as a deeply religious woman who was quick with a smile and invariably pleasant to others—the epitome of a loving grandmother. However, her fate was irreversible. When she died by lethal injection in 1984, Margie Velma Barfield—a Black Widow whose real motives remain an unresolved issue—became the first woman to be executed in this country since 1976.

JEALOUSY AND REJECTION

Without question, the predominant motive for the Black Motive serial killer who is not suffering from an obvious psychological disorder is profit. However, there are exceptions to this common characteristic. For example, the murders committed by Vera Renczi resulted from this Hungarian Black Widow's pathological and lifelong fear of rejection. Even more unusual than her singular motive, Renczi had a gruesome and unique ritual of preserving the remains of her victims, which has yet to be duplicated by any Black Widow (see Table 2.15).

Vera Renczi was born just after the turn of the century to an established and wealthy family in Bucharest. Despite her privileged childhood, Renczi was a wild teenager and mature beyond her years, especially in matters of the heart. By the age of sixteen, the young woman had run away with a number of local men considerably her senior; however, none of these relationships lasted for more than a brief period of time, generally because of Renczi's pathological jealousy and the endless fits of anger that she directed at her unworthy paramours.

Table 2.15: Vera Renczi

Classification	Black Widow.
Birth Information	Born in 1903, in Hungary.
Active Period	Throughout her adult life.
Victim Information	Murdered thirty-five individuals, including husbands, lovers, and her son.
Method	Poison (arsenic).
Motive	A Black Widow murderer who could not deal with rejection.
Disposition	Renczi confessed to her crimes and led investigators to her basement, where thirty-five zinc coffins were discovered. The coffins contained the bodies of her victims. Renczi was convicted of her crimes and sentenced to life imprisonment. She subsequently died while in custody.

While still a teenager, Renczi married a local businessman who was much older than she. To her husband's delight, the couple soon gave birth to what was to be their only child—a son. However, the marriage was not a happy one. Apparently, Renczi's raging jealousy and unbridled mistrust had doomed the relationship from the start.

Within a few years of their wedding day, Renczi's husband suddenly disappeared. Appearing angry and bereaved, she explained to neighbors that her unfaithful spouse had abandoned her—he had simply left his devoted wife and young son without reason or warning. As time passed, she amended the story to add more permanency to her loss by declaring that her unworthy husband had been killed in an automobile crash.

Renczi soon remarried but quickly became convinced of her second husband's persistent unfaithfulness. Like his predecessor, Renczi's new mate inexplicably disappeared from the household, and once again, the Black Widow complained to sympathetic neighbors that an unfaithful, unworthy man had maliciously abandoned her.

Throughout the coming years, Renczi raised her son without a husband; however, she engaged her passions with incredible gusto and acquired thirty-two different lovers. Amazingly, each lover would suddenly disappear from Renczi's life, usually prompting the Black Widow to complain about the infidelity and unfaithfulness of men. Even Renczi's son mysteriously vanished while still a young man, with little details provided by his mother to curious neighbors. In truth, her son had inadvertently stumbled upon the mystery of Renczi's missing husbands and lovers—that she had dispatched each one with a lethal dose of arsenic. In what the angered Black Widow could only have viewed as the ultimate act of male treachery, her son had attempted to blackmail her. However, rather than pay for his loyalty, Vera Renczi eliminated her own son with the same poison that had proven so effective with her husbands and lovers.

Renczi's last lover was the husband of a local woman who knew about the affair, which was destroying her marriage. After her straying husband failed to return home from an evening at Renczi's side, the angry woman contacted police and demanded that they investigate his disappearance. When the police arrived at the Renczi home to make their routine inquiries, the Black Widow suddenly confessed to a lifetime of serial murder and led the stunned officers to the basement of her home. There, in her basement, were the remains of thirty-five men, each preserved in an expensive zinc coffin.

Vera Renczi had poisoned virtually every man in her life who had come close to her in any way, including her son, two

husbands, and thirty-two lovers. To this tenacious and pathological Black Widow, each of the victims proved unfaithful,
uncaring, and unwilling to provide the depth of love and loyalty she demanded. Hence, each was dispatched with one or
more homemade meals generously spiked with arsenic.

Based on her confession and the evidence contained in
the thirty-five zinc coffins in her basement, Renczi was found
guilty of murder and sentenced to life in prison. She died
many years later while still in custody, closing one of the
most bizarre cases of a Black Widow serial murderer in the
history of criminology.

MIXED AND UNCERTAIN MOTIVES

It is unusual for a Black Widow to attack her victims for
more than a single, typically clear, reason; however, there
are cases in which a female serial killer has demonstrated
complex, multiple motives for homicide. For example, Maria
Velten, a classic German Black Widow, murdered five individuals with at least two distinct motives. Velten dispatched
her two husbands in attacks that were clearly motivated by
profit. However, she also killed at least two other relatives because they proved to be too ill for the Black Widow to effectively manage (see Table 2.16).

The most notorious of the mixed-motive American
Black Widows was Blanche Taylor Moore, who murdered
five individuals by poisoning them with arsenic between
1966 and 1989. Moore, as portrayed by actress Elizabeth
Montgomery in the movie adaptation of her life, *Black
Widow,* proved to be a most uncommon and tenacious serial
murderer—a Black Widow with a dual purpose who resorted
to murder, assault, and arson for the sake of both revenge and
profit (see Table 2.17).

Moore was born Blanche Kiser in Tarheel, North Carolina, on February 17, 1933. Kiser's childhood was utterly destroyed by her father, an alcoholic and self-righteous country
minister who regularly enlisted his daughter as a prostitute to

help pay off his perennial gambling debts. Young Blanche was left with one overwhelming wish for her future—to leave her perverse, sermonizing father and begin a new life that was far away from his abuse. In the meantime, Blanche's childhood prison of despair was brightened only by her own deep religious convictions.

Table 2.16: Maria Velten

Classification	Black Widow.
Birth Information	Born in 1916, in Germany.
Active Period	1963 to 1980. Active from age forty-seven to age sixty-four.
Victim Information	Murdered her father, aunt, two husbands, and a lover.
Method	Poison.
Motive	Velten's father and aunt were murdered for convenience and because she was unable to care for them. Her two husbands and lover were murdered for profit.
Disposition	Velten was arrested in 1983. She confessed to her crimes, was tried, and received a sentence of life imprisonment.

In May 1952, at the age of nineteen, Blanche Kiser married twenty-four-year-old James Taylor, a furniture refinisher. The Taylor marriage appeared to be a happy one, and the following year, Blanche gave birth to her first child, Vanessa. Shortly after her daughter's birth, Blanche began work as a clerk at Kroeger's Supermarket in Burlington, North Carolina. Getting compensated in her first "legitimate" job only added to Taylor's growing happiness and self-esteem, and for a time, she settled into a quiet family life.

Six years later, in 1959, Taylor gave birth to her second daughter, Cindi, and was promoted to the position of head cashier at Kroeger's. However, all was not well in the Taylor household. James Taylor had proven to be a hard drinker who was also addicted to gambling—vices that must have been painfully reminiscent of Blanche Taylor's father. The extra money that Blanche now earned at her new position barely kept the Taylor family clothed and fed, with much of it going to pay off her husband's gambling debts.

Frustrated and angry about her deteriorating home life, Blanche began a series of romantic affairs with a number of male supervisors at the supermarket. By 1962, she was aggressively pursuing Kroeger's assistant store manager, twenty-seven-year-old Raymond Reid. Married and the father of two children, Reid resisted Taylor's tenacious flirtations for three years before finally giving in to her advances. By the end of 1965, however, Reid and Taylor were meeting clandestinely on a regular basis.

In September 1966, Taylor unexpectedly expressed a desire to initiate a reconciliation with her hated father, Parker Kiser, and called at his home. Within days of her arrival, Kiser suddenly fell desperately ill. Assuming the role of a loving daughter, Taylor remained at her father's side to nurse him back to health; however, despite his daughter's ministrations, Kiser's condition continued to worsen and he began to suffer from violent stomach cramps, diarrhea, vomiting, and delirium. In less than a week, Taylor's father was dead. A local physician was called in to determine the cause of death; however, he failed to recognize the telltale signs of arsenic poisoning and decided that the aging man's demise was due to a heart attack. At long last, the father who had abused Blanche Taylor throughout her childhood had become only a painful memory.

Two years after the death of Parker Kiser, James Taylor suffered a near-fatal heart attack. Frightened and remorseful about how he had been neglecting his family, Taylor turned to Christianity, gave up gambling and drinking, and became a model husband and father. However, his new approach to family life came too late for his bitter wife. Although Blanche remained with her husband, she could not forgive or forget the suffering that she had endured over the past ten years—nor could she forget Raymond Reid.

Table 2.17: Blanche Taylor Moore

Classification	Black Widow.
Birth Information	Born in 1933, in North Carolina, as Blanche Kiser.
Active Period	1966 to 1989. Active from age thirty-three to age fifty-six.
Victim Information	Murdered two husbands, her father, her mother-in-law, and her lover.
Method	Poison (arsenic).
Motive	Most of the murders were committed for the profit derived from life insurance proceeds or the victim's assets. A few of the murders were motivated by revenge.
Disposition	Moore was arrested in 1989. She was subsequently tried, found guilty of murder, and sentenced to death in 1991.

In 1970, Blanche's eighty-six-year-old mother-in-law, Isa Taylor, became bedridden. Taylor, who had never particularly cared for her mother-in-law, inexplicably rushed to the woman's bedside, allegedly to make her as comfortable as possible. However, Isa Taylor soon suffered the same fate as Parker Kiser. Once again, had an autopsy been performed, medical personnel would have discovered the unmistakable signs of poisoning, including undigested arsenic in the woman's stomach. Instead, however, Blanche Taylor once again got away with murder when Isa Taylor's death was ruled to be due to natural causes.

By 1971, Raymond Reid had become convinced that his future should be with Blanche Taylor and filed for divorce.

Also by this time, Taylor and Reid's affair had become legendary among the Kroeger's employees. For the next two
years, until Reid's divorce was finalized in 1973, the couple
carried on with their torrid affair, showing little concern
about the growing scandal, which certainly even reached into
the Taylor household.

In September 1973, James Taylor was suddenly struck
down with what his doctor believed to be influenza. However,
Taylor's symptoms were extreme and ranged from swollen
glands and a sore throat to bloody stools and hair loss. In a
matter of days, Taylor was sufficiently ill that he had to be
hospitalized. On October 2, 1973, less than an hour after eating a dish of ice cream that his wife had brought from home
to his hospital bedside, forty-five-year-old James Taylor died.
Incredibly, attending physicians certified that Taylor's death
was attributable to a heart attack.[1]

James Taylor's death left his grieving widow with a small
inheritance, which she quickly used to move to nearby Burlington, where Raymond Reid lived. Taylor and Reid began to
date openly and discuss marriage. However, each time a wedding date was set, Taylor found an excuse to postpone the event.
It seemed that the Black Widow was happy with the relationship as it was. Eventually, it became clear to all but Raymond
Reid that a wedding would never be forthcoming. Although
the couple continued dating, Blanche kept her options open by
spending time with several other men in Burlington and assess-
ing her possibilities for the future.

On January 23, 1985, Blanche Taylor's house in Burlington was destroyed by fire. Officials who investigated the blaze
confirmed that the fire was deliberately started and accepted
Taylor's story of an unidentified male who had been loitering
around her residence shortly before the fire broke out. With
the settlement that Taylor received from her fire insurance
policy, she was able to purchase a new, more expensive mobile home. Unbelievably, less than a month later, her new
home also burned to the ground and Taylor received yet another insurance settlement.

In the same year her homes were destroyed, Taylor filed a sexual harassment suit against Kroeger's Supermarket and the store manager, Kevin Denton, with whom she had had a flirtatious relationship. Denton was promptly terminated, and two years later, Kroeger's settled the suit out of court by paying Taylor $275,000.

For Blanche Taylor, 1985 must have proven a momentous year in a number of ways. On Easter Sunday of that year, the deeply religious Taylor attended sunrise services at the Carolina United Church of Christ. It was at the conclusion of the service that Blanche introduced herself to the church's fifty-one-year-old pastor, Reverend Dwight Moore. True to her nature, Taylor soon began calling on the Reverend Moore regularly, engaging him in long conversations after the Sunday services. Unknown to Raymond Reid, it was not long before the couple was meeting for casual outings. Reverend Moore would later recall that it was on his second date with Blanche Taylor that he first "felt the chemistry between them."[2]

Early in 1986, Reid, who was still hoping to marry Taylor, developed a severe case of shingles—a viral infection of the nervous system. By April, his condition had deteriorated significantly and he was hospitalized. His physicians diagnosed Reid as suffering from Guillain-Barre syndrome, a nonfatal inflammatory condition of the nervous system and muscles that results in a general loss of sensation and symptoms that are similar to arsenic poisoning. Although complete blood and urine tests were ordered at the time of his admission to the hospital, Reid's laboratory results were inexplicably delayed in reaching his doctor. Had they been provided to the medical staff in a timely manner, the test results would have informed doctors that six times the normal amount of arsenic had settled into the ailing man's system.

Over the next six months, culminating with Reid's death on October 2, 1986, Blanche Taylor made daily visits to the hospital, always bearing her paramour gifts of home-cooked meals. On one visit, Taylor assisted Reid in drawing up a new will that named her as beneficiary of one-third of her lover's estate. When he finally died, Reid's demise was attributed to Guillain-Barre syndrome and the attending physicians believed that no autopsy was necessary. The apparently bereaved Taylor mourned her longtime lover and quietly pocketed $50,000 from his estate.

The next few years brought Blanche Taylor and the Reverend Moore closer together. Finally, on April 21, 1989, the two wed, with Blanche proudly taking her new husband's name. However, the couple's happiness was incredibly short-lived. While returning from their honeymoon, on April 26, 1989, Dwight Moore fell violently ill after eating pastry on the Cape May ferry. Moore rushed her ailing husband home, where she cared for him for two more days before taking him to the Alamance County Hospital. Shortly after his admission to the hospital, having just dined on his wife's homemade soup, Moore took a sudden turn for the worse. However, apparently looking for a prosaic explanation for Moore's sudden illness, his physician diagnosed severe indigestion and sent him home with his wife.

Once home, Moore began to feel a bit better and settled in for the day with his new bride. However, shortly after ingesting his next meal, Reverend Moore became severely ill once again. This time, Blanche drove her husband to North Carolina Memorial Hospital but, in what proved to be a comedy of errors, the hospital refused to admit Moore without a written reference from the Alamance County Hospital. Once again, the couple returned home.

On April 30, 1989, Moore's symptoms radically worsened. Within a twenty-four-hour period, Moore had retained forty pounds of excess fluids and was close to death. Blanche again made the trip to Alamance County Hospital with her desperately ill husband. This time the paperwork seemed to be in order and Moore was referred to the North Carolina Memorial Hospital. Upon his arrival, a toxic-screening test was immediately ordered. Two weeks later, on May 13, 1989, the startling test results were finally made available. It was a miracle that Moore had survived—his system contained twenty times the amount of arsenic considered lethal. Hospital administrators immediately notified local police of the results of Moore's medical tests, now certain of what had caused his life-threatening illness.

Law enforcement personnel were quick to respond to the concerns of hospital staff and soon questioned Blanche Moore about her husband's last few days. During their investigation, the police became quite interested in the many mishaps that had befallen their suspect. In particular, investigators were suspicious of the similarities between Dwight Moore's symptoms and those described in the medical files of Raymond Reid and James Taylor.

On June 13, 1989, police exhumed the bodies of Blanche Moore's deceased lover and first husband. Autopsies confirmed the presence of arsenic and, on July 18, 1989, Moore was arrested for first degree murder in the deaths of Reid and Taylor. Although traces of arsenic were also found in the exhumed bodies of Moore's father and mother-in-law, there was insufficient evidence in either case to warrant an indictment for murder.

The trial for the murder of Raymond Reid began on October 21, 1990, in Winston-Salem, North Carolina. Throughout the proceedings, Moore persisted in her claim of innocence, saying, "I know arsenic was found in these people, but it's not because I put it there."[3] However, her appeals were unconvincing to the jury and she was found guilty of murder. On January 18, 1991, Blanche Taylor Moore was sentenced to death by lethal injection for the murder of Raymond Reid.

Prosecutors eventually dropped possible subsequent charges for the murder of James Taylor and the assault charges in the case of Reverend Dwight Moore. Their decision was succinctly explained to reporters by Tom Keith, district attorney of the county in which the cases would have been tried: "You can't kill the woman more than once."[4]

"They All Died on Me"

In 1972, Alfred Steinschneider, a doctor of pediatric medicine at Upstate Medical Center in Syracuse, New York, published a groundbreaking paper on sudden infant death syndrome (SIDS). Steinschneider had undertaken a study of infants with a familial history of breathing disorders, and in his publication, he postulated the possibility of a genetic basis for SIDS because it so often attacked members of the same family. His study included the case histories and medical treatment of five babies from four different families. Steinschneider discovered that each of the babies had passed routine medical examinations and was considered normal and healthy, despite the fact that their parents had claimed that each suffered from prolonged apnea. At the time of Steinschneider's study, this form of apnea was believed to be a precursor to SIDS.

Prolonged apnea is a condition in which an infant suddenly and inexplicably stops breathing, turns blue, and subsequently resumes normal breathing without any apparent cause. Among the deceased patients included in Steinschneider's study were a brother and sister, whom he identified only as "N.H." and "M.H." The study noted that three other children from the same "H." family had previously died from SIDS, although the details of these earlier deaths were not provided. Steinschneider's 1972 study not only proved to be remarkable for its insight into SIDS but later provided the clues necessary for two determined public officials to uncover the heinous actions of a classic Black Widow serial murderer who had been relentlessly preying on her own children for six years.

In 1986, William Fitzpatrick, an assistant district attorney employed by Onondaga County, New York, was deeply involved in the prosecution of a complex child murder case. It was during the course of his investigation into that crime that he and Dr. Linda Norton, a Texas pathologist who was consulting on the case, happened to read Steinschneider's original SIDS study. Norton was stunned by the similarities between the case they were investigating and the deaths of the "H." family children that had played such a prominent role in Steinschneider's publication. Discussing the striking coincidences of the two cases with Fitzpatrick, Norton came to believe that it was possible that the children of the "H." family had actually been the victims of a serial murderer.[5]

By 1992, Fitzpatrick had become the District Attorney of Onondaga County. However, despite his workload, he had not forgotten his conversation of six years earlier with Linda Norton. In fact, he was so troubled by the possible implications of the "H." family deaths that he began his own investigation to determine the real identity of the individuals mentioned in Steinschneider's paper. As Fitzpatrick became more involved in the investigation, he also became increasingly suspicious of the improbability of five unexplained infant deaths in one family—three of whom had apparently died of SIDS even prior to Steinschneider's study.

After a thorough investigation, Fitzpatrick was convinced that the deaths of the "H." family children were, in fact, homicides. He had also learned the true identity of the children's mother and, armed with the case file, Fitzpatrick alerted Robert Simpson, the district attorney of Tioga County, New York (where the deaths had taken place), of his suspicions. Simpson immediately began a local investigation supported by the expertise of two eminent pathologists and the extensive information that had already been collected by Fitzpatrick. The combined efforts of the two district attorneys eventually led, on March 23, 1994, to the arrest of Waneta Hoyt, a forty-seven-year-old housewife from Oswego. Within days, Hoyt was formally charged with the murder of five of her own children between 1965 and 1971 (see Table 2.18).

The long saga of the deaths of Hoyt's children proved to be one of misdiagnosis and missed opportunities on the part of local authorities and medical personnel. The five children, ranging in age from six weeks to two years, had each unexpectedly died over a six year period, despite the fact that none suffered from a serious medical ailment or had even had a significant prior illness. Remarkably, the cause of each child's death had been determined to be sudden infant death syndrome (SIDS), based exclusively on the explanations of Waneta Hoyt.

Table 2.18: Waneta E. Hoyt

Classification	Black Widow.
Birth Information	Born in 1946, in New York.
Active Period	1965 to 1971. Active from age nineteen to age twenty-five.
Victim Information	Murdered five of her six children. Her victims ranged in age from six weeks to two years old.
Method	Suffocation.
Motive	Hoyt may have suffered from Munchausen syndrome by proxy. She stated that she murdered her children because they would not stop crying.
Disposition	More than twenty years after the death of her last child, a pathologist (Dr. Linda Norton) and a district attorney (William Fitzpatrick), worked to reopen the case of the deaths of Hoyt's young children. A reexamination of the deaths eventually led to multiple charges of murder against Hoyt. She was subsequently tried, found guilty of five counts of murder, and sentenced to seventy-five years to life in prison.

Eric, the first infant to die, was only three months old when he stopped breathing for no apparent reason on January 26, 1965. His mother, who gave every indication of profound anguish and sorrow to local authorities, claimed that she had found the baby lifeless in his crib. Unfortunately, no autopsy was performed on the infant and his death was assumed to be a routine case of SIDS. The second Hoyt child to die, Julie, was six weeks old on September 5, 1968, when her mother reported to the local medical examiner that the baby had choked, turned blue, and suddenly stopped breathing while she was being fed. Once again, no one questioned Julie's death; nor were any questions raised when Hoyt's oldest child, James, died later that year in the same manner.

Like the other Hoyt children, two-year-old James had been in good health when he awoke on the morning of September 26, 1968. However, before noon, James was dead. This time, Hoyt told the local medical examiner that James had suddenly called out to her in fright and then inexplicably stopped breathing. Incredibly, no one seemed suspicious of the unfortunate circumstances that continued to plague the Hoyt children. In fact, Hoyt's friends were most sympathetic to the bereaved mother, who kept dozens of her children's pictures prominently displayed throughout the house and who lovingly laid flowers on their graves each Memorial Day, saying to her friends: "I miss my children. They all died on me—you know, that crib disease."[6]

Molly Hoyt was born in March 1970, and her brother, Noah, was born in 1971. By then, electronic monitors were being extensively tested on high-risk babies in an effort to forewarn caretakers when an infant's breathing became irregular or stopped altogether. The apnea monitor promised new hope for children who were prone to SIDS; however, in 1970, the device was still experimental and meant for use by medical personnel who could provide rapid intervention for an infant who stopped breathing. Because Hoyt had already lost three infants to SIDS, her daughter, Molly, was accepted into a federally funded SIDS study and Hoyt was permitted to use the new device. Within a year, Hoyt's youngest child, Noah, was also accepted into the same program.

After a period of time under medical supervision, the apnea monitor seemed to be working well for Molly—so well, in fact, that the persistent Hoyt eventually convinced physicians that she could monitor Molly at home without the assistance of hospital personnel. The medical staff finally agreed and, on May 8, 1970, Molly Hoyt made medical history by being the first baby to be placed on an apnea monitor at home without medical supervision. However, the success of the device was short-lived. Hoyt soon began complaining that the monitor was inexplicably malfunctioning—a situation that quickly led to the next tragedy to strike the Hoyt children.

According to Hoyt, on June 10, 1970, Molly mysteriously died in her sleep. The apnea monitor, she said, had never made a sound, or if it did, she had been unable to hear it. Incredibly, within a year, Molly's younger brother, Noah, died in precisely the same manner, with the same explanation from his mother. No autopsy was performed in either case since both infants were considered to be at high risk for SIDS. There was also no police investigation into these, or any other, of the Hoyt children's mysterious deaths—that is, until two decades later, when Fitzpatrick and Simpson would learn the horrifying truth about the Hoyt children.

On March 23, 1994, Waneta Hoyt was arrested for the murder of her children and quickly admitted her role in each death. Her only explanation to law enforcement personnel was that she had killed her children because of their incessant crying. Providing the details of her egregious crimes, Hoyt went on to admit that she had suffocated Eric, Molly, and Noah with pillows as they slept. She had suffocated James with a towel and stopped Julie's breathing by forcing the infant's face against her shoulder during a feeding. Although remorseful and cooperative at first, Hoyt later recanted her entire confession and denied any culpability in the deaths of her children. However, the authorities had accumulated more than enough evidence to bring her to trial. On April 21, 1995, Waneta Hoyt was found guilty on all five counts of murder and received a sentence of seventy-five years to life in prison.

The confluence of the early medical work of Alfred Steinschneider and the later investigations by Fitzpatrick, Norton, and Simpson, redefined the possibilities of family serial murder and brought a new focus on the question of sudden infant death syndrome. Medical experts now believe that between 1 and 20 percent of the 7,000 to 8,000 American babies who are annually diagnosed as having died of SIDS may have actually died of other causes.[7] Research also indicates that there is a discomforting connection between mothers who make use of home apnea monitors and children who are later determined to be the victims of homicidal smothering.[8] Although the great majority of infant deaths are due to genuine medical complications, hundreds of these children die inexplicably each year. Sadly, many of these infants may die at the hands of their mothers. Psychiatrists believe that many of the mothers who compulsively kill their young suffer from Munchausen syndrome by proxy—a psychological disorder than can go unnoticed and undiagnosed for years until the murderer is apprehended or there are no more children to harm.[1]

It is possible that mothers who kill their young often go undetected because they are the most unlikely of suspects. Our culture is rooted in the concept of family—a fundamental unit of survival that is predicated on love and trust. To the majority of Americans, it is inconceivable that the symbolic embodiment of love and trust—a mother—could, in fact, be a brutal serial murderer. Beyond this social bias lies another obstacle to prevention: medical misdiagnosis is common in cases of sudden infant death because the determination of the cause of death is often in the hands of a coroner who may have little or no medical experience in dealing with the complex issues of such a tragedy. Unless the cause of death is blatantly obvious, many coroners understandably choose to rely on the statements of supposedly bereaved parents rather than view them as possible suspects in an apparently motiveless homicide.[9] This combination of social bias and the inexperience of key medical personnel allowed Waneta Hoyt to un-

---

I. See Appendix III for an explanation of this psychological disorder.

remittingly murder her children and remain undetected for over three decades.

District Attorney Fitzpatrick expressed the inherent unwillingness of Americans to recognize the potential of a mother as a serial murderer when he said, "We have prejudices about what killers look like, and they don't look like nice middle-class moms from the suburbs."[10] Sadly, to all who knew her, Waneta Hoyt fit this description perfectly—even after she had murdered five of her own children.

NOTES

1. "Poisoning Investigation Expands," *Charlotte* (North Carolina) *Observer* (Internet edition), 23 June 1989.

2. "Arsenic Follows the Men in Her Life," *Akron* (Ohio) *Beacon Journal* (Internet edition), 14 November 1990.

3. Julia M. Klein, "On Stand, Woman Denies Poisoning Lover and Husband," *Philadelphia Inquirer* (Internet edition), 9 November 1990.

4. "Further Charges against Poisoner to Be Dropped," *Charlotte Observer* (Internet edition), 6 March 1994.

5. Anastasia Toufexis, "Medicine: When Is Crib Death a Cover for Murder?" *Time,* 143, no. 15 (11 April 1994, Internet edition).

6. Ibid.

7. Ibid.

8. Todd Lighty, John O'Brien, and Charles B. Hickey, "Upstate Study of SIDS Hides Homicides," *Syracuse On Line* (undated Internet edition).

9. "Defining the Scope and Nature of Fatal Abuse and Neglect," *Virtual Hospital* (Internet edition), 15 September 1995.

10. Anastasia Toufexis, "Medicine."

3

ANGELS OF DEATH

The Angel of Death has been abroad throughout the land, you may almost hear the beating of [her] wings.

—John Bright
In a speech to the House of Commons on February 23, 1855

Throughout the recorded history of many Western cultures, Azrael, the Angel of Death, has long claimed a significant and foreboding place in literature and in the collective consciousness of those who have even fleetingly considered the roots of their religious convictions. For two millennia, the archetypal quality of this transcendental symbol has proven both pervasive and irresistible. No matter what form it takes, the presence of the Angel of Death represents the ultimate adjudication of life—it is a symbol that is quintessential to the fleeting, tremulous, and uncontrolled nature of our mortality. It is the Angel of Death who invariably presides over the manner and time in which we all must relinquish that which we treasure most. In any of its many incarnations, the image of Azrael is timeless, profound, troubling, inevitable, and evolving. Few other symbols among those in our Western culture bear such a penetrating impact on the mind or cast such incisive fear into the heart.

To our civilization, the symbolic significance of the Angel of Death is especially powerful and recondite because it is fundamental to a shared liturgy known to millions of people. In ancient religious doctrine, it was Azrael who presided over the ultimate retribution against the firstborn sons of Egypt when their pharaoh persistently refused to release his Jewish captives from their imprisonment. In the mid-twentieth century, this symbol took on its darkest meaning when Josef Mengele, a Nazi physician who came to be known as the *Angel of Death,* supervised and participated in the execution of countless thousands of Jews who had been cruelly imprisoned in the notorious concentration camp at Auschwitz. Between these extremes of purpose, the Angel of Death has been present among us in endless manifestations that have transformed its meaning into something profoundly archetypal—a symbol that is inherently understood to a greater depth than even the most erudite attempts at description.

In recent decades, a new incarnation of the Angel of Death has appeared as a fearsome, final life-partner to the very young, the elderly, the ill, and the innocent. She is the lethal caretaker.[1] This contemporary Angel of Death embodies an especially pernicious darkness in our humanity by systematically attacking the weak and defenseless who have been involuntarily placed into her care or must rely on her for comfort and support. She carries out her serial crimes almost exclusively within institutions that are committed to those in need of the life-giving support of medical personnel or professional caretakers such as hospitals, sanitariums, or nursing homes. In carrying out her lethal mission, the Angel of Death compulsively seeks out victims who are at the extreme of their inability to withstand any assault—the very young, the elderly, and the frail. She persistently targets those who are in the greatest physical need and least able to mount an effective defense against such an onslaught.

Ego and a compulsion for domination frequently motivate the Angel of Death. She is obsessed with the need to con-

---

1. Angel of Death serial murderers are not limited to women. There are recorded incidents of this type of serial killing perpetrated by males who occupy the role of caretaker or nurse. However, the emphasis in this book is on the female serial murderer; hence, the use of feminine pronouns.

trol the lives of those who are completely dependent on her for care. In a few cases, this killer may suffer from a significant psychological disorder (such as Munchausen syndrome by proxy) which has remained undetected and unrecognized for some time. If so, she will be compulsively driven to attract the attention of medical personnel in order to gain recognition and self-aggrandizement through her heroic efforts to save the lives of those she has marked for injury or death. In any case, the Angel of Death is a fearsome predator who prefers to attack defenseless victims and enjoys the merciless power to make and carry out life and death decisions.

The victims of this serial murderer invariably exhibit two characteristics that make them especially attractive to the Angel of Death: (1) they are incapable of warding off any significant physical assault, and (2) they have come to believe that their attacker is a concerned and supportive caretaker. Because of this relationship with her victims, the Angel of Death only strikes when she is confident of complete control over her prey; she is typically unwilling to engage in a protracted struggle to accomplish her heinous mission and will choose victims who she believes are already doomed to die or, in her mind, have no further rights of survival.

The Angel of Death prefers to murder her victims in a way that is subtle, covert, and difficult to detect. When the intended victim is an adult, her favored weapon is often a lethal injection of potassium, potassium chloride, insulin, or a similar substance. These chemicals are abundant in her workplace and her unquestioned actions in caring for a patient naturally include routine injections. When the Angel of Death preys on young children or infants, she may resort to suffocation to simulate apnea or a similar breathing disorder in addition to the use of lethal injections. Whatever the method of attack, this serial killer will carefully weave the actions and tools of her crime into the routine of her work environment and responsibilities. She will appear to be going about her business in an efficient and caring manner, while in reality, she is determining who is to live and who is to die.

It is common for the actual number of victims of an Angel of Death to be uncertain. Because she usually carries out her activities in an environment where death is a regular occurrence (such as a hospital or nursing home), it may take a significant period of time or an alarming increase in the number of deaths before administrators or law enforcement personnel become suspicious of foul play. In particular, hospital administrators are often reluctant to suspect that an Angel of Death is operating among their staff because of the liability and loss of confidence that inevitably results from her crimes. Even after such a possibility has been recognized and an investigation begun, it may be difficult to apprehend a suspect because of the number of medical personnel who are frequently involved in a victim's care and the subtle methods of attack favored by the perpetrator.

Despite the difficulties inherent in apprehending an Angel of Death killer, this perpetrator may exhibit three characteristics that are invaluable to investigators: (1) she is compulsive in her need to kill and will attack repetitively within her own area of responsibility, thereby creating a discernable pattern of murder; (2) the perpetrator may be tempted to discuss her misadventures with others because she will often rationalize her crimes as acts of mercy; (3) some victims may survive the attack and be able to assist in a subsequent investigation of the perpetrator's activities.

Even without the benefit of survivor testimony, the combination of a localized pattern of murders that can be linked to a discrete area of responsibility and the propensity of the murderer to discuss her crimes can lead to a successful apprehension once an investigation is underway. Unfortunately, these criminal patterns may only become evident after the Angel of Death has claimed a significant number of victims because of the typically slow response of institutional administrators in recognizing the possibility of a serial murderer in their midst. Because of this protracted cycle of recognition and investigation, it is not unusual for the Angel of Death to claim at least eight identifiable victims before she is finally apprehended. Unfortunately, in many cases, the likely number of actual victims may be more than double this figure.

The number of institutionalized patients who are injured or die at the hands of an Angel of Death each year is uncertain. If the perpetrator is mobile and moves from position to position on a regular basis, it may be nearly impossible to recognize a pattern of murder or identify a primary suspect. Institutions that experience inexplicable waves of injuries or fatalities that cease without explanation should at least consider the possibility of an active serial murderer on their staff. Although this situation is generally nothing more than a statistical aberration, in some cases it may indicate that something far more sinister is going unrecognized or being ignored. Because the Angel of Death is able to prey on victims who have given over their unquestioned trust—and because the methods of this perpetrator are designed to be consistent with the environment in which she carries out her crimes—this serial murderer is among the most formidable from the perspective of law enforcement personnel. This is particularly true if her crimes occur in an organization that is reluctant to even consider the possibilities of such a perpetrator operating among the staff.

The crimes of an Angel of Death serial murderer are both morally egregious and among the most difficult to recognize. This perpetrator is often trusted and highly regarded by her supervisors, coworkers, and victims. Like Azrael, she has the outward appearance of a caring benefactor; however, like that messenger from God, she carries a weapon of lethal destruction at her side and is willing to preside over the question of life or death for even the most innocent of her charges.

TO BE A HEROINE

In March 1982, Genene Jones resigned her job as a licensed vocational nurse at the Bexar County Medical Center Hospital in San Antonio, Texas, to take a new position at the Kerr County clinic, which was headed by a local physician,

Kathleen Holland. A year later, in February 1983, Jones received a subpoena to appear before a special grand jury that had been convened in San Antonio to investigate the mysterious deaths of nearly fifty children at the Bexar County hospital. That same month, both Jones and Holland received subpoenas from a Kerr County grand jury investigating the inexplicable deaths of eight other infants who had apparently succumbed to lethal injections of a muscle relaxant while being treated at the Kerr County clinic. At the same time, Jones and Holland were also named as defendants in a massive lawsuit filed by the parents of fifteen-month-old Chelsea McClellan, who had mysteriously died after routine medical treatment at the Kerr County clinic. By early 1983, it had become obvious to the family of Chelsea McClellan, law enforcement authorities, and the grand juries in two counties that a prolific Angel of Death serial murderer had been active in at least two Texas medical facilities for several years and, as far as they could discern, that she was still targeting infants and young children even as the investigation was underway.

The common link and primary suspect in most of the inexplicable deaths at both medical facilities was Genene Jones, a native of Texas, who was born in 1951 (see Table 3.1). While in her early twenties, Jones had been employed as a beautician; however, in 1977 she earned a vocational-nursing license in order to pursue her long avowed desire to work with children—particularly those who were desperately ill. For the next four years, Jones worked at several hospitals in the San Antonio area until, in 1981, she accepted a nursing position at the Bexar County Medical Center Hospital.

As of vocational nurse, her new job brought Jones into daily contact with dozens of infants and young children who had been hospitalized for a variety of ailments. That same year (shortly after Jones joined the staff), hospital administrators noticed an alarming increase in the number of deaths of their young patients. To their horror, most of the unexplained deaths seem to be linked in some way to nurse Jones.

By the end of 1981, the unusual number of infant deaths had not abated, and in November, hospital administrators began the first in a series of formal investigations that would eventually culminate in the grand jury actions of 1983. Eventually, even the U.S. Centers for Disease Control (CDC) would be called in to help with the Bexar County hospital investigation. CDC personnel would later confirm the worst fears of hospital administrators after they discovered that many of the victims had received lethal injections of the cardiac medication digoxin—a method of attack that had the effect of interrupting or stopping the children's normal heart rhythm. However, within a year (while the investigation was still underway), Jones had already moved on to a new venue in which to pursue her lethal career.

In March 1982, Kathleen Holland resigned from the Bexar County hospital staff for the opportunity to practice private medicine and head the Kerr County clinic. Genene Jones was asked to join the clinic staff and quickly agreed, following Holland on to her new responsibilities. However, a series of inexplicable events plagued the clinic shortly after Jones's arrival and threw the medical practice into turmoil. In August and September of that year, at least seven young children suffered unexplained respiratory attacks while visiting the clinic for routine medical procedures and were rushed for emergency treatment to nearby Sip Peterson Hospital. In September, Chelsea McClellan was brought to the clinic by her mother for a routine visit and, while there, suffered an unexpected and severe respiratory attack. The young child was rushed to the hospital for emergency treatment but tragically died before she arrived.

By this time, medical personnel at the Sip Peterson Hospital had become extremely suspicious of the number of coincidental and mysterious incidents of respiratory arrest that had plagued Holland's clinic. Once again, Genene Jones came under suspicion because of her obvious involvement in each case. To worsen the case against Jones, Holland had discovered that a bottle of succinylincholine (a powerful muscle relaxant that could account for the respiratory failures in the clinic's patients) had inexplicably disappeared from the clinic stores and was mysteriously located several weeks later by Jones when her employer persisted in questioning its disappearance. Concerned about Jones's suspicious behavior and her possible involvement in the tragedies at the clinic, Holland fired Jones on September 26, 1982. However, county prosecutors could not easily dismiss the doctor's possible knowledge about the mysterious deaths of her patients. On February 24, 1983, Holland appeared before the grand jury in San Antonio in answer to a subpoena; however, she invoked

Table 3.1: Genene Jones

Classification	Angel of Death.
Birth Information	Born in 1951.
Active Period	1978 to 1982. Active from age twenty-seven to age thirty-one.
Victim Information	The actual number of victims is unknown. It is believed that she is responsible for at least eleven homicides but may have been responsible for many more. Some investigators believe that she may have been involved in the deaths of forty-six babies and children while working as a nurse. The victims, who were all children, were generally not seriously ill or in danger of death at the time they were murdered.
Method	Injections of lethal agents (typically, digoxin).
Motive	Ego motive—these were crimes motivated by issues of power and control.
Disposition	Jones was convicted of murder in 1984 and sentenced to ninety-nine years in prison.

her Fifth Amendment rights and refused to testify.[1] Despite her refusal to cooperate with the grand jury, prosecutors and the jury members had already made the connection between Genene Jones and the mysterious attacks on so many children at the two medical institutions that had employed her over the prior years.

For the next five months, Jones was under intense investigation for murder by two grand juries. On May 26, 1983, she was indicted on two counts of first-degree murder by the Kerr County grand jury. In both cases (including that of Chelsea McClellan), the complaint alleged that Jones had deliberately induced the death of her victims by injecting them with a potent muscle relaxant, thereby causing fatal respiratory arrest. Six months later, on November 21, 1983, Jones was also indicted for assault against a four-week-old infant by injecting him with an anticoagulant medication that caused severe hemorrhaging.

On January 15, 1984, Genene Jones was brought to trial in Georgetown, Texas, on a charge of murder in the case of Chelsea McClellan. The argument for the prosecution claimed that Jones had deliberately induced life-threatening symptoms in her young victims in order to be recognized as a heroine when her quick intervention brought them miraculously back from the brink of death. Sadly, in an unknown number of instances, Jones's ability to save the lives of her victims fell far short of her willingness to put them in lethal jeopardy. The trial lasted for a month before the jury found her guilty of murder on February 15, 1984, after only three hours of deliberation. Three months later, on May 15, 1984, at the age of thirty-three, Genene Jones received a sentence of ninety-nine years in prison.[2] In the state of Texas, such a sentence is the equivalent of a life sentence with the possibility of parole, allowing for her potential release from prison after a minimum of twenty years served. Later that year, in October, Jones was also convicted of attempted murder in the case of Rolando Santos, the month-old infant whom she had injected with an anticoagulant. For that attack, Jones received a concurrent prison term of sixty years.

In an unexpected twist of justice, Genene Jones was never charged with any further crimes, despite the fact that she was a prime suspect in at least ten additional murders. The vital documents that would have been necessary to bring additional charges against her suddenly became unavailable after the Bexar County hospital shredded over four tons of pharmaceutical records in March 1984, eliminating any trace of Jones's activities during her employment at the hospital.[3]

Ultimately, the final victim count attributable to Genene Jones's crimes of serial murder can never be known; however, some investigators believe that the number of her victims may have been between forty and fifty, making her the most lethal Angel of Death in the history of Texas.

Uncertain Guilt

As in the case of Genene Jones, the number of victims who were claimed by Nurse Terri Rachals remains uncertain. In fact, many believe that Rachals never attacked any of her patients, despite the fact that statistical and circumstantial evidence overwhelmingly indicates that she did. The state of Georgia was so convinced of her guilt that Rachals was eventually charged with six counts of first degree murder and an additional twenty counts of aggravated assault against a variety of intensive care patients. However, in what proved to be an unexpected twist in the course of justice against this alleged Angel of Death, Terri Rachals was never convicted of a capital crime (see Table 3.2).

Born in 1962, Rachals's childhood years were the subject of controversy at her later trial for murder. Rachals claimed that she had been repeatedly molested by her adoptive father for over five years, experienced frequent fugue states in which she "blacked out" and was unaware of her actions, and was finally forced to leave her home at the age of sixteen because of many years of sexual abuse. Rachals's adoptive father strongly denied this portrayal of her childhood (and himself); however, there was some evidence to suggest that Rachals had suffered from a significant psychological disorder that may have first become apparent in her teenage years.

Table 3.2: Terri Rachals

Classification	Angel of Death.
Birth Information	Born in 1962.
Active Period	1985 to 1986. Active from age twenty-three to age twenty-four.
Victim Information	Attacked a wide range of victims from age three to eighty-nine years. All the victims were attacked between October 1985 and February 1986. It is believed that as many as nine patients may have died from these assaults.
Method	Injections of potassium chloride.
Motive	Ego motive—these were crimes apparently motivated by issues of power and control by a person who may have suffered from a psychological disorder.
Disposition	Indicted on six counts of murder in 1986, Rachals was later determined to be guilty of aggravated assault. She was acquitted on all of the murder counts and sentenced to seventeen years imprisonment for a single count of aggravated assault.

By the early 1980s, Terri Rachals appeared to be living a quiet and unexceptional life. She had managed to find a position as a nurse in surgical intensive care at the Phoebe Putney hospital in Albany, Georgia. Her work record at the hospital was exemplary, and Rachals was considered to be both reliable and caring with her patients. Domestically, Rachals was married to a local man who suffered from cerebral palsy, had a young son who was the apparent center of her universe, and was an active member of her local church. One of Rachals's neighbors described her this way: "Mrs. Rachals would be the last person one would suspect of harming anyone."[4] This was a sentiment that seemed to be shared by all who knew Terri Rachals. However, that opinion was to change for many individuals by early 1986.

For reasons that still remain controversial, it is believed that Rachals abruptly turned to the serial murder of patients under her care between October 1985 and February 1986. During those few months, it is believed that Rachals committed at least twenty acts of aggravated assault against her patients by injecting them with potassium chloride. Although most of the victims were able to recover from these attacks (because they occurred in the intensive care unit of a hospital), it is thought that Rachals may have been responsible for as many as nine cases of fatal cardiac arrest because of the injections that she administered to her patients.

Alarmed by the sudden surge in patient deaths in November 1985, hospital administrators launched an investigation into the operations of the intensive care unit to which the individuals had been assigned. Even a preliminary review of hospital records clearly indicated that the afternoon shift nurse, Terri Rachals, was present and attending to most of the patients who had succumbed to inexplicable bouts of cardiac arrest—a statistical improbability so high as to leave little doubt as to Rachals's involvement in the incidents. However, even before the investigation had reached a final conclusion, Terri Rachals resolved any lingering doubts when she voluntarily approached the Georgia Bureau of Investigation to offer a confession that she had injected at least five of her patients with the lethal medication. Three of the patients had died from these injections.

On March 16, 1986, three days after her confession, the Albany grand jury indicted Terri Rachals on six counts of murder and twenty counts of aggravated assault. A day later, she was arraigned on the charges in an Albany courthouse. However, shortly after her arraignment, Rachals recanted her entire confession, claiming that she was confused and disoriented at the time that she made the condemning statements to investigators.

Rachals went to trial in the summer of 1986, where she was described by the prosecutor as "the murderess of the century."[5] The case against Terri Rachals appeared strong; however, it was also highly circumstantial and based largely on the statistical probability of her involvement in so many inexplicable incidents of cardiac arrest. Her defense team was tenacious and well prepared, portraying Rachals as a gentle woman who had suffered for many years from a debilitating psychological disorder. While the prosecution claimed that the serial murders committed by Rachals were ego-driven acts of control and domination, the defense countered that Rachals had actually only attacked one elderly patient who had pleaded with her to help him die. In fact, the single attack to which the defense team admitted had not been lethal. The defense further argued that their client was plagued by continuing fugue states in which she was completely unaware of her own actions. During the course of the trial, both the prosecution and defense provided expert testimony to bolster their opposing positions on the mental state of Terri Rachals.

On September 25, 1986, the jury reached a verdict that shocked the prosecution and many observers of the trial. They found Terri Rachals not guilty on all murder counts, not guilty on nineteen of the twenty counts of aggravated assault, and guilty on the single count of assault to which the Rachals defense team had already conceded. In finding Rachals guilty of aggravated assault, the jury noted that she was mentally ill yet clearly culpable and aware of her actions. Two weeks later, Rachals was sentenced to seventeen years' imprisonment for assault against an eighty-nine-year-old patient by the injection of potassium chloride. The sentence imposed on Rachals made her eligible for parole after serving only twenty-four months in prison.

That the findings of the jury were controversial was expressed most vehemently by the district attorney who prosecuted the case: "I hope every juror is willing to go into intensive care with Rachals as their nurse."[6] Clearly, the prosecutor felt that a serial killer who had been well aware of her crimes failed to receive the punishment that she deserved. However, those who knew Terri Rachals personally, as well as those who weighed the testimony at her trial, were convinced that this woman could never be the insidious Angel of Death who apparently had prowled the intensive care unit of the Phoebe Putney hospital for more than three terrifying months.

The Deaths at Grantham

Born in Britain in 1968, Beverley Allitt seemed an unremarkable child to all who knew her. However, by the age of thirteen, Allitt's personality had undergone a significant and profound change. She had been transformed from a happy and well-adjusted child to one who relentlessly demonstrated cruelty and violence toward others.

As a young adult, Allitt's propensity for cruelty and odd behavior became more self-directed. While completing a two-year nursing course, she missed more than 130 days of work, always claiming an endless variety of baffling physical and psychological symptoms, which generally defied successful medical treatment. Because of her persistent unreliability, Allitt found it difficult to find work, even though she had successfully completed the nursing course. Finally, in 1991, at the age of twenty-three, Allitt was hired as a full-time nurse in a small, short-staffed hospital. However, as her employers would soon learn, the Grantham and Kesteven Hospital would have been much better off had they remained short-staffed. Over the ensuing fifty-eight days after she was employed, Allitt would be responsible for at least twenty-six vicious attacks on a variety of children; four of these attacks would prove fatal and nine would result in irreparable physical or brain damage to her young patients (see Table 3.3).

Table 3.3: Beverley Allitt

Classification	Angel of Death.
Birth Information	Born in 1968, in Great Britain.
Active Period	1991. Active at the age of twenty-three.
Victim Information	All of the victims were children who had been treated at Grantham and Kesteven Hospital in England. There were at least twenty-six known attacks and four deaths attributed to Allitt.
Method	Lethal injections of insulin and potassium; in one instance, suffocation.
Motive	Allitt suffered from Munchausen syndrome by proxy.
Disposition	Allitt was convicted of multiple counts of murder in 1993 and sentenced to thirteen terms of life imprisonment.

Beverley Allitt had already attacked more than twenty children at the Grantham Hospital before Paul Crampton, a five-month-old, was admitted to her ward in March 1991. It was his inexplicable illness that would finally prompt an investigation into the series of bizarre mishaps that had plagued the hospital's young patients. Shortly after Crampton arrived at the hospital, he was found to be near death for no apparent reason. Routine blood samples were drawn and sent for analysis in an effort to reach a meaningful diagnosis of the baffling ailment that threatened the boy's life. The test results indicated that Crampton had received a large dose of insulin, despite the fact that he was not diabetic and had no need for the medication. Fortunately for Paul Crampton, this diagnosis saved his life.

Based on the unsettling blood test results in the Crampton case, hospital administrators finally decided that it was time to investigate the dozens of recent, inexplicable illnesses and deaths of their young patients. Unfortunately, it took fifteen days for the hospital to receive the initial test results for Crampton and another eighteen days before the hospital administrators informed law enforcement officials of their suspicions. Because of the long delay in recognizing what had happened to Paul Crampton, Allitt was able to continue her attacks on the Grantham children. Over the intervening weeks, she victimized three more young patients, and unfortunately, one of the children died before the official investigation began.

Allitt's first fatality was seven-week-old Liam Taylor, who was admitted to Grantham Hospital on February 23, 1991, with a simple chest cold. Thirty-six hours later, he was dead. A postmortem examination revealed that the infant had suffered serious heart damage, much like what would normally be attributed to the effects of years of heavy smoking or drinking. Taylor's death baffled the hospital staff; however, they were not sufficiently concerned about the circumstances to begin an immediate investigation. At the time, there was little reason to suspect foul play in a hospital populated by employees and patients who shared the comfort of a small town with a long and unquestioned history of peaceful surroundings and an unusually low crime rate.

Just ten days after Liam Taylor's death, tragedy struck the hospital once again. Eleven-year-old Tim Hardwick had been admitted to Ward 4—Beverley Allitt's station—after a bout of epilepsy. When the young boy unexpectedly died, the attending physicians decided that the cause must have been a prolonged epileptic seizure. Unfortunately, no postmortem examination was performed and there were apparently no suspicions about Allitt's role in the child's death.

Shortly after Tim Hardwick died, Becky Philips was admitted to the hospital and assigned to Ward 4. Philips was a three-month-old twin who arrived at Grantham Hospital during the week of March 5, 1991, suffering from difficulty breathing. The hospital staff easily stabilized her breathing and released her to return home with her parents. However, later that night the girl unexpectedly lapsed into a coma and died. Because the cause of Becky Philips's breathing disorder was unknown, her terrified parents feared that the tragedy might foreshadow the worst for their surviving daughter. As a result, the Philipses decided to have Becky's sister, Kate, immediately admitted to Grantham Hospital for a complete physical examination. Much to the Philipses short-lived relief, all of Kate's test results confirmed that she was a normal, healthy infant. However, before the baby could be released to her parents, she suffered three serious attacks of arrested breathing. The last of these unexplained episodes stopped her heart, causing hospital staff to struggle for an extended period of time to save the child. Even though they were eventually successful, Kate suffered permanent brain damage long before her breathing was restored.

Allitt's last fatality was Clare Peck, a fifteen-month-old asthmatic child who was admitted to Ward 4 on April 22, 1991. Two hours after being placed in Allitt's charge, Peck was dead. Despite the fact that the child's blood indicated an unusually high level of potassium, hospital physicians attributed her death to asthma. It would be another eight days after the child's death before the police would begin their investigation into the series of bizarre events that had descended on quiet Grantham hospital.

Once the investigation had begun, law enforcement officials soon discovered that the common denominator in all twenty-six attacks on Grantham's children was their attending nurse, Beverley Allitt. Moreover, officials were able to determine that all the victims had been injected with dangerously high levels of insulin or potassium. In one instance,

Allitt later admitted to suffocating an infant when her lethal injection failed to produce the expected results.

Much too late to help any of her hapless victims, Allitt's personal medical history was closely examined by law enforcement personnel. It was learned that the nurse had long suffered from Munchausen syndrome by proxy.[1] This crippling psychological disorder had impelled Allitt to relentlessly attack the defenseless Grantham patients in an effort to gain the attention and appreciation of the hospital staff and physicians that she so desperately craved. The investigation into Allitt's background also disclosed that she had harbored persistent destructive tendencies toward others since the age of thirteen. Had her medical history been more carefully examined before she was employed, it might have become clear to hospital administrators that Allitt should never have been allowed near the patients at Grantham. Sadly, that failed to happen.

Allitt was eventually charged with four counts of murder, eight counts of assault, and ten counts of grievous bodily harm with intent to kill. In an ironic postscript to her arrest, which underscored Allitt's significant psychological impairment, her legal proceedings were delayed for an unusually long time because of a series of inexplicable illnesses that kept her from attending the scheduled hearings. Nonetheless, on May 28, 1993, Beverley Allitt was found guilty on all counts and sentenced to thirteen terms of life imprisonment.

---

1. See Appendix III for an explanation of this psychological disorder.

NOTES

1. "Doctor Refused to Testify on 42 Child Deaths," *Philadelphia Inquirer* (Internet edition), 25 February 1983.

2. "US/World News in Brief," *Boston Globe* (Internet edition), 15 May 1984.

3. "Subpoenaed Documents Shredded," *Philadelphia Inquirer* (Internet edition), 11 March 1984.

4. "Hunting Humans—Terri Rachals," in Kozel Multimedia, *Mind of a Killer,* CD-ROM (Chatsworth, CA: Cambrix, 1995), Section: "Hunting Humans."

5. "Nurse Acquitted on Six Murder Charges," *San Jose* (California) *Mercury News* (Internet edition), 26 September 1986, 15A.

6. Ibid.

4

SEXUAL PREDATORS

Predator: an organism that lives by preying on other organisms.

Webster's New Universal Unabridged Dictionary

The title of this book, *Murder Most Rare,* applies especially to the female sexual serial killer who acts alone in carrying out her egregious crimes. So unusual is this crime that America has only experienced a single female sexual serial killer in its history—Aileen Wuornos. Although it is not unusual for a woman to partner with a male sexual predator as a member of a serial-killing team, the female sexual predator who acts alone unquestionably represents the most extraordinary of perpetrators in the history of this crime. Indeed, her crimes are murder most rare.

Despite the fact that we have a growing knowledge of the male sexual predator and his crimes, it is uncertain if any of this knowledge is applicable to the female sexual serial murderer. To draw conclusions about this type of perpetrator from what is known about the male counterpart may or may not prove to be valid; it is, at best, risky guesswork. In the final analysis, male and female serial murderers differ in fundamental ways that make workable comparisons difficult and uncertain. Likewise, female sexual predators who are members of a serial-killing team do not provide a sure point of comparison for the obvious reason that their motives are shared and intermingled with their murderous partners.

The questions raised by the crimes of Aileen Wuornos are complex and troubling. Since her case is unique in the history of criminology, very little of what has been learned from her background and criminal activities can be generalized. It is certainly impossible to even begin to profile such a murderer. The only other female sexual predator whose crimes approximate those of a male sexual serial killer was Marti Enriqueta, who was active in Spain shortly after the turn of this century (see Table 4.1). Unfortunately, far less is known of Enriqueta and her crimes than of Wuornos, who claimed her victims less than a decade ago in America.

Table 4.1: Marti Enriqueta

Classification	Sexual Predator.
Birth Information	Born in Spain.
Active Period	Uncertain. Known to be active until 1912.
Victim Information	Murdered at least six children. Each of her victims was sexually molested and tortured in satanic rituals.
Method	Ritualistic murders that included boiling the bodies of her victims.
Motive	The murders involved sexual encounters, violence, and cannibalism.
Disposition	Enriqueta was convicted of murder in 1912 and sentenced to death.

An obvious question that arises in the context of the rarity of the female sexual serial killer is one of significance. Were the crimes of Wuornos an anomaly, as many criminologists believe, or was she the first of a new category of lethal criminal with which future law enforcement personnel must grapple? Today, the answer to this question is unknown. However, a longer view of the crime of serial murder leads to a different answer. The crime of serial murder is evolving in lockstep with its perpetrator and the complexities of our society. The serial killer of today is more pernicious, diverse, and active than in the past. The crimes committed by this perpetrator are more complex today than in previous decades; and they are also more numerous. There is no reason to exclude the possibility of other female sexual serial killers in the coming decades. However, the history of serial murders committed by women indicates that sexual motivations for this crime are rare. Therefore, it is reasonable to assume that there will be other female sexual killers in the future, but it is also reasonable to assume that they will be few in number. Since any definitive answer obviously lies in the future, the best one can know of this most rare of murderers can be learned from the crimes of Aileen Wuornos.

SERIAL MURDER OR SELF-DEFENSE?

Aileen "Lee" Carol Wuornos clearly stands apart from all the other American female serial killers who have been profiled in this book. She has been persistently, and mistakenly, portrayed in the media and on television as the first American female serial killer. In reality, she was neither the first such murderer nor the most prolific. However, Wuornos could be the first female sexual serial killer who acted alone in committing her crimes, if one discounts the possibility that she acted in self-defense when she murdered seven men in Florida in 1989 and 1990 (see Table 4.2).

Wuornos has remained steadfast in her position that each of the murders that she committed was necessary in order to protect her own life. Because Wuornos worked as a prostitute for over twenty years, she had any number of violent and abusive encounters with men. Each man Wuornos murdered had become involved with her for sexual reasons, and in at least one instance, the victim was known to be an extremely violent individual with a history of rape. However, most of her victims did not have such a background, and there would have been little or no reason for Wuornos to suspect a violent outcome to the encounter. All of Wuornos's victims were shot with a .22-caliber handgun that she kept constantly in her possession, and each of her victims was robbed of personal effects, their automobile, or both. Each crime scene indicated that Wuornos was able to gain control over her victim and shoot him to death. In each instance, she had the presence of mind to rob her victim and make some attempt to secret the body. Given the method and pattern of her crimes, it is difficult to accept an argument of self-defense in each crime. However, Wuornos's background and long history of abusive encounters with men must have played a major role in her later crimes.

Table 4.2: Aileen Carol Wuornos

Classification	Sexual Predator.
Birth Information	Born in 1956, in Michigan, as Aileen Carol Pittman.
Active Period	1989 to 1990. Active from age thirty-three to age thirty-four.
Victim Information	Murdered at least seven men who had been involved with her for paid sex.
Method	Each victim was shot multiple times with a .22-caliber pistol and robbed of their personal effects, automobile, or both.
Motive	Sexual homicide connected to the crime of prostitution.
Disposition	Wuornos confessed to the murders but claimed self-defense. In 1992, she was tried and convicted of her crimes, receiving multiple death penalty sentences.

The evidence and testimony surrounding the crimes of Aileen Wuornos overwhelmingly point to a series of conscious and brutal attacks against her victims—attacks predicated on some form of sexual encounter for money. However, it seems clear that the murders were not motivated by a drive for bizarre sexual satisfaction, as is often the case with male serial killers. Rather, Wuornos lashed out against her victims in a rage that originated in decades of abusive and debilitating encounters with men that began in her early childhood.

A Childhood of Horrors

It is difficult to image a more horrendous childhood than the one experienced by Aileen Pittman Wuornos. Fathered by a psychopathic child molester and rejected by her mother as a toddler, Wuornos was raised by her grandparents and older sister. She was physically abused by her grandfather and subjected to even more physical and sexual abuse by older boys and young men throughout her childhood years. It was not until the age of thirteen that Wuornos learned the truth about her parents. (She had long been told that her grandparents were, in fact, her birth parents.) By the age of fifteen, Wuornos had been rejected by her grandfather, her grandmother was dead, and she was a ward of the court. In 1971, at that young age, she began a life of petty crime, prostitution, and drifting that eventually led to a year of serial killing in Florida. Nothing came easy for Wuornos, who struggled throughout her childhood with the kind of physical and sexual abuse that would be inconceivable to most individuals.

February 29, 1956. Aileen Pittman (Wuornos) is born to teenage parents, Diane Pratt and Leo Pittman, in Rochester, Michigan. Pratt and Pittman had separated several months prior to Wuornos's birth. Leo Pittman was a habitual sex offender who suffered from significant psychological problems. He would later be jailed for molesting a seven-year-old girl and eventually institutionalized in mental hospitals in Kansas and Michigan. Pittman played no role in Wuornos's childhood and later committed suicide while institutionalized for his crimes.

January 1960. Diane Pratt, Wuornos's birth mother,

claims that she can no longer tolerate the demands and incessant crying of her two young children, Aileen and her older brother, Keith. Pratt leaves her children in the care of her parents and Wuornos's older sister, Lauri.

March 18, 1960. Wuornos's maternal grandparents legally adopt Aileen and Keith. Wuornos would later describe her grandfather as an abusive alcoholic who beat his wife and the children regularly. According to Wuornos, she was thirteen years old before she was told the truth about her birth parents and her true relationship with Mr. and Mrs. Wuornos.

1962. At the age of six, Wuornos is severely burned while she and Keith set fires with lighter fluid. Although she recovers, she is permanently scarred on her face.

June 1970. Wuornos, who later claims to have been sexually active for over a year by 1970, becomes pregnant after being raped. According to Wuornos, her grandparents refuse to believe that she was raped and begin to incessantly refer to her as a "whore." She is only fourteen years old.

March 23, 1971. Wuornos gives birth to a son at a Detroit maternity home for unwed mothers. She immediately gives the infant up for adoption.

July 7, 1971. Grandmother Britta Wuornos dies, allegedly of liver cancer. However, Diane Pratt (Wuornos's birth mother) believes that her father actually murdered her mother. By the time of Britta Wuornos's death, Grandfather Wuornos had incessantly threatened to kill both Aileen and Keith if they were not removed from his home. Shortly after her grandmother's death, Wuornos and her brother become wards of the court.

1971. Wuornos begins a life of drifting and prostitution that will span nearly twenty years. She is completely alone, destitute, unskilled, virtually uneducated, and only fifteen years old. Her only close personal relationship is with her brother, Keith.

1974. Wuornos celebrates her eighteenth birthday. She would later state that she was raped at least five times before she turned eighteen.

May 1974. Using the alias Sandra Kretsch, Wuornos is jailed in Jefferson County, Colorado, for disorderly conduct, drunk driving, and firing a .22-caliber pistol from a moving vehicle. She skips town before her trial date.

July 13, 1976. Wuornos is arrested in Antrim County, Colorado, for assault and disturbing the peace after she throws a cue ball at the head of a bartender with whom she has been arguing. She is also served with outstanding arrest warrants from Troy, Michigan, for driving without a license and consuming alcohol in a motor vehicle. Her brother, Keith, helps her pay a $105 fine to clear the cases.

July 17, 1976. Keith Wuornos dies of throat cancer, devastating Aileen Wuornos. To her surprise, Wuornos receives $10,000 from the proceeds of his life insurance. Within two months, she has spent all the money and is again destitute and drifting.

Florida

When Aileen Wuornos arrived in Florida at the age of twenty, she was destitute, angry, and had a lengthy history of minor criminal activities. Although she had long demonstrated a propensity for violence against men, Wuornos was certainly not yet a killer. However, the bitter experiences of her childhood and adolescence continued into her adulthood in Florida. Wuornos was unable to sustain a meaningful relationship with any man. Although she did briefly marry while in Florida, the relationship was with a man who was some fifty years her senior, and it was brought to a sudden end when each accused the other of physical abuse. For well over a decade, Wuornos continued to earn a meager living as a prostitute. Eventually, she met another woman in a bar, with whom she began a relationship that would last throughout her year of serial killing.

September 1976. Wuornos hitches rides to Florida and sporadically continues to earn money through prostitution. Sometime during the next few years, she marries a seventy-year-old man; however, the marriage quickly fails when the two partners accuse each other of physical abuse. Wuornos then drifts through a series of short-lived heterosexual relationships. Two years after her divorce, she attempts to commit suicide by shooting herself in the stomach.

May 20, 1981. Wuornos is arrested in Edgewater, Florida, for the armed robbery of a convenience store. On May 4, 1982, she is sentenced to prison for the robbery; she is released thirteen months later, on June 30, 1983.

May 1, 1984. Wuornos is arrested for trying to pass forged checks at a bank in Key West, Florida.

November 30, 1985. Wuornos is named as a suspect in the theft of a pistol and ammunition in Pasco County, Florida.

December 11, 1985. Using the alias Lori Grody (the name of her aunt in Michigan), Wuornos is cited for driving a motor vehicle without a valid license.

January 4, 1986. Wuornos is arrested in Miami, Florida, under her own name and charged with automobile theft, resisting arrest, and obstruction of justice by giving false information to a law enforcement officer. A .38-caliber handgun and ammunition are impounded from her car at the time of her arrest.

June 2, 1986. Wuornos is detained as Lori Grody after a male companion accuses her of threatening him with a gun and demanding $200. At the time she is detained, law enforcement personnel discover a .22-caliber handgun and ammunition in Wuornos's automobile. Wuornos later denies that the incident ever took place.

June 9, 1986. While using the alias Susan Blahovec, Wuornos is ticketed for speeding in Jefferson County, Florida.

June 1986. Wuornos meets Tyria Moore in a South Daytona, Florida, bar. The women soon become homosexual lovers and begin a relationship that will last for the next four years. The couple is supported by Wuornos's prostitution.

July 4, 1987. Using the alias Susan Blahovec, Wuornos and Moore are detained for assaulting a man with a beer bottle.

December 18, 1987. Using the alias Susan Blahovec, Wuornos is cited for walking on the interstate and possessing a suspended driver's license.

January 11, 1987. Using the alias Susan Blahovec, Wuornos writes a threatening letter to a circuit court clerk regarding her citation of December 18, 1987.

February 9, 1988. Using the same alias, Wuornos writes a second threatening letter to the circuit court clerk.

March 12, 1988. Using the alias Cammie March Green, Wuornos accuses a Daytona Beach bus driver of assault, claiming that he pushed her off his bus after an intense verbal argument. Tyria Moore is listed as a witness to the incident.

July 23, 1988. A Daytona Beach landlord accuses Tyria Moore and Susan Blahovec (Wuornos) of vandalizing their apartment.

November 1988. Using the alias Susan Blahovec, Wuornos attempts to buy lottery tickets at a Zephyr Hills, Florida, supermarket and becomes embroiled in a heated argument with the store manager. For the next six days she makes incessant threatening telephone calls to supermarket employees.

A Year of Murder

Aileen Wuornos began her lethal career at the age of thirty-three. By this age, she was clearly a hardened and angry woman who had experienced two decades of debilitating abuse and horror, which in retrospect seemed to inevitably impel her to murder. However, her first victim was a man who proved to be a brutal rapist—a fact that lends credence to Wuornos's later claims of self-defense. Unfortunately, the background of this victim was never disclosed by law enforcement personnel, and in fact, was never brought to light until well after Wuornos had been convicted of murder and given the death penalty.

Wuornos has relentlessly claimed that she acted in self-defense in attacking each of her male victims. Although this argument was considered completely specious until 1992—the year in which the violent background of her first victim was made known—it now seems likely that Wuornos may have acted to protect her own life in at least one instance. Is it possible that Wuornos's first murder was an act of self-defense that led to a compulsion to attack future victims? Although it seems unreasonable to believe that each of her murders was an act of self-defense, one cannot discount the possibility that Wuornos's first victim may have threatened her life and prompted an ultimate act of retaliation. Given her long history of abusive relationships with men, could this incident have triggered Aileen Wuornos's short, but spectacular, career as a serial murderer?

November 30, 1989. Richard Mallory, a fifty-one-year-old electrician from Clearwater, Florida, is last seen alive by his coworkers. Those who know Mallory consider him a volatile and difficult character. He has been divorced five times, has a reputation as an unusually heavily drinker, is considered extremely paranoid, and exhibits an insatiable obsession with pornographic material. Despite his unsavory reputation with coworkers, Mallory had no criminal record, according to local police.

December 1, 1989. Mallory's 1977 Cadillac Coupe de Ville is found abandoned at Ormond Beach, in Volusia County, Florida. Nearby, law enforcement personnel discover his wallet (without any cash) and personal papers, along with several condoms and a half-empty bottle of vodka.

December 13, 1989. Mallory's partially decomposed body is found in the woods northwest of Daytona Beach by two men who are searching the area for junkyard scrap to sell. The body is naked from the waist up. Investigators on the scene determine that Mallory was shot three times in the chest with a .22-caliber pistol, thus becoming Wuornos's first known victim.

According to later testimony, Wuornos claimed that the encounter started as a routine proposition for sex. However, Mallory soon became physically abusive and began to attack the woman. As they struggled, Wuornos pulled the

.22-caliber pistol from her handbag and shot him a single time in the chest. Seeing that he was injured, she considered what to do next. Fearing that if the incident was discovered, she would be arrested for attempted murder, Wuornos fired two more shots, killing Mallory. She then wrapped the victim's body in a piece of carpet and drove off in his car, after relieving Mallory of the valuables in his possession.

May 19, 1990. Forty-three-year-old David Spears, a construction worker from Sarasota, Florida, leaves his workplace to visit his ex-wife in Orlando. However, he neither arrives in Orlando nor reports back to work.

May 25, 1990. David Spears's supervisor happens on his pickup truck on interstate I-95, south of Gainesville, Florida. However, law enforcement officials are unable to discover Spears's whereabouts.

May 31, 1990. Charles Carskaddon, a forty-year-old part-time rodeo worker from Missouri, is reported missing after he leaves Booneville, Missouri, to drive interstate I-95 to meet his fiancée in Tampa, Florida.

June 1, 1990. The nude body of a male is discovered in a wooded area forty miles north of Tampa, in Citrus County, Florida. The victim has been shot six times with a .22-caliber pistol. Law enforcement personnel recover a used condom near the body. Less than a week later, on June 7, 1990, the body of David Spears is identified from dental records; he is Wuornos's second known victim.

June 6, 1990. The naked body of Charles Carskaddon is discovered thirty miles south of the location of David Spears's corpse. He has been shot nine times with a .22-caliber weapon. The next day, Carskaddon's abandoned automobile is located. Missing from the vehicle is the victim's .45-caliber automatic pistol and his personal effects. Carskaddon is Wuornos's third victim.

June 7, 1990. Peter Siems, a sixty-five-year-old missionary and former merchant mariner, is last seen leaving his home in Jupiter, Florida, to visit relatives in Arkansas. On

June 22, 1990, a missing person report is filed with Florida law enforcement personnel. Siems would later be identified as Wuornos's fourth victim, although his body was not located.

July 4, 1990. Siems's automobile is involved in an accident in Orange Springs, Florida. Although the vehicle is quickly abandoned, witnesses describe the occupants as two women—one blonde (Wuornos) and one brunette (Moore)—and provide sufficient information to produce police-artist sketches. The occupants of the automobile were injured in the crash but fled. However, the driver left a bloody palm print behind, on the trunk of Siems's car.

July 30, 1990. Eugene Burress, a fifty-year-old sausage deliveryman, leaves his workplace in Ocala, Florida, to start his normal rounds of commercial deliveries. He never returns to work, and a missing person report is filed early the next morning after his abandoned delivery van is located.

August 4, 1990. Burress's body is discovered by picnickers in the Ocala National Forest. He has been shot twice with a .22-caliber pistol. Near the body, law enforcement personnel find some of his personal effects, credit cards, and an empty cash bag in which he carried the cash receipts from his deliveries. Burress is later identified as Wuornos's fifth victim.

September 11, 1990. Richard Humphreys, a fifty-six-year-old retired police chief from Alabama, fails to return home from his job as a child abuse claims investigator in Ocala, Florida. The next day, his body is found in an empty lot, shot seven times with a .22-caliber pistol. All Humphreys's pockets are empty and his personal effects are missing. A week later, on September 19, Humphreys's car is found abandoned and missing the license plates. A month later, on October 13, 1990, his badge and some personal effects are discovered in Lake County, Florida, seventy miles south of where his body had been found. Humphreys is Wuornos's sixth victim.

November 19, 1990. The body of Walter Antonio is discovered in the woods northwest of Cross City, Florida. Antonio was a sixty-year-old truck driver from Merrit Island, Florida, who also worked as a reserve police officer for Brevard County, Florida. The victim had been shot three times in the back and once in the head with a .22-caliber pistol. His body was found nude except for his socks. Antonio had been robbed of his police reserve badge, handcuffs, cash, and a gold ring. His car is located five days later in Brevard County. Antonio is Wuornos's seventh victim.

Arrest and Trial

By any standards, Aileen Wuornos was not a precise, methodical serial murderer, unlike the vast majority of female serial killers. Whatever their causes, these murders were opportunistic in nature and brutal in their commission. Although it is true that Wuornos made some efforts to hide the corpses of her victims, she repeatedly used their automobiles, flaunted their personal effects, and attempted to publicly pawn their assets. Wuornos made only feeble attempts to avoid apprehension and gave little or no thought to planning her crimes. Because these murders were spontaneous and her activities after each killing continued to be flagrant, it was only a matter of time before law enforcement personnel caught up with their prey. By the end of November 1990, the police were well aware that they had a pernicious serial killer operating in their area, and they were beginning to close in on Aileen Wuornos.

November 30, 1990. Law enforcement personnel release sketches of the suspect they believe has been involved in some or all of the seven related homicides that occurred over the past twelve months. Over the next month, police receive several tips regarding two women identified as Tyria Moore and "Lee" Blahovec.[1] Investigators soon discover the aliases used by Aileen Wuornos (Grody, Green, and Blahovec) and

---

I. "Lee" is the nickname used by Aileen Wuornos.

are able to link Moore and Wuornos to the accident involving Peter Siems's automobile.

December 6, 1990. Wuornos, using the alias Cammie Green, pawns items belonging to Richard Mallory in Daytona Beach, Florida; she later pawns articles belonging to Richard Spears in Ormond Beach.

January 9, 1991. Aileen Wuornos is apprehended at a bar known as the Last Resort in Ormond Beach, Florida. The next day, Tyria Moore is located at a relative's home in Pennsylvania and agrees to cooperate with law enforcement personnel. Subsequently, police arrange for Wuornos and Moore to talk on the telephone; during these conversations, Moore pleads with Wuornos to confess to the murders.

January 16, 1991. Wuornos confesses to six murders, claiming that each was an act of self-defense. She denies murdering Peter Siems, whose body was never located, as well as another male victim who had been discovered in 1990 but never identified. Explaining her crimes to police, Wuornos made this statement:

I shot them because, to me, it was like a self-defending thing. Because I felt if I didn't shoot them and didn't kill them, first of all . . . if they had survived, my ass would be getting in trouble for attempted murder, so I'm up shits creek on that one anyway; and if I didn't kill them, you know, of course, I mean I had to kill them . . . or its like retaliation, too. It's like, you bastards, you were going to hurt me.[1]

January 13, 1992. Wuornos's trial for the murder of Richard Mallory begins. During her testimony, Wuornos explains that her actions were necessary to defend herself after Mallory threatened her life. However, Wuornos's former lover, Tyria Moore (who was not a participant in any of the murders), testifies against her and discloses conversations that took place after the murder of Richard Mallory that prove harmful to the defense. These conversations indicate that Wuornos was probably not acting in self-defense when she shot Mallory.

On January 27, 1992, the case is handed over to the jury, which deliberates for less than two hours before finding Wuornos guilty of first-degree murder. After hearing the verdict, Wuornos shouts at the jurors: "I'm innocent! I was raped! I hope you get raped! Scumbags of America!"[2] On January 29, 1992, the same jury recommends the death penalty for Aileen Wuornos.

April 1992. Wuornos pleads guilty to the murders of Burress, Humphreys, and Spears.

May 7, 1992. Wuornos receives a second death penalty for the murders to which she confessed the preceding month.

November 10, 1992. A nationally televised program (*Dateline NBC*) airs information about the Wuornos murders and various law enforcement investigations surrounding the case. During the program it is disclosed that Richard Mallory had served ten years in prison for rape—a fact that had not been discovered by law enforcement personnel and that would have lent credence to Wuornos's statements at her trial, in which she claimed to have been acting in self-defense. However, no information about any of Wuornos's other victims has ever been brought forward to substantiate her longstanding claim that she acted only in self-defense in attacking her other victims.

Epilogue

Throughout 1992, Aileen Wuornos underwent a series of legal proceedings and was involved in one of the most sensational media events ever to surround such a case. However, to law enforcement officials, officers of the court, and the majority of the public, her guilt was clear and her motives obvious. Since that time, while awaiting her fate on death row, Wuornos has become a born-again Christian. Facing multiple death sentences and now (as of this writing) involved in the last of her mandatory appeals, Aileen Wuornos remains unshakable in her assertion that she acted in self-defense, despite the near-universal belief that she was America's first female sexual serial murderer.

NOTES

1. "Hunting Humans—Aileen Wuornos," in Kozel Multimedia, *Mind of a Killer,* CD-ROM (Chatsworth, CA: Cambrix, 1995), Section: "Hunting Humans."
2. Ibid.

5

REVENGE

> If you prick us do we not bleed? If you tickle us do we not
> laugh? If you poison us do we not die? And if you wrong us
> shall we not revenge?
>
> —William Shakespeare
> Shylock, in *The Merchant of Venice*, act 3, scene 1

The insatiable drive for revenge and retribution is arguably
one of the most familiar and pernicious of human emotions.
Unfortunately, homicides that are motivated by a compulsive
sense of retribution are commonplace in most Western societies. In general, however, they represent crimes that are
easily solved by law enforcement personnel. These felonies
are often straightforward because of the obvious relationship
that usually exists between the perpetrator and his or her victims or because the murderer's statements and actions made
the intent of the crime obvious. A murder that is motivated by
revenge is typically a crime of passion that is both blatant in
its intent and relatively unplanned in its commission. However, there are exceptions to this broad profile. Some revenge
murders are carefully planned and carried out with startling
calm and precision.

Serial murder motivated by revenge is a rare occurrence.
Because the crime of serial murder incorporates a discrete
cooling-off period between homicides, the familiar emotional characteristics of revenge do not easily translate into a
sustainable motivation for aggression over a long period of
time. In order for revenge to be the moving force behind a

crime of serial murder, the emotional intensity of the compulsion must be maintained throughout several cooling-off periods and simultaneously balanced with the organizational ability to plan multiple homicides with, at least, some care. In other words, the unique and overpowering sense of revenge needed to accomplish serial murder must be both deeply pathological and at least somewhat manageable in order for the perpetrator to succeed at her crime. To subordinate the impetus of such a pervasive emotional state to a planned homicidal attack against multiple victims implies an especially foreboding intensity to this emotion—a dark quality that is certainly foreign to most individuals.

Even though the victims of a person who is motivated by revenge may be numerous, the emotion itself is highly personalized. In response to this intense personalization, the revenge murderer will usually carry out her crimes alone. The victims of this perpetrator may be the individuals who are held responsible for an affront that is deeply experienced and unforgivable, or they may be incidental (but related) to the offending party. In some instances, the victims are not even personally connected with the affronting individual or entity but are viewed by the perpetrator as symbolic of an organization or institution that has been targeted for retribution. In cases of serial murder motivated by revenge, attacks against individuals who are incidental, but meaningful, to the primary target of retribution are common.

Although serial murder motivated by revenge is rare, there is an obvious consistency among the victims of this perpetrator. In carrying out her acts of retribution, the female serial revenge murderer overwhelmingly targets members of her own family. Sadly, these victims are often her own children. Even though this perpetrator may be obsessed with an unmitigated sense of revenge against her spouse (the most common scenario), she frequently strikes out against her own children in what she perceives to be the ultimate act of retribution. In other instances, the perpetrator may attack family members who have questioned her decisions or relationships; such an attack may include her spouse, who may be targeted in an attempt to fulfill a clandestine relationship with a lover.

The woman who commits serial murder because of a compulsion to exact retribution generally favors the same methods and weapons as the Black Widow, such as poison or suffocation. Since the targets of her wrath are usually family members, there are clear similarities between this perpetrator and the Black Widow. However, there are also significant differences between the Black Widow serial murderer and the revenge murderer. Whereas the Black Widow is a patient, precise, and cunning adversary, the perpetrator who is motivated by revenge is generally impassioned and often fails to plan her crimes with great care. Although she is sufficiently organized to commit multiple homicides over an extended period of time, this murderer is basically driven by an emotion that she is unable to control and unwilling to accept. For these reasons, the revenge murderer usually claims fewer victims and is active for a significantly shorter period of time than the typical Black Widow.

The average revenge murderer claims three or four victims over a period of two years or less; however, there are cases of revenge murders that have gone on for as long as five years before either the perpetrator was apprehended or the killings ceased. In general, the revenge serial murderer attacks her victims in a relatively short period of time and often lashes out after a triggering event that renews and deepens her pathological compulsion for retribution. For example, a mother who attacks and murders her children over a period of time may target each child only after a bitter argument with her spouse or some similar triggering event of rejection.

As is typical of most female serial killers, the revenge murderer usually claims her first victim while she is in her twenties, although there are some exceptions to this profile. The revenge murderer is generally not a cunning adversary for law enforcement personnel, and her crimes rarely escalate to the point of serial murder. However, when they do, it is often because the deaths that surround her have been dismissed as unfortunate but explainable—a situation reminiscent of that which often surrounds the lethal activities of the Black Widow. When she is finally apprehended, the revenge murderer will usually admit to her crimes in short order and generally demonstrates a genuine sense of remorse.

In the final analysis, this perpetrator is a victim of her own emotions and is often driven to murder by an overwhelming sense of rejection or abandonment. Unable to deal with such an emotional crisis yet still capable of planning and organizing her attack, the revenge murderer lashes out in a pathological attempt to regain some measure of control in a life that has become unbearably painful and chaotic.

An early twentieth century case of revenge serial murder was that of Martha Hasel Wise, who came to be known in the press as the *Borgia of America* (see Table 5.1). Born in Ohio, in 1885, Wise was widowed by the age of thirty-five and left penniless. However, by 1924, at the age of thirty-nine, Wise had met Walter Johns, a man considerably younger than she, with whom she had fallen deeply in love. Johns was quick to reciprocate the emotion and asked Wise to marry him as soon as possible.

When Wise announced her intention to marry Johns, her family condemned the plan and harshly criticized her romantic involvement with such a young man. Regardless of her pleading, Wise's family was adamant that she should immediately break off the engagement. Frustrated and angered, Wise devised a plan of revenge to eliminate her entire family and set herself free to marry Walter Johns.

On January 1, 1925, Wise initiated her plan to revenge and successfully poisoned her aging mother with arsenic. To her short-lived satisfaction, the death of the old woman was attributed to natural causes and aroused no suspicion among the surviving family members. Convinced that she had found a way to eliminate all opposition to her marriage, Wise went on to poison other members of her family. A month after murdering her mother, Martha Wise successfully poisoned her aunt and uncle in the same manner. However, her attempts at murdering several other members of the family failed.

After recovering from their illnesses, the surviving family members became convinced that Wise had attempted to murder them and expressed their suspicions to the local authorities. When Wise was questioned about the recent illnesses and deaths in her family, she quickly confessed to murdering her mother, aunt, and uncle. However, she was not prepared to take full responsibility for her actions, telling police: "It was the devil who told me to do it. He came to me while I was in the kitchen baking bread. He came to me while I was working in the fields. He followed me everywhere."[1] Wise then went on to confess to a long list of other felonies, which included arson and a number of burglaries.

Table 5.1: Martha Hasel Wise

Classification	Revenge.
Birth Information	Born in 1885, in Ohio. Wise would later become known as the *Borgia of America* because of her crimes.
Active Period	1925. Active at the age of forty.
Victim Information	Murdered three members of her own family, including her mother, aunt, and uncle. Attempted to murder other family members.
Method	Poison (arsenic).
Motive	Revenge for the opposition to her marriage by family members.
Disposition	Wise confessed to three murders and a variety of other felonies. She was tried, found guilty, and sentenced to life imprisonment. Wise subsequently died of natural causes while in custody.

The year after she murdered three members of her family, Wise was brought to trial on a variety of charges and pled insanity as a defense. Despite supporting testimony that seemed to lend credence to her questionable state of mind, the jury found the defendant guilty of first-degree murder. Wise was sentenced to life imprisonment for her crimes and eventually died of natural causes while in custody.

A decade before Martha Wise murdered three members of her family, a woman in Texas committed a similar series of crimes. However, the victims of Ellen Etheridge's revenge were all children (see Table 5.2).

Table 5.2: Ellen Etheridge

Classification	Revenge.
Birth Information	Born in Texas.
Active Period	1913.
Victim Information	Murdered four of her eight stepchildren.
Method	Poison.
Motive	Dissatisfied with her marriage and jealous of the children's relationship with her husband, Etheridge struck out against her stepchildren.
Disposition	Etheridge confessed to the murders and was sentenced to life in prison.

In 1912, Ellen married J. D. Etheridge and inherited an instant family. Etheridge was a wealthy Texas entrepreneur who had recently lost his wife and had been left with sole responsibility for their eight young children. J. D. Etheridge was obvious in his devotion to his children—far too obvious for Ellen Etheridge to ignore. After only a year of marriage, Ellen had become incurably jealous of the relationship between her husband and her stepchildren and decided that her rivals must be eliminated.

In June 1913, Etheridge poisoned two of her stepchildren

with arsenic and succeeded in convincing her grieving husband (and local authorities) that the deaths were natural. In October of that same year, she poisoned two more of the children, again arguing for natural causes. However, few people believed in the possibility of such a pair of coincidental tragedies occurring within a year and autopsies were ordered. The authorities soon learned that the latest victims had been administered a lethal dose of arsenic. When the police confronted Ellen Etheridge with the evidence, she quickly confessed to all four murders. Etheridge was subsequently sentenced to life imprisonment and died while in custody.

In recent years, a similar case of revenge serial murder against children claimed ongoing headlines in the state of Georgia. In 1989, it was discovered that Martha Ann Johnson, a local woman, had murdered four of her own children over a five-year period and had managed to avoid apprehension for over a decade (see Table 5.3).

Martha Ann Johnson was born in 1955, in Georgia. By the age of twenty-five, she had given birth to four children by three different husbands: Jennyann Wright, born in 1971; James William Taylor, born in 1975; Earl Wayne Bowen, born in 1979; and Tibitha Janel Bowen, born in 1980.

Johnson's third marriage, to Earl Bowen, was stormy and bitter from the first. Although Bowen was a caring provider to all four children, the couple argued constantly and often fiercely. By 1977, Johnson and Bowen had been married for over a year and the relationship was clearly dysfunctional. Their marriage was punctuated by repetitive cycles of arguments that were usually followed by Bowen leaving the family home to regain his calm. On several occasions, the couple separated for days at a time; each time, however, they would ultimately make up and vow to give the relationship another chance.

On September 25, 1977, after a particularly vicious argument, Johnson brought two-year-old James Taylor to the Clayton County hospital, claiming that she had been unable to awaken him early that morning. Sadly, by the time Taylor arrived at the hospital, he was already dead. Taylor's attending physicians attributed the boy's death to sudden infant death syndrome (SIDS) and no investigation was ordered. The tragedy of the child's death brought Johnson and Bowen back together—but only for a time.

Table 5.3: Martha Ann Johnson

Classification	Revenge.
Birth Information	Born in 1955, in Georgia.
Active Period	1977 to 1982. Active from age twenty-two to age twenty-seven.
Victim Information	Murdered four of her children.
Method	Suffocation. Johnson, who weighed about 250 pounds, would roll her weight onto the children while they slept.
Motive	Revenge. Each murder followed an argument with her husband in which he would leave the family home to "cool off."
Disposition	Johnson went to trial in 1990 and was convicted of multiple counts of homicide. Her sentence was death.

In 1980, after Johnson and Bowen had again temporarily separated because of their continuing disagreements, Johnson brought Tibitha Bowen to the same hospital and told the same horrifying story. Once again, physicians determined that the three-month-old infant had died of SIDS, and no autopsy was performed. The following year, on February 15, 1981, two-year-old Earl Wayne Bowen was pronounced dead from what physicians thought had been an inexplicable seizure. Since Earl's death was also deemed to be from natural causes, no further investigation was considered necessary.

Incredibly, the following year, on February 21, 1982, eleven-year-old Jennyann Wright also died under mysterious circumstances. As in the other three tragedies, Johnson claimed that her latest victim had simply stopped breathing and could not be awakened. However, the police were suspicious of the circumstances surrounding the death of the child and ordered an autopsy. The medical examination revealed that the child had probably died of asphyxia and labeled the death suspicious. Despite these findings, no inquest was held and local prosecutors declined to file any charges against Martha Johnson.

The murders of Johnson's children went unacknowledged for nearly seven more years until a reporter at the *Atlanta Journal-Constitution* launched an investigation in December 1988. This public investigation prompted officials to reexamine the four children's deaths and revive the medical examiner's report on the demise of Jennyann Wright. Responding to considerable public pressure, officials were eventually able to reconstruct enough evidence to issue a murder warrant for Martha Johnson, based largely on the autopsy of Jennyann Wright in 1982.

On July 3, 1989, Johnson was arrested for murder and held without bail. She quickly confessed to murdering Jennyann Wright and James Taylor by rolling her body onto the small children while they slept. However, she denied any responsibility for the deaths of her other two children. Johnson made it clear that the murders were an act of revenge committed to punish her husband after the couple had argued.

Johnson went to trial on April 30, 1990, for multiple counts of murder, having retracted her confession of a year earlier. However, a condemning piece of evidence presented at her trial was a videotape of the original confession, which could not be ignored by the jury. In the end, Johnson's trial was a short one that clearly evidenced her guilt. By May 5, 1990, Martha Johnson has been found guilty and sentenced to death for the murder of her children.

NOTE

1. "Hunting Humans—Martha Hasel Wise," in Kozel Multimedia, *Mind of a Killer,* CD-ROM (Chatsworth, CA: Cambrix, 1995), Section: "Hunting Humans."

6

FOR PROFIT OR CRIME

> Crimes of which a people is ashamed constitute its real history. The same is true of man.
>
> —Jean Genet
> Notes for *The Screens*, (1961; tr. 1973)

In order to be classified in the Profit or Crime category, a serial murderer must exhibit two characteristics that differentiate her crimes from that of a Black Widow: (1) she must clearly murder for profit, and (2) she must focus her lethal efforts on individuals who are not members of her family. In other words, to meet the criteria for this classification, the serial murderer must be in the business of killing for profit and willing to seek out nonfamily members as victims in order to accomplish her crimes. Finally, she must be willing to undertake her crimes alone and not have been brought into a criminal career by a partner. Therefore, the following definition applies to the Profit or Crime category of serial killer: *a woman who systemically murders individuals in the course of other criminal activities, or for profit, but who is not a member of a team of killers.*

In many respects, the woman who kills for profit and the Black Widow are similar in their perpetration of serial murder; however, there are also some interesting differences in how these two categories of criminal pursue their felonies. Whereas the Black Widow will focus her lethal activities on family members as primary targets, the Profit or Crime killer consciously establishes herself in the business of murdering for profit and will actively pursue victims who may, at first, be unknown to her. Although both categories of killer will strike against nonfamily members, the Black Widow will generally look first (or even exclusively) to family members, whereas the Profit or Crime killer will seek her victims outside the family structure. Regardless of how these two serial murderers select their victims, they share many fundamental behavioral characteristics. Like the Black Widow, the Profit or Crime killer is typically organized, intelligent, resourceful, and careful in carrying out her crimes; consequently, she is slow to be suspected of foul play and will often prove to be a difficult adversary for law enforcement personnel.

Also like the Black Widow, the Profit or Crime killer can be a patient predator whose crimes demonstrate maturity and forethought. She is usually precise in planning her activities and gives serious attention to avoiding apprehension. It is important to remember that the Profit or Crime killer views her criminal activities as akin to a career and is strongly motivated by financial gain. Therefore, she is able to structure her crimes to be as covert as possible and able to organize all the details necessary to avoid drawing attention to herself. As

Figure 6.1: Victims for Profit or Crime

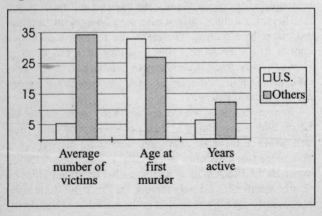

one would expect, the woman who murders for profit is mature—usually over twenty-five years of age when she begins her lethal career. If she is an American, the perpetrator may be over thirty years of age before she commits her first murder (see Figure 6.1).

Profit or Crime killers tend to target two types of victims: (1) those with whom they have developed a relationship as a caretaker or a trusted friend, and (2) those who can be easily manipulated or controlled and who represent the opportunity for profit. In the first instance, the typical relationship may be that of a housekeeper or caretaker for the elderly or infirm. Unlike the Angel of Death, who will pursue a murderous role that is based on her medical training and responsibilities, the Profit or Crime killer who acts as caretaker will fill the role of a trusted companion or support person outside the arena of medicine. The second category of victims—those who are subject to control or manipulation by the perpetrator—are targeted because they represent an opportunity for profit that derives from a third party. These unfortunate victims are pawns in a crime of profit that takes the form of a transaction between the Profit or Crime killer and an individual who seeks her services for some form of compensation. Examples of these victims are spouses who are murdered by a Profit or Crime killer at the request of their mates for a fee or the murder of infants who were entrusted to the Profit or Crime killer for services such as adoption.

It is difficult to be certain of the number of victims who are claimed by the typical Profit or Crime killer. The available statistics regarding non-American perpetrators of this crime are terribly skewed by selective and sensationalized reporting in the United States. However, the data available for American Profit or Crime killers is generally more reliable and indicates that typically, the killer claims between five and ten known victims during her active period. However, as in the case of Angel of Death killers, the actual number of victims of this classification of perpetrator is likely to be much greater. Since the victims of the Profit or Crime killer may not leave behind family members who can be easily traced and since this murderer tends to select individuals who are unlikely to be missed by friends, it is often extremely difficult to quantify the killer's criminal activities with any certainty. This perpetrator specializes in murdering for profit, so one can be sure she will pursue the course of her crimes with a great deal of attention to secrecy and a strong desire to avoid apprehension.

The Profit or Crime killer will usually be active between five and ten years before she is apprehended or her crimes cease for other reasons. The length of her criminal career is generally shorter than that of the Black Widow because she typically murders more frequently and may be somewhat more willing to kill in a risky manner. However, the Profit or Crime killer typically maintains a criminal career longer than that of the average female serial killer and is second only to that of the Black Widow (in cases where sanity is not an issue). Once again, this protracted period of activity is evidence of the planning and attention to detail that is characteristic of the Profit or Crime killer. It is also evidence of her organized psychological state.

The Profit or Crime killer is perhaps the most dispassionate and callous of the various categories of female serial murderer. Although the crimes of the Angel of Death killer are especially egregious because they focus on victims who are typically defenseless, the Profit or Crime killer takes her crimes to an even higher level of horror by placing a monetary value on the life of her victims. Beyond this comparison, the Angel of Death often suffers from a psychological disorder that can be linked to her activities, whereas the Profit or Crime killer is typically quite sane, highly manipulative, and extremely calculating in her activities.

Like many female serial murderers who act alone, the Profit or Crime killer prefers poison as a weapon. However, unlike the Angel of Death, who strongly favors a single method of execution (the lethal injection), the Profit or Crime killer will sometimes use a variety of methods to accomplish her mission. Nonetheless, the overwhelmingly favored weapon of this perpetrator is poison that is introduced into the food or drink of her victims (see Figure 6.2).

Because the Profit or Crime killer is precise, dispassionate, and careful, she is often able to murder for several years before she is apprehended. However, her Achilles' heel is the same characteristic that motivates her to murder in the first place—greed. The Profit or Crime killer derives her income from murder and is often driven to obtain profit far beyond her needs. Because of this compulsion for profit—and because she may become increasingly brash after several successful murders—this perpetrator will eventually take risks that would be unthinkable to the Black Widow. Over time, the Profit or Crime killer may become less careful in identifying and attacking her victims—behavior that can lead to suspicion about her activities and the number of unexplained disappearances or deaths of individuals near her. Since this perpetrator is generally not a mobile murderer, she will often attack in a localized area and may eventually draw attention to herself simply because of the number of victims that she claims. When she is eventually apprehended, the Profit or Crime killer will remain a difficult adversary for

Figure 6.2: Weapons and Methods—Profit or Crime

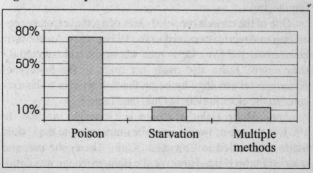

law enforcement personnel because she will be reticent to admit her crimes and usually unwilling to cooperate in any investigation.

The Profit or Crime killer is in the business of murder for an ancient and straightforward reason—to enhance her income. She is also organized, mature, meticulous, and manipulative. Although her numbers are not great among the ranks of female serial murderers, the Profit or Crime killer is a fearsome predator because of her intense motivation and highly dispassionate approach to murder. What will never be known is the actual number of Profit or Crime killers who have managed to avoid detection of their crimes because they were eventually able to overcome their compulsion for endless profit and cease their murderous behavior.

LETHAL CARETAKERS

It is difficult to imagine a more callous murderer than the lethal caretaker who claims her victims in the name of profit. This serial killer deliberately seeks out individuals who are often completely dependent on her for care and support. In her morbid obsession with profit, she will carefully plan her crimes and dispassionately slay individuals who have come to trust her completely. In her actions, the lethal caretaker who murders for profit is a close cousin to the Black Widow, except that she primarily targets individuals outside her family circle.

One of the earliest recorded cases of a lethal caretaker operating in America occurred in the 1930s, when Anna Marie Hahn murdered five elderly men whom she had targeted for their assets. Hahn also made her mark in the history of American criminology by being the first woman to be executed in the electric chair in Ohio (see Table 6.1).

Anna Marie Hahn was born in Germany, in 1906. In 1927, at the age of twenty-one, she immigrated to the United States and settled in Cincinnati, Ohio. There, she met and married Philip Hahn. However, the Hahn marriage was childless and unhappy; it ended in divorce after Philip Hahn expressed fear that his wife had tried to poison him in an effort to collect his assets.

Table 6.1: Anna Marie Hahn

Classification	Profit or Crime.
Birth Information	Born in 1906, in Germany. Immigrated to the United States at the age of twenty-one.
Active Period	1932 to 1937. Active from age twenty-six to age thirty-one.
Victim Information	Murdered five elderly men. Attempted to murder another elderly man, who survived. Each of the victims had employed her as a live-in attendant.
Method	Poison. Each victim was administered a different poison.
Motive	Murdered her victims for life insurance proceeds and their assets.
Disposition	Hahn was arrested in 1937 and subsequently found guilty of her crimes. She was executed in 1938.

After the collapse of her marriage, Anna Hahn struck on a scheme of lethal profit that would eventually result in her execution. Catering to the large German population in the Cincinnati area, Hahn began to offer her services to elderly men as a live-in attendant. Over the next five years, she would claim five victims with her brutal scheme of murder for profit.

Hahn officially began her killing career on May 6, 1932, when Ernest Koch, a man in his seventies who had come to rely on his attendant's care, suddenly died without explanation. Amazed at how easy it had been to dispatch her charge and pocket his assets, Hahn went on to find other victims. Over the next few years, Hahn murdered another four elderly men:

Albert Parker, Jacob Wagner, George Gsellman, and George Obendoerfer. In each case, the lethal and greedy caretaker would bilk her victims of their assets in a variety of ingenious ways, but the profits were never sufficient to accommodate her growing desires. Hahn was also creative in the manner in which she dispatched her elderly charges, using a different poison for each victim.

Anna Hahn's killing career came to an end with the death of George Obendoerfer in 1937, when the serial murderer was discovered diverting money from her victim's bank account and arrested on a charge of fraud. While investigating her activities, suspicious police also ordered an autopsy on Obendoerfer's body. The results of the medical examination disclosed that the old man had died from arsenic poisoning. The truth about Obendoerfer's death prompted an investigation into the demise of Hahn's previous employers, including the exhumation of their remains. Within a few months of her arrest, Anna Hahn was charged with five counts of homicide.

At her trial, Hahn claimed that she had murdered her employers as an act of mercy to prevent them from further suffering. However, the facts soon made it clear that, before their deaths, the men she had murdered were typically in good health. At the end of her trial, Anna Hahn was found guilty on all counts and sentenced to death. On June 20, 1938, she became the first woman in Ohio's history to die in the electric chair.

More deadly than Anna Marie Hahn was Antoinette Scieri, who murdered at least twelve elderly patients for whom she provided private nursing services in the 1920s, in France. Scieri's method of operation was nearly identical to that of Hahn and most other lethal caretakers: after gaining the trust of her victims, she would dispatch them with poison (see Table 6.2).

Scieri was born in Italy before the turn of the century and emigrated to France as a young woman. By 1915, she had already launched a life of crime that included forgery, fraud, and theft, and that would eventually culminate in serial murder. The same year, she was arrested and imprisoned for her first felony after she defrauded a wounded soldier of his cash.

At the end of World War I, Scieri married, divorced, remarried, and had a number of different affairs, resulting in the birth of two children by different fathers. She also developed a reputation as an aggressive and violent woman who was frequently thrown in jail for assaulting her neighbors. By 1920, in an effort to find new opportunities for her life of crime, Scieri moved to a small French village and established herself as a live-in nurse in search of elderly clients.

Table 6.2: Antoinette Scieri

Classification	Profit or Crime.
Birth Information	Born in Italy. Emigrated to France while still a child.
Active Period	1924 to 1926.
Victim Information	Convicted of murdering twelve individuals; probably responsible for many more.
Method	Poison (various).
Motive	Victims were murdered for their assets.
Disposition	Scieri confessed to a dozen murders in 1926 and went to trial. She was convicted on all counts and sentenced to death. Her death sentence was later commuted to life imprisonment, and Scieri eventually died of natural causes while in custody.

For the next two years, Scieri carried on her lethal trade by offering her services to a variety of aging individuals in and around the village of St. Gilles. Among her long list of victims was her last husband, Joseph Rossignol, and an uncertain number of elderly male and female patients. Scieri's favorite method of dispatching her prey was to prepare meals generously laced with a variety of poisons. She would then steal whatever assets she could find and move on to the next victim.

Scieri's felonious career was brought to a sudden end in 1926, when the spouse of her last victim became suspicious of the nurse's behavior. Local police were dispatched to investigate the matter and were stunned when the lethal caretaker voluntarily confessed to more than a dozen murders over the previous two years. Scieri was bound over for trial and quickly found guilty on all counts. On April 27, 1926, she was condemned to death for her crimes. In pronouncing sentence, the presiding judge said this about the condemned:

You have been called a monster, but that expression is not strong enough. You are debauched. You are possessed of all the vices. You are also a drunkard, vicious, and a hypocrite. You have no shame. I do not believe judicial history contains the records of many criminals of your type.[1]

However, despite the judge's anger and his sentence of death, Antoinette Scieri managed to avoid the gallows. Her sentence was commuted to life imprisonment and she subsequently died of natural causes while in custody.

Although the crimes of Anna Marie Hahn and Antoinette Scieri were both brutal and sensational, the most infamous lethal caretaker in history claimed her victims in Sacramento, California, a mere decade ago. Her name was Dorothea Puente, and she was made famous by the unprecedented press and media coverage that surrounded her gruesome activities and subsequent trial.

The Victorian on F Street

Richard Ordorica had worked for eight hard years as a graveyard-shift janitor before saving enough cash for a down payment on an aging Victorian house located at 1426 F Street in Sacramento, California. His dream was to provide a more stable financial future for his family by renting out the home and moving his wife and children to the less crowded suburbs of Sacramento. In 1986, Ordorica was convinced that he had found the perfect tenant for his Victorian—Dorothea Puente, a fifty-seven-year-old single woman with a pleasant smile, a great gift of gab, and an apparently gentle disposition.[2] Ordorica was immediately impressed with Puente and more than happy to let her take charge of the premises. However, within two years, Ordorica and the rest of the nation would harbor a much different view of Dorothea Puente when she was accused of defrauding and brutally murdering at least nine of her lodgers in the Victorian on F Street (see Table 6.3).

Table 6.3: Dorothea Montalvo Puente

Classification	Profit or Crime.
Birth Information	Born in 1929.
Active Period	1986 to 1988. Active from age fifty-seven to age fifty-nine.
Victim Information	Murdered at least nine individuals for whom she was caretaker. Her number of victims may have been as high as twenty-five.
Method	Various (mostly poison).
Motive	The victims were murdered for the proceeds of their Social Security checks and other assets.
Disposition	Puente went to trial in 1993, charged with multiple counts of murder, and was found guilty. She was sentenced to life imprisonment without the possibility of parole.

Puente was born in Mexico in 1929, to an early life of poverty and abandonment. She was given up to an orphanage while still an infant and had no family to whom she could turn. Over the next forty years, Puente married four times but had only a single child—a daughter whom she gave up for

adoption at birth. In 1982, at the age of fifty-three, Puente
was arrested, charged, and convicted of robbery after she victimized a variety of elderly men whom she met in local bars
or who were introduced to her by friends. Puente's method of
attack was to drug her victims and then rob them of their cash
and valuables. Among her victims were two men over the age
of eighty whom she drugged and then defrauded of all their
assets. For her crimes, Puente spent the next two and a half
years in prison, finally winning her freedom in 1985. Several
months after her release from prison, Puente met Richard Ordorica and rented his home on F Street. Clearly, her years in
prison had not changed Puente's most favored way of generating income.

In 1986, Puente convinced a Sacramento, California, social worker that she could care for a number of elderly and
frail persons living on fixed incomes by boarding them at her
F Street home. She agreed to provide housing and meals,
along with any reasonable support her tenants might require,
at rents that would be acceptable to the social worker and her
clients. The offer appealed to the social worker, who was
hard-pressed to find reasonably priced accommodations for
her many clients, and Puente was soon receiving referrals for
new tenants. Over the next two years, Puente was sent at least
nineteen social service clients to be housed and provided
with care. Sadly, many of these needy individuals would
never be heard from again.

By the summer of 1988, after two years of referring
clients, the social worker became concerned about the unusual number of Puente's boarders who had suddenly disappeared. To worsen matters, the neighbors on F Street had
complained to law enforcement and local health department
officials about the persistent stench from Puente's property
and the constant presence of vermin and flies in the area. By
November of that year, a missing person report had been filed
for one of Puente's tenants, Bert Montoya, and police had visited the landlady to investigate the matter. Puente explained

that Montoya had suddenly returned to his native Mexico without any explanation to her or the other residents at F Street. At first, the police were willing to accept Puente's explanation; however, a few days later, the social worker also contacted them to report that another of the landlady's residents had unexpectedly disappeared. The two coincidental reports to the police, combined with the continuing complaints of neighbors about the stench from Puente's backyard, were enough to arouse a good deal of suspicion. Within a few days, law enforcement officials went once again to the F Street residence to try to learn the truth about a growing number of inexplicable disappearances.

On November 11, 1988, investigating officers located a corpse buried in the backyard of the old Victorian. The next day, two more bodies were uncovered and the police were now prepared to arrest Puente on charges of murder. However, she escaped that afternoon and fled to the Los Angeles area. Despite her absence, and with an arrest warrant outstanding, investigators continued to dig around the Puente premises. By November 14, 1988, they had discovered a total of seven bodies. Law enforcement officials would later estimate that as many as twenty-five of Puente's tenants had been reported missing over the two year period from 1986 to 1988. In each case, Puente had apparently attacked her victims in order to divert their Social Security payments or other personal income to her own uses.

On November 17, 1988, Dorothea Puente was located in Los Angeles and arrested after being recognized by a man she had met in a local bar. Apparently, Puente had created a good deal of suspicion in the gentleman's mind when she persistently inquired about his Social Security income. When she boldly offered to immediately move into the gentleman's house and prepare a special Thanksgiving dinner, he notified the police and she was quickly arrested.

By the following month, law enforcement officials had positively identified four of Puente's victims from their remains; however, the identification of many of the other victims was a difficult and slow process. In addition to the bodies buried in the backyard, police also identified a corpse that had been stuffed into a wooden box and dumped near the Sacramento River. In the end, Puente was charged with nine counts of murder, although even at that time, law enforcement officials believed that the actual number of Puente's victims may have exceeded a dozen. In June 1990, at the age of sixty-one, Dorothea Puente was arraigned on multiple murder charges.

Two years later, in November 1992, Puente's trial finally began after incessant legal wrangling and a change of venue to Monterey, California. The prosecution portrayed Puente as an evil-hearted woman bent on obtaining profit at the ultimate expense of her elderly, and often frail, tenants. The defense countered by developing an image of Puente as kind, caring, and misunderstood, which her gentle physical appearance seemed to bolster. The complex questions of how Puente managed to murder her victims and how many she had attacked were never satisfactorily answered. Much of the evidence against the aging woman was circumstantial yet clearly implicated her in the murders. On a victim-by-victim basis, it was difficult to prove Puente's role in the murders; overall, however, the prosecution's case was a strong one.

The Puente trial was a marathon affair that went on for over six months before the issue was finally handed to the jury. On July 16, 1993, the jury began deliberations; however, it did not reach a verdict quickly or easily. It was not until August 27, 1993, that the jury found Puente guilty of three counts of murder, dismissing all other capital charges for lack of evidence. A month later, on September 21, 1993, the penalty phase of the trial to determine Dorothea Puente's fate began. Once again, a variety of delays marked the proceedings, including juror illness and an eventual deadlock on the issue of whether Puente should be given life imprisonment or condemned to death. Finally, on October 14, 1993, at the age of sixty-four, Puente was sentenced to life imprisonment without the possibility of parole.

It will never be known how many individuals fell victim to Dorothea Puente's insatiable greed and remorseless methods. It is possible that as many as two dozen elderly citizens were victimized by her brutal scheme. However, for the jury that was charged with the ultimate determination of guilt, it was a difficult task to be sure of her complicity beyond a reasonable doubt. Ultimately, it proved impossible for the jury to agree upon her punishment. With the deadlock that ensued in the penalty phase of the trial, Puente's fate was placed in the hands of the superior court judge who heard the case and, by law, his only option was the sentence that Dorothea Puente ultimately received.

THE BUSINESS OF MURDER

Although rare, the female serial killer will occasionally escalate her profit-motivated crimes into a business operation that relies on homicide to generate income. When this bizarre form of serial murder occurs, it is typically undertaken with one or more partners who cooperate in a lengthy series of serial killings that are committed in a systematic manner. Because of the highly organized methods used by this type of serial killer, many lethal crimes may occur before law enforcement officials become involved in the case.

Those who commit serial murder as a business share some of the qualities of a Team Killer because of the common goals and intimacy of the partners. However, there are at least two significant differences between the Team Killer and the Profit or Crime killer who has elected to transform her crimes into a business venture. Whereas the Team Killer rarely commits murder for purely monetary reasons, the serial killer who murders as a business has profit as a singular motivation for her crimes. Moreover, the members of a killing team are often disorganized in committing their crimes, whereas the business serial murderer is an especially well-organized perpetrator.

The first recognized case of a female serial killer who had organized her efforts into a structured business was that of a Russian, the notorious Madame Popova. Unfortunately, little is known about this infamous serial murderer because her crimes took place shortly after the turn of the century and occurred in a society that until recently has remained highly cloistered (see Table 6.4).

Table 6.4: Madame Popova

Classification	Profit or Crime.
Birth Information	Born in the 1800s, in Russia.
Active Period	1879 to 1909.
Victim Information	Popova confessed to the murder of over 300 men.
Method	Poison.
Motive	Popova ran a business that would liberate married women from their cruel husbands for a modest fee.
Disposition	Arrested in 1909, Popova confessed to the incredible number of murders. She was executed by firing squad.

What is known about Madame Popova is that she operated an incredibly lethal serial-killing business in Czarist Russia between 1880 and 1909. According to her own confession, Popova was responsible for the murder of approximately 300 men in a surprisingly efficient operation that specialized in eliminating unwanted husbands for a profit.

Popova's business was allegedly a bustling and profitable one, to which distressed Russian wives could turn to eliminate a brutish or undesirable spouse with complete confidentiality. For a relatively small sum, Popova would arrange to have the victim poisoned, either by her own hand or with the help of an accomplice.

In 1909, law enforcement officers discovered Popova's serial-killing business after receiving a tip from one of Popova's clients who had experienced an unexpected attack of remorse. When the police interrogated Popova, she eventually confessed to the murder of some 300 husbands over a thirty-year period. However, she apparently refused to disclose the names of any of her accomplices. Popova's punishment from the Czarist courts for three decades of serial murder was her own death before a firing squad.

Twenty years after the execution of Madame Popova, another serial-killing business was in full operation near the city of Halifax, Nova Scotia. However, rather than attacking unwanted husbands for profit, this business, which was run by Lila Gladys Young and her husband, William, specialized in the murder of infants (see Table 6.5).

In 1928, Lila Gladys Young and her husband, William, opened the Ideal Maternity Home in the town of Chester, Nova Scotia, near Halifax. Young and her husband were both devoted Seventh Day Adventists who had been raised by strict and religious parents. Married in 1925, William Young was a chiropractor, while Lila claimed to be an experienced midwife. Together, they established the Ideal Maternity Home to cater to unwed mothers and provide adoption services for their clients.

The Youngs advertised their confidential services in newspapers throughout the eastern seaboard and were soon operating a busy and highly profitable business. In addition to the maternity operation that was the heart of their business, the Youngs offered a host of other confidential services, which included infant care and adoption arrangements—all for a variety of fees that could range from a few hundred to several thousand dollars. Unfortunately, with the growth of their business, the Youngs also discovered that many more babies were born at the Ideal Maternity Home than could be accommodated by adoption. In order to maintain their profit margin and avoid the cost of caring for infants who could not be quickly adopted, the Youngs murdered an undetermined number of babies by starvation and buried their remains in an open field that was owned by a relative.

Table 6.5: Lila Gladys Young

Classification	Profit or Crime.
Birth Information	Born in 1899, in Nova Scotia.
Active Period	1927 to 1946. Active from age twenty-eight to age forty-seven.
Victim Information	Young and her husband ran a maternity home that proved to be a multimillion-dollar business. They also engaged in a number of illegalities related to child-care and adoption services. It is believed that their neglect and maltreatment of newborns may have resulted in the deliberate death of one hundred or more infants.
Method	Neglect and mistreatment of infants; intentional starvation of some infants.
Motive	Profit generated from a "baby-farming" operation.
Disposition	Young became entangled in persistent legal difficulties throughout the 1940s. Finally bankrupt, she died of leukemia in 1967, over twenty years after her infamous maternity home had been closed.

The Ideal Maternity Home operated continuously from 1928 to 1946, generating a tremendous income for its owners. However, it was often investigated by the authorities and the Youngs became increasingly involved in a number of legal difficulties that arose because of the appalling conditions at the home. Despite the steadily worsening situation over the home's many years of operation, the Youngs found their services in continuous demand by hundreds of unwed, teenage mothers from Canada and the United States.

Investigations into the baby farming operation were especially intense during the mid-1940s. These probes resulted in testimony by one of Lila Young's workers that he had buried the remains of well over one hundred infants who had died at the Ideal Maternity Home. However, officials were never able to prove that homicide had occurred at the hands of Lila or William Young; consequently, the maternity home continued in business.

During its eighteen years of operation, the Ideal Maternity Home generated several million dollars in revenue for the Youngs. However, despite its financial success, the business was a gruesome affair that profited by the callous murder of countless infants whose mothers believed that their babies had been successfully adopted. In 1946, Lila and William Young were finally arrested and convicted of selling infants and the Ideal Maternity Home was officially ordered closed. However, the Youngs were not incarcerated for their crimes and still continued to provide private maternity and adoption services on a limited basis. By this time, the murderous couple was the target of a number of investigations on a variety of fronts, including the media.

By the end of 1947, the Ideal Maternity Home had closed its doors for good. The Youngs ceased all operations and moved to Quebec in order to escape the persistence of authorities and the press. However, the couple had squandered away all their assets and were now bankrupt. For the next several years, the Youngs lived quietly. During the 1960s, they both died from natural causes, five years apart. Neither Lila nor William Young ever faced criminal prosecution for their two decades of serial murder for profit.

NOTES

1. "Hunting Humans—Antoinette Scieri," in Kozel Multimedia, *Mind of a Killer,* CD-ROM (Chatsworth, CA: Cambrix, 1995), Section: "Hunting Humans."

2. "Landlord Left with Bill in Sacramento Slayings," *San Jose* (California) *Mercury News* (Internet edition), 18 July 1989, 8B.

7

TEAM KILLERS

Team: a group organized to work together.
Webster's New Universal Unabridged Dictionary

When a woman commits serial murder, she is more likely to do so as a member of a killing team than to act alone. In fact, we estimate that approximately one third of all female serial killers have operated only as a member of a team and never committed a homicide except in the context of the team's criminal activities. A Team Killer is defined as *a woman who systematically murders others or participates in the systematic murder of others in conjunction with another person.* The perpetrator is considered a Team Killer even if she does not personally murder others but participates in the homicidal activities of the team.

We have identified three distinct types of serial-killing teams: (1) *male/female teams,* (2) *female teams,* and (3) *family teams.* Each of these teams enacts its crimes in a somewhat different manner. The team characteristics are defined by the individual activities of the dominant team member, the number of perpetrators on the team, the team's sexual makeup, and the individual relationships among team members. By definition, the male/female team is comprised of only two members, one of each sex. The female team is comprised of two or more women, and the family team is comprised of three or more members of both sexes.

The male/female team is the most common serial-killing unit, particularly in the United States. This team is comprised of a male and a female who are jointly active serial murderers. The homicides committed by the male-female team generally tend to be sexual in nature, although such a team may occasionally come together for a crime spree that involves nonsexual homicides in combination with other felonies. In the male/female team, the female Team Killer is usually younger relative to other categories of female serial murderers, averaging slightly over twenty years of age at the time of her first murder. The female member of this team is often sexually involved with her male partner, who is often an active sexual predator and serial murderer in his own right. Since the crimes of the male/female serial-killing team are usually sexual in nature and undertaken in a cooperative way, the partners may be loosely organized in their activities; or, alternatively, they may be capable of systematically planning their crimes, depending on the degree of cooperation between the partners and their individual capacities for organization. In either case, their murders are often extremely vicious, opportunistic, and sometimes highly reckless when the team is unable to effectively organize its activities. The period of lethal activity of male/female killing teams tends to be relatively short (typically one year) because the team is often poorly organized and may commit very public and flagrant felonies. However, there are cases in which well-organized male/female serial-killing teams have been criminally active for several years before they were apprehended. Finally, it is typical for the male perpetrator to be the dominant character in a male/female serial-killing team; however, there have been significant and interesting exceptions to this rule.

Exclusively female killing teams are the second largest category of Team Killers. By definition, they are comprised of two or more women who are jointly active serial killers. The majority of female killing teams are comprised of only two women, although there have been notorious teams comprised of as many as four perpetrators, each of whom were active serial murderers. Unlike the male/female team, which overwhelmingly specializes in brutal sexual homicides, the female killing team can form for a variety of motives, such as Profit or Crime or Angel of Death killings. In general, the average age of the members of a female serial-killing team is somewhat older than that of a member of a male/female team. The typical member of a female killing team commits her first murder in her mid-twenties. In addition, a female serial-killing team is typically active for about two years before the members are apprehended or the murders cease—an active period that is twice as long as that of the average male-female serial-killing team. Whereas the murders committed by the typical male/female serial-killing team involve a variety of weapons and are frequently gruesome, the murders committed by members of a female killing team are generally consistent with those committed by a female serial killer who acts alone. Lethal injections, poison, and smothering or suffocation are the preferred weapons and tactics of exclusively female serial-killing teams. Like the male/female team, there is typically a dominant individual who leads the members of the female serial-killing team and acts as the organizer of their combined criminal activities.

Family serial-killing teams are comprised of three or more individuals of both sexes. The team may be comprised of actual members of the same family or it can be made up of unrelated individuals who have come together to form a family-like structure that specializes in criminal activities. Although most family teams are dominated by a male, this is not always the case. Family serial-killing teams share many of the characteristics of male/female killing teams. The family team may engage in crime sprees or be active in a string of sexual serial murders, or both. These teams can range from highly organized in its activities to very disorganized. However, regardless of their ability to organize the details and commission of their crimes, these family teams tend to be extremely violent and undertake activities that are often very public in nature. For these reasons, the period of lethal activity of such a team is relatively short—usually about one year. The female members of a family team are typically young, with their age paralleling the average age of the members of male/female killing teams.

Overall, female members of an American killing team exhibit these general characteristics: (1) an average age of between twenty and twenty-five years at the time of the first murder; (2) an average number of known victims that ranges between nine and fifteen; and, (3) an average active period of one to two years (see Figure 7.1). In general, contemporary killing teams outside the United States share these fundamental characteristics; however, much of the information about historical Team Killers outside this country has been sensationalized in the press and is not as reliable as contemporary, domestic data.

The weapons of choice for the Team Killer tend to vary widely depending on the nature of the homicides that are

Figure 7.1: Victims of the Team Killer

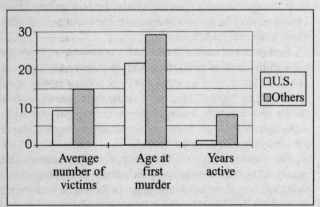

committed. For those teams that specialize in sexual homicides, the method of murder often parallels the activities of a male serial killer who operates alone. These crimes tend to be especially egregious and may involve torture of the victims or dismemberment of the bodies in addition to sexual abuse and rape. However, exclusively female killing teams tend to use methods and weapons that are more consistent with the female serial murderer who operates alone, such as poison or lethal injections (see Figure 7.2).

Figure 7.2: Weapons and Methods of the Team Killer

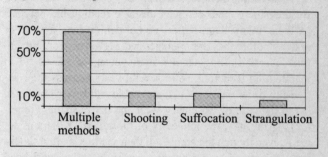

The dynamics of team killers are complex and frequently volatile. Regardless of the type, each team will be dominated by a single individual who attempts to organize the criminal activities of the team and will take a leadership role in most, if not all, the homicides. (However, this leadership role is not held exclusively by males in a male/female or family serial-killing team.) In addition, the nondominant members of any team may be quite active in the actual commission of the murders and not merely relegated to entrapping victims for the more aggressive partner.

Many male/female serial-killing teams are comprised of partners who share a sexual relationship, which may be unusual or bizarre; the same situation may occur in family serial-killing teams. Killing teams comprised of two or more females may also involve intimate sexual relationships among the members; however, the team may also be comprised of individuals who share no intimate relationship other than their criminal activities.

Certain Team Killers tend to garner shocking and persistent headlines in the press. Because their crimes are often brutal in nature, and because the most common team is comprised of a male and a female sexual predator, these perpetrators have managed to capture the attention of the media in a unique way. This fascination with the male/female killing team is often enhanced by the dynamics of the relationship between the partners, which itself may be brutal and bizarre. Because there tends to be an unstable relationship between partners, many Team Killers do not exhibit long periods of activity before they are apprehended. However, from time to time a serial-killing team proves unusually successful at maintaining its activities for several years because the relationship of its members is more stable and better organized (as in the case of Rosemary West and her husband, Frederick). Thankfully, the longevity of most Team Killers is not great, even though the number of their victims is often shocking. Perhaps the most notorious example of a short-lived serial-killing team in recent American history was that of the teenage Nebraska lovers Charles Starkweather and Caril Ann Fugate.

CONSPIRATOR OR VICTIM?

In the late 1950s, the names of Charles Starkweather and Caril Ann Fugate became instantly known to millions of Americans because of their brutal crime spree, which terrorized residents of Nebraska and the surrounding states for nearly a month. Unlike the romanticized exploits of the notorious killing team of Bonnie Parker and Clyde Barrow, the murders attributed to Starkweather and Fugate were unusually random and gruesome, apparently often carried out for the sheer pleasure of killing. However, after their arrest it became increasingly uncertain whether the murders attributed to Starkweather and Fugate were really the crimes of a serial-killing team or those of a single sociopath who held his partner as a terrified hostage throughout a month-long lethal rampage (see Table 7.1).

Table 7.1: Caril Ann Fugate

Classification	Team Killer (with Charles Starkweather).
Birth Information	Born in 1944, in Nebraska.
Active Period	1958. Active at the age of fourteen.
Victim Information	As part of a team, participated in the murders of ten adults and one child. Three of the victims were members of her own family.
Method	Various. Most of the victims were shot by Charles Starkweather. At least two female victims were stabbed, and one other was mutilated with a knife.
Motive	Victims were slain during an extended crime spree.
Disposition	Fugate and Starkweather were arrested in 1958. Both were found guilty of their crimes, and Starkweather was subsequently executed, in 1959. Fugate received a life sentence and was eventually paroled in 1976.

At the time the couple began their short-lived killing careers, Starkweather was seventeen years old and Fugate only fourteen. Even at his young age, Starkweather was an individual who had gained an unquestioned reputation as being impulsive, aggressive, and often out of control. With significant physical problems (myopia and severely bowed legs) and a short stature (he was five feet, two inches tall), Starkweather had suffered a childhood marked by endless taunting from his peers and rejection by his family. A perpetually angry teenager, Starkweather was unable to complete high school and instead dropped out to support himself as a garbage collector. At work he was known to be argumentative with his colleagues and abusive to customers. Persistently hostile without reason, Starkweather would often intimidate others with a rifle, which was always within his reach.

On the other hand, Caril Ann Fugate had no history of violence and seemed both happy and successful in school. However, when she met Starkweather at the age of fourteen, she fell immediately and irrevocably under his spell. In fact, she would later state that the diminutive and moody Starkweather was the most attractive man that she had ever met. For his part, Starkweather was equally smitten with Fugate, whom he considered mature and sophisticated for her young age. Predictably, Fugate's parents were not at all pleased by her infatuation with Starkweather, whom they viewed as wild and dangerous.

That Fugate fell under the control of the older teen is unquestioned. However, even decades after their infamous crime spree, it remains unclear what role she played in the murders of many individuals, including the members of her own family. According to the statements made by Starkweather at his trial, Caril Ann Fugate was a willing partner in crime and a heinous murderer in her own right. However, Starkweather was notorious for changing his story and legendary in his ability to exact retribution against others, including the girl he claimed to love more than his own life.

Fugate has consistently claimed that the crime spree in which she was involved began and ended with Charles Starkweather. To many people, her version of events is both compelling and consistent with the facts. Given the fact that many male/female serial-killing teams are dominated by an aggressive and murderous male, it is reasonable to believe that Starkweather was certainly the primary, if not the sole, source of mayhem in a series of murders that captured the attention of the American public in 1958. No matter which version of this crime spree is the most accurate, nothing can diminish its overt brutality.

The Crime Spree

December 1, 1957. Charles Starkweather robs a neighborhood gas station in his hometown of Lincoln, Nebraska. In the course of the robbery, Starkweather abducts twenty-one-year-old Robert Colvert (the station attendant) at gunpoint and forces him to drive to the outskirts of town. There, he executes Colvert with a shotgun. With no witnesses and little evidence at the crime scene, police are unable to immediately identify the perpetrator. Caril Fugate is not involved in this crime.

January 21, 1958. Starkweather drives to Fugate's home in the afternoon to wait for the teenager to return from school. Before Fugate arrives home, Starkweather becomes involved in a violent argument with Caril's mother, Velda Bartlett, about his relationship with the fourteen-year-old. The argument escalates into physical violence and ends with Starkweather shooting Velda Bartlett and her husband to death. By this time, Caril has returned home from school and allegedly witnesses Starkweather's murder of her two-year-old sister, Betty Bartlett, who is killed when he jams the barrel of his rifle down her throat, choking her to death. Fugate then prepares a handwritten note and posts it on the front door of the home; it reads: "Stay a Way. Every Body is Sick With the Flu."[1] According to his later court testimony, Starkweather now conceals the three bodies of his victims while Fugate watches television. Fugate's testimony contradicts many of the statements made by Starkweather; however, there is no question about the fact that three members of her family were brutally murdered on this day.

January 22–January 27, 1958. According to Starkweather, the couple remains at the Bartlett home for the next several days, watching television and making love. Eventually realizing they are low on provisions and in fear of discovery by inquisitive neighbors who have not seen any family members in several days, the pair decides to flee the crime scene.

January 28, 1958. While trying to escape the area, Starkweather's car stalls in the soft soil on a nearby farm. The couple is approached by the owner of the property, seventy-year-old August Meyer, who is apparently upset about discovering the automobile and its occupants on his land. The two men begin to argue and Starkweather settles the dispute by shooting the aging farmer and his dog. Now forced to flee on foot, Starkweather and Fugate make their way to a nearby road to hitchhike a ride and continue their escape.

The couple is seen by two high school students, Robert Jensen (seventeen years old) and Carol King (sixteen), who offer them a ride. Once in the car, Starkweather abducts the teenagers at gunpoint and forces them to drive to a nearby abandoned schoolhouse. Inside the cellar of the building, Starkweather shoots Jensen six times in the head, killing him instantly. He then rapes and shoots King, also killing her instantly. After her death, King's genitals are severely mutilated with a knife; however, it is never determined who committed this heinous act. In later trial testimony, Starkweather claimed that Fugate committed the mutilation in a jealous rage. However, Fugate denied this testimony and claimed that Starkweather was responsible.

The couple now steal Jensen's automobile to continue their escape. According to Starkweather's testimony, the lovers argue about surrendering to authorities but, at Fugate's insistence, decide to return to Lincoln instead. Fugate would later testify that she continued to be in fear for her life as a kidnapping victim of her sociopath lover.

January 30, 1958. Starkweather and Fugate are back in Lincoln and in need of money to continue their escape. They force their way into the home of C. Lauer Ward, a local businessman of some wealth. At the time of the invasion, the home is occupied by Ward's wife, Clara, and the family maid, Lillian Fencl. Starkweather binds both women, moves them into a bedroom, and then stabs each to death. The couple then waits in the home for Ward to return from work in the evening. As he steps through the front door of his home, Ward is immediately killed by multiple shots from Starkweather's rifle.

The pair now steals the Ward's limousine and decides to drive to Washington state. Law enforcement officials are aware of the couple's ongoing crime spree and have mobilized members of the Nebraska National Guard to patrol their possible escape routes. However, despite their efforts, authorities are unable to locate Starkweather and Fugate.

February 1, 1958. The couple arrives in Douglas, Wyoming, and attempts to steal another vehicle. Starkweather spots a salesman, Merle Collison, asleep behind the wheel of his car on the side of the road. Approaching the vehicle from the driver's side, Starkweather murders Collison by shooting him nine times in the head. However, he is unable to remove the victim's body from the car before a passing motorist stops at the bizarre scene to lend assistance. Starkweather turns his rifle on the passerby, and the two men begin to struggle for the weapon as a local deputy sheriff also arrives on the scene.

As the officer approaches the two men, Fugate rushes toward the police car, screaming, "He [Starkweather] killed a man!" Seeing the officer draw his weapon, Starkweather retreats to the Ward limousine and flees the scene. A high-speed chase ensues that involves a number of police vehicles. Starkweather is finally forced off the road by pursuing police and taken into custody along with Caril Fugate, who had been detained at the scene of the shooting.

Controversy

Charles Starkweather immediately confessed to the crime spree that had claimed eleven lives. He also insisted that Caril Ann Fugate had been a willing partner in each of the murders, which began with the Bartlett family triple homicide. According to his testimony, Starkweather insisted that he had argued with Fugate about surrendering to authorities but eventually agreed with her demands that the couple continue with their gruesome rampage. However, Fugate argued that she had been a victim of her uncontrollable lover, in fear for her life and unable to escape from the gun-wielding maniac.

Regardless of the controversy that surrounded the perpetrators' statements, their mutual presence and involvement in the crime spree was unquestioned at the time of their arrest and trial. Both Charles Starkweather and Caril Ann Fugate were quickly found guilty of murder; however, their respective sentences indicated a perceived difference of their roles in the murder spree: Starkweather was given the death penalty, while Fugate received a life term in prison. On June 24, 1959, Charles Starkweather died by electrocution at the Nebraska state prison.

Over the ensuing years, Caril Ann Fugate proved to be a cooperative and model prisoner. Throughout her incarceration, she also consistently, and often convincingly, denied her complicity in one of the most notorious murder sprees in American history. Those who came to know Fugate during her imprisonment, including correctional authorities, universally considered her a sincere individual who expressed a genuine sense of remorse for the crimes committed in 1958. After nearly twenty years in prison, Fugate was able to win parole, having been strongly supported in her bid for freedom by the warden of her prison. Two decades after her release from prison (and forty years after the notorious crime spree), Fugate continues to maintain her version of the events of 1958—that in reality, she, too, was a victim of a lethal sociopath of the first magnitude.

"I BELONG TO THE FOLSOM WOLF"

Nearly thirty years after the notorious crime spree of Charles Starkweather and Caril Ann Fugate, a similar, but less lethal, rampage occurred in California and Arizona. In 1986, the killing team of James Marlow and Cynthia Coffman claimed four victims in a brutal five-week murder spree,

which included robbery and sexual assault. However, unlike
Caril Ann Fugate, Coffman was clearly an active participant
in the murders and eventually received both a death sentence
and life imprisonment for her role in the serial-killing spree
(see Table 7.2).

Table 7.2: Cynthia Coffman

Classification	Team Killer (with James Gregory Marlow).
Birth Information	Born in 1962, in St. Louis, Missouri.
Active Period	1986. Active at the age of twenty-four.
Victim Information	Participated in the murder of at least four women to rob them of their assets. At least two of the victims were sexually molested.
Method	Strangulation.
Motive	Coffman participated with Marlow in murders that were primarily motivated by robbery during an extended crime spree.
Disposition	Both Coffman and Marlow were arrested and tried in 1989. Both were found guilty and sentenced to death. Coffman received an additional sentence of life imprisonment at a second murder trial in 1992.

Coffman was the daughter of a wealthy, well-respected
family from St. Louis, Missouri. Born in 1962, she was
raised in a deeply religious environment and provided with a
full and stable home life. Nonetheless, by the age of seventeen, Coffman was pregnant by her teenage boyfriend and
had been forced into a marriage punctuated by arguments and
turmoil. Despite its difficulties, Coffman's marriage lasted
for five years before she finally left her home and family to
begin a new life in Arizona.

In 1985, Coffman found a job as a waitress in an Arizona café and, within a few months, had moved in with a local man. Her new relationship proved chaotic and marked by drunkenness and drug use. By the end of 1985, the couple had been evicted from their apartment because of their incessant propensity for wild, all-night parties and disruptive behavior. The following year, Coffman and her lover were arrested for possession of illegal drugs. Although the charges against Coffman were eventually dismissed, her paramour received a short sentence in the county jail. It was during one of Coffman's visits to her lover that she first met another inmate, James Marlow.

The attraction between Marlow and Coffman was immediate and intense. Marlow was five years older than Coffman and a white supremacist who had a lifelong history of offenses, including theft, robbery, and assault. Despite his unsavory background, Coffman found Marlow irresistible and immediately abandoned her former lover when Marlow was released from prison.

After James Marlow gained his freedom the couple began to drift throughout the South, borrowing money from his relatives and committing a variety of minor offenses to make ends meet. The pair was unable or unwilling to find work and eventually turned to more serious crime to make money. On July 26, 1986, Marlow and Coffman burglarized a home in Kentucky, taking cash, valuables, and weapons. Within a week they had fled to Tennessee, where they were married in an impromptu ceremony. To show her unending commitment to Marlow, Coffman had the phrase, "I belong to the Folsom Wolf," tattooed on her buttocks.[2] This was a point of intense pride for James Marlow, who had long been known to his cellmates in California by that moniker.

Emboldened by their successful robbery in Kentucky, Marlow and Coffman headed back west, to more familiar surroundings. On October 11, 1986, the couple committed their first known murder when, that night, they attacked a thirty-two-year-old woman who had just withdrawn cash from an automated teller machine (ATM) in Costa Mesa, California. The couple brutally beat the woman, robbed her of the cash, and strangled her to death. They then transported the body to Riverside County, where it was discovered several weeks later.

The murderous team then traveled back to Arizona to commit a second killing. There, on October 28, 1986, Marlow and Coffman attacked, robbed, and murdered a thirty-five-year-old woman who had also just withdrawn cash from a nearby ATM. Less than two weeks later, the couple was back in California, in the town of Redlands. On November 7, 1986, Marlow and Coffman repeated their previous murders by abducting a twenty-year-old woman who had just used an ATM in a shopping center. Five days later, the couple claimed their last victim, a nineteen-year-old female student, in the same manner. The last two victims of the murderous couple had also been brutally sexually assaulted.

Throughout their crime spree, Marlow and Coffman had been disorganized and careless in each of their murders, leaving a good deal of evidence in their wake. Police were soon able to link the couple to one of the homicides after they located a checkbook belonging to a known victim. Incredibly, the victim's checkbook had been carelessly discarded by the perpetrators inside a sack that contained their full names. Authorities now knew the identities of the suspects and were able to circulate information about the perpetrators to the media. On November 14, 1986, Marlow and Coffman were arrested near a motel in Big Bear City, California, where they had registered under their own names and been recognized by the motel owner.

After the arrest, Cynthia Coffman confessed to her role in the murders and led authorities to the location of one of the victims, who had remained missing since the previous month. However, for nearly three years a series of legal maneuvers kept Marlow and Coffman from going to trial. During that period, the relationship between the lovers disintegrated and each accused the other of solely perpetrating the four murders.

Finally, on July 18, 1989, Marlow and Coffman went to trial in San Bernardino, California, each charged with a single count of murder. The prosecution's case against the pair was irrefutable, and the two were quickly found guilty of the charge against them. On August 30, 1989, both James Marlow and Cynthia Coffman were sentenced to death. Coffman's death sentence was the first of its kind in California since capital punishment was reinstated in 1977.

On May 14, 1992, Cynthia Coffman was tried on a second charge of murder in Orange County, California. This trial lasted for six weeks and again resulted in a guilty verdict. However, Coffman's jury did not recommend the death penalty in the case, opting instead for life in prison without the possibility of parole. On September 26, 1992, the presiding judge accepted the recommendation of the jury and sentenced Cynthia Coffman to life imprisonment.

THE LONELY HEARTS KILLERS

One of the strangest male/female serial-killing teams to capture national headlines in this country was that of Raymond Fernandez and Martha Beck. Active for two years in the late 1940s, this murderous pair accounted for at least twelve murders (and probably as many as twenty) in a crime spree that escalated from fraud to homicide (see Table 7.3).

Raymond Fernandez, a native of Hawaii, considered himself the epitome of the irresistible Latin lover. However, from an early age, Fernandez was really nothing more than a second-rate con man who specialized in wooing lonely females in order to bilk them of their assets. Throughout the course of his criminal career, Fernandez drifted continuously, plying his trade as a gigolo and engaging in bigamous relationships across the United States. In 1947, Fernandez was in Pensacola, Florida, continuing his fraudulent ways by placing personal advertisements in newspapers and joining various lonely hearts clubs in an effort to locate new victims willing to trade their assets for companionship.

Table 7.3: Martha Beck

Classification	Team Killer (with Raymond Martinez Fernandez).
Birth Information	Born in 1920.
Active Period	1947 to 1949. Active from age twenty-seven to age twenty-nine.
Victim Information	Murdered at least twelve and possibly as many as twenty women.
Method	Various. Many murders were sexual in nature.
Motive	Fernandez and Beck were known in the press as the *Lonely Hearts Killers*. Fernandez would attempt to start a love relationship with the victims in order to bilk them of their assets. If the victim demonstrated any resistance, she would be murdered. Beck posed as Fernandez's sister.
Disposition	The team was arrested and confessed to their crimes. They were tried in 1949 and, despite their insanity defense, were found guilty. Both were executed in 1951.

One of the women who responded to Fernandez's news-paper advertisements in 1947 was Martha Beck, a lonely registered nurse who weighed nearly 300 pounds and significantly overshadowed the smaller, stylish Fernandez. Given her background and personal characteristics, everything about Martha Beck indicated that she would hold no interest for Raymond Fernandez. It had long been his method of operation to lure older, passive, and, often, petite women to his side, ensuring as much as possible that each had assets she was willing to sacrifice. On the other hand, Beck met none of these qualifications. She was five years younger than Fernandez, was obviously physically powerful and domineering, and clearly had little to offer in the way of beauty or assets. Nonetheless, as both Fernandez and Beck would persistently claim, their initial meeting was a classic story of love at first sight.

Rather than targeting Beck for his usual fraudulent treatment, Fernandez openly confessed his years of crime and enlisted her as an accomplice. For her part, Beck was enthralled with her new Latin lover and excited by the opportunity to join him in a life of sex, travel, and easy money. Shortly after their first meeting, Beck quit her job to join Fernandez in his exploits. In short order the unlikely pair had devised a new method of operation that called for Martha Beck to pose as Fernandez's sister while he continued to lure lonely women into a web of fraud.

Over the next two years, Beck and Fernandez proved to be an unusually successful and lethal serial-killing team. Their personal relationship was comprised of regular periods of marathon sex, while they worked in partnership to attract other women to the polished and suave Fernandez. However, Beck soon became jealous of the endless relationships required by her lover's profession and unwilling to simply move on when their fraud was discovered. Obviously changed by the torrid relationship, Fernandez was unwilling or unable to check Beck's propensity for violence and rages of jealousy. For her part, Beck had made it very clear that she would not tolerate any woman who presented a threat to her status with Fernandez. The result of this intense emotional chemistry proved to be lethal in the extreme. In short order, the pair began to resolve any threat to the relationship by murdering their prey whenever Fernandez's role as a lover proved to be ineffective or problematic.

From 1948 to 1949, this serial-killing team murdered as many as twenty women, whom they entrapped through a variety of advertisements and announcements in lonely hearts clubs publications. Both Fernandez and Beck took an active role in the murders, using a variety of means such as shooting, poison, drowning, bludgeoning, and strangulation. In most instances, the couple was careful and organized in eliminating the victims, typically weaving a web of lies that accounted for the sudden disappearance of each new lover. However, they were also aided by the fact that many of their victims were not in contact with other family members and were often spinsters who were typically well past middle age.

The victims of Fernandez and Beck often met their fate in ways that were gruesome and brutal. For example, a sixty-six-year-old woman, Janet Fay, was not only bilked of her assets by the smooth-talking Fernandez, but murdered in an especially heinous manner: Fay was repeatedly bludgeoned over the head with a hammer wielded by Beck while her lover strangled the unfortunate woman with a scarf. Other victims disappeared in less brutal, and more mysterious, ways. One of Fernandez's many wives vanished while on their honeymoon in Spain, the supposed victim of a train wreck that never occurred. Another of his unfortunate lovers was reported to have died of exhaustion after a marathon sexual encounter with the insatiable Fernandez.

Despite their relatively organized approach to murder, Fernandez and Beck ran afoul of the law in January 1949 after the murder of their youngest victim, twenty-eight-year-old Delphine Dowling. Dowling had invited the lethal couple to move into her home in order to be closer to Fernandez while she considered his offer of marriage. Dowling was irrevocably smitten with this older man and pleased to discover that his sister, Beck, had shown a special fondness for Dowling's two-year-old daughter, Rainelle. However, Fernandez and Beck were impatient to collect from their latest prey and Dowling failed to part with her assets as quickly as planned. Deciding to take matters into their own hands, Fernandez shot Dowling while Beck drowned her daughter in the bathtub. The couple than buried the bodies of their victims in the basement of the Dowling home, carefully laying new concrete over the site of their remains.

Shortly after the murders, neighbors became suspicious when they noticed that Dowling and her daughter had suddenly disappeared, while Fernandez and Beck still occupied her home. The police were contacted and soon called at the Dowling home to make inquiries. Greeted at the door by Martha Beck, the officers asked for permission to look around the home and were given access by the overconfident Beck. In short order, however, one of the policemen discovered the new patch of concrete in the basement and began to question the murderous couple. Not satisfied with their evasive answers, officers excavated a portion of the basement floor and discovered the bodies of Dowling and her daughter.

Based on the gruesome discovery, Fernandez and Beck were quickly arrested on suspicion of murder. Once in custody, Fernandez immediately confessed to the Dowling murders. Over the next few days, both Fernandez and Beck continued to confess their crimes, eventually accounting for twelve murders that could be confirmed by authorities and their probable involvement in several other homicides. In July 1949, Fernandez and Beck went to trial on multiple charges of murder, countering the prosecutor's overwhelming case with an insanity defense. Throughout the trial, the couple occupied their time by holding hands and whispering loving phrases to each other while the stunned jury tried to comprehend the true horror of their crimes. In the final analysis, the case for the prosecution was never in doubt and the pair was found guilty on all counts.

On August 22, 1949, Fernandez and Beck were sentenced to death. Despite appeals that eventually reached the United States Supreme Court, Raymond Fernandez and Martha Beck were executed on January 2, 1951. The Lonely Hearts Killers' final moments were spent together, in a pair of electric chairs at Sing Sing prison, with each murderer expressing undying love for the other at the moment of death.

SEXUAL TEAM KILLERS

Most serial-killing teams that are comprised of a single male and a single female member commit sexual homicides as their primary criminal activity. Like those mixed teams that engage in crime sprees, sexual killing teams tend to be dominated by the male partner. However, in these teams the male member is often much more than a career criminal—he is frequently a sexual serial killer in his own right. In many male/female sexual killing teams, the female member is easily dominated and manipulated by her male partner and, in a certain sense, may also be one of his victims. However, there are cases in which the female member is also an active murderer and a sexual psychopath of a magnitude that rivals her male counterpart.

Male/female teams that specialize in sexual homicide are maintained by the synergy of the sexual relationship between the partners and their combined pathological obsession with sexual domination and control. Such teams often commit extremely brutal crimes that tend to garner a great deal of media attention. Sadly, the victims of a male/female sexual-killing team are often children or young adults who experience gruesome sexual torture before they are finally murdered.

The Moors Murders

"If I came face to face with Myra Hindley, she's just dead," growled Danny Kilbride, referring to his brother's murderer.[3] Kilbride's words were aired on the 1994 British Broadcasting Corporation (BBC) production of "Witness Programme," a current affairs telecast in which the victim's murderer, fifty-two-year-old Myra Hindley, also made a public plea for her freedom. After nearly thirty years behind bars, Hindley was the longest serving woman prisoner in British history on the day that the program aired (see Table 7.4).

Table 7.4: Myra Hindley

Classification	Team Killer (with Ian Brady).
Birth Information	Born in 1942, in England.
Active Period	1963 to 1965. Active from age twenty-one to age twenty-three.
Victim Information	Murdered at least five young (teenage) individuals. Believed responsible for as many as ten additional slayings.
Method	Strangulation, stabbing, shooting, and torture.
Motive	All of the crimes were sexual homicides.
Disposition	Both Brady and Hindley were convicted of murder in 1966. Both received a sentence of life imprisonment.

Myra Hindley was born in July 1942, in Groton, England. With the birth of her sister, four years later, the Hindley household became hopelessly overcrowded and Myra was sent to live with her grandmother. Her early life was unremarkable until 1961 when, at the age of nineteen, Hindley found work at a chemical supply company in Manchester. It was while employed as a clerk-typist that Hindley met her coworker and future partner in murder, Ian Brady. The illegitimate son of a Scot, Brady was four years Hindley's senior and considerably more experienced in the dark ways of the world. With an extensive criminal record and an obvious propensity for antisocial behavior, Brady was also an enthusiastic sexual sadist and a compulsive devotee of fascism and the historical leaders of Nazi Germany.

Hindley was immediately impressed by the older Brady, whom she often found reading Hitler's *Mein Kampf* (in the original German) during his lunch break. Her obvious curiosity about this apparently multifaceted man was not lost on

Brady, who thrived on his ability to impress others in any way possible. When Brady invited her to a local theater to take in a film about the Nuremberg war crimes trials, the shy and self-conscious Hindley was more than willing to accept.

From that first date, Hindley and Brady became insepara-ble partners. They would often spend a leisurely afternoon picnicking on the moors and reading aloud to each other about their favorite heroes, such as the Marquis de Sade or Adolf Hitler. Hindley soon developed a particular fascination with Irma Grese, a sadistic administrator of the infamous Nazi concentration camp at Belsen. To complete her identifi-cation with Grese and enhance her appeal to the bizarre whims of her lover, Hindley bleached her hair and began to wear black leather outfits and Nazi-style jackboots. To show his approval, Brady began to refer to his lover as "Myra Hess."[4]

In early 1963, the couple started to dabble in pornography in an effort to enhance their income along with their sexual thrills. Using an automatic camera, Hindley and Brady would pose in various sexual acts while using props such as whips, chains, and even a bewildered canine. However, despite their obvious enthusiasm, the newly formed business venture never turned a profit and the couple soon went looking for fresh forms of excitement.

Brady had long been fascinated with the movie *Compul-sion,* a taut drama about the infamous child murderers Leopold and Loeb. The couple would often discuss this movie (and the crime on which it was based) in minute detail and eventually convinced each other that a perfect act of mur-der could be the basis for the ultimate romantic encounter. These discussions soon carried Hindley and Brady well be-yond fantasy—into planning and, eventually, to action. So it was, that from 1963 to 1965, Hindley and Brady acted out their perverse fantasies by abducting and murdering at least five children, who ranged in age from ten to seventeen years.

The couple's first murder was that of sixteen-year-old

Pauline Reade, who vanished on July 12, 1963. Reade was last seen at her own home, which was located only two doors from the house of Hindley's brother-in-law. Despite the fact that Reade was probably a victim of convenience in a poorly planned crime, the murder went undetected for over two decades. Finally, in 1986, Hindley (already incarcerated for three other murders at the time) confessed to killing the young woman twenty-three years previously and burying her body on Saddleworth Moor. However, because of the moor's treacherous terrain, there were numerous unsuccessful attempts at locating Reade's gravesite even after Hindley's confession. Finally, on June 30, 1987, investigators were able to discover Reade's remains near the location that Hindley had specified. The following month, pathologists determined that the teenager had been sexually assaulted before her throat was slit.

On November 23, 1963, four months after the disappearance of Pauline Reade, twelve-year-old John Kilbride was returning home from the cinema when he accepted a ride from Hindley in the market town of Ashton-under-Lyne. It was the last time Kilbride was seen alive. Police unearthed his body on Saddleworth Moor two years later, on October 21, 1965. Like Reade before him, Kilbride was sexually molested before he was murdered.

The couple's third victim, twelve-year-old Keith Bennett, left his home on the night of June 16, 1964, to spend the night at his grandmother's house. Along the way he accepted a ride from a woman who later proved to be Myra Hindley. Like John Kilbride, Bennett never reached his destination; and, like Pauline Reade, Bennett's murder went unsolved until Hindley confessed to the crime in 1986. Sadly, Keith Bennett's body was never located.

Hindley and Brady's next victim, ten-year-old Lesley Ann Downey, died on December 26, 1964, after inexplicably vanishing from the streets of Manchester. Ten months later, on October 16, 1965, her remains were found buried on Saddleworth Moor, not far from the gravesite of John Kilbride. As with the previous victims, Downey had been tortured and sexually assaulted before she was murdered.

By early 1965, with no solid forensic evidence and an absence of witnesses, police were perplexed by what they assumed to be a series of unrelated child abductions that had occurred over the prior eighteen months. Meanwhile, Hindley and Brady had come to believe that their crimes were nearly perfect but not sufficiently satisfying. By the fall of 1965, Brady was ready for a change. With at least four children already murdered, and no suspicion pointed in his direction, Brady came to the conclusion that it would be entertaining to corrupt Hindley's eighteen-year-old brother-in-law, David Smith, by bringing him into the couple's sadistic and murderous games. Smith, a petty criminal, had always been in awe of Brady, and the couple agreed that it would be easy to recruit him into their next act of mayhem.

The victim selected for Smith's indoctrination into murder was Edward Evans, a seventeen-year-old homosexual who was last seen at a local pub on October 6, 1965. Planning to involve her brother-in-law in a sexual attack on Evans, Smith was lured to the house that Brady shared with Hindley and her grandmother under the pretext of walking Hindley home from her sister's house. When Hindley and Smith arrived, her brother-in-law was startled by a scream emanating from inside the house. Unwittingly, Smith walked through the front door and was confronted with the macabre scene of Ian Brady, hatchet in hand, hacking away at the head of the prone Evans. Caught up in the chaos of the moment, Hindley screamed for Smith to help Brady finish his gruesome task. However, Smith could only watch in horror as Evans struggled and screamed for help. In a fury, Brady finally ended the young man's life by strangulation, with a stunned David Smith standing over him in disbelief.

Hindley and Brady were so sure of themselves that they never considered that the horrified Smith might inform the police of their most recent escapade. However, by eight o'clock on the morning of October 7, 1965, police officers arrived at Hindley's residence after hearing Smith's incredible story of the previous night. Unprepared for the intrusion and convinced that she was beyond the reach of the law, Hindley politely ushered the policemen into her home. Within moments, however, the bloodied body of Edward Evans had been discovered in her bedroom.

With information provided by David Smith, police also located a luggage locker rented by Brady at Manchester Central Station. From the locker police recovered two suitcases that contained nude photographs of Leslie Ann Downey, a tape recording of her screams and pleas for her life while being tortured, and several snapshots of a location on Saddleworth Moor. Later that month, using the photographs of Saddleworth Moor, authorities were able to locate the final resting places of Leslie Ann Downey and John Kilbride.

Hindley and Brady were arrested for the murders of Evans, Downey, and Kilbride. Dubbed by the media as the *Moors Murderers,* the crimes attributed to Hindley and Brady provoked a surge of public outrage that had not been seen in England since Jack the Ripper.[5] Not surprisingly, the couple's trial came to be known in the press as the "trial of the century."

The case against Hindley and Brady was a strong one. Perhaps most compelling for the jury was the tape recording of the screams of Leslie Ann Downey as she was being tortured and murdered. The impact of such evidence was clearly immeasurable and easily convinced the stunned jurors of the murderous couple's guilt. On May 6, 1966, Myra Hindley and Ian Brady were sentenced to life imprisonment without the possibility of parole—the maximum penalty possible in their case.

Despite the overwhelming evidence disclosed at their trial, neither defendant confessed to the crimes until 1986. However, during her many years of imprisonment, Myra Hindley experienced a religious conversion and finally decided to cooperate with the authorities. Claiming she had been deeply moved by a letter from the mother of murder victim Keith Bennett, Hindley agreed to assist Detective Chief Superintendent Peter Topping in his decades-long search for the remains of Bennett and Pauline Reade.

Today, Myra Hindley continues to spend her days at Durham prison, often writing to the British Home Secretary and pleading for her release from prison. Ian Brady is serving out his sentence in a hospital for the criminally insane, having been diagnosed as suffering from schizophrenia. Tragically, Saddleworth Moor still holds the secret location of the body of Keith Bennett.

Number 25 Cromwell Street

To the neighbors of the couple who lived at 25 Cromwell Street, Gloucester, England, they were known as *Motherly Rose* and *Friendly Fred*.[6] From these innocuous monikers it is difficult even today to conceive of Rosemary West, a mother of eight, as Britain's most prolific female serial killer. However, she and her husband, Frederick, were partners in a life of unparalleled pathological sexual sadism and murder that went on for nearly twenty years (see Table 7.5).

Rosemary Pauline Letts, was born on November 29, 1953, in Devon, England, to a blatantly dysfunctional family of six brothers and sisters. Her father was both tyrannical and abusive, introducing Letts to bizarre sexual encounters at an early age. Letts's mother, who was weak-willed and compli- ant, finally abandoned the family home with all her children except young Rose, who was left behind to become the object of her father's sexual obsessions. The child's abandonment to her father probably set the stage for Rosemary's later fixation with the much older Frederick West, which started in 1968 while she was still in her teenage years. Twenty-seven-year- old Frederick West, who had claimed to have recently sepa- rated from his first wife, appealed to Rosemary's penchant for older men. After a torrid sexual encounter, he quickly convinced the young woman to live with him as his lover and take on the role of nanny to his two daughters.

Table 7.5: Rosemary West

Classification	Team Killer (with Frederick West, her husband).
Birth Information	Born in 1954, in England.
Active Period	1971 to 1987. Active from age seventeen to age thirty-three.
Victim Information	Murdered at least ten women and young girls. The number of victims may have been as high as eighteen.
Method	Various. The victims were brutalized, tortured, and sexually molested. After their deaths, the bodies were mutilated.
Motive	Sexual homicide.
Disposition	The Wests were arrested in 1994 and charged with multiple counts of murder. Frederick West committed suicide by hanging himself on New Year's Day of 1995. Rosemary West was convicted of ten counts of murder in 1995, resulting in the imposition of ten life sentences in prison.

Letts's father despised Frederick West and, in a jealous rage, ordered his daughter to never see her lover again. However, Letts was headstrong and deeply angered at her father for his many years of abuse. She refused to give up West and continued her sexual liaison until her father had her taken into protective custody by British social services. However, a year later Rosemary turned sixteen and could no longer be legally held by the Crown. She quickly moved in with Frederick West; his daughter, Anne Marie, and his stepdaughter, Charmaine. Letts soon lost any remaining inhibitions. Sex became the center of her existence, and she began using the name Rosemary West in a final act of defiance against her cruel and pathological father.[7]

In October 1970, the Wests moved into their first home, at

25 Midland Road, Gloucester, and began involving their acquaintances and neighbors in an increasingly bizarre life of
sex and drugs. By this time, Rosemary was already far advanced in her first pregnancy and spent her days aiding her
husband in luring unsuspecting neighbors to their home for
sex. In an early, notorious case, a female neighbor was unexpectedly drugged by the Wests and woke up the following
morning to find herself naked, in bed, between the couple. To
her horror, she realized she had been sexually violated—part
of a pattern of sex and violence that would soon become an
insatiable compulsion for the Wests.

Heather West, the first of eight children born to the couple, arrived on October 17, 1970. With the birth of her own
child, Rosemary's jealously wheeled out of control, and she
began to single out her husband's stepdaughter, Charmaine,
for incessantly cruel and debilitating treatment. Charmaine's
young playmates often witnessed scenes' of frightening
intimidation and abuse, which were endlessly meted out by
the girl's vicious stepmother. This behavior continued until
May 22, 1971, when eight-year-old Charmaine inexplicably
disappeared while Frederick was serving a term in prison for
theft. Whenever Rosemary was asked about Charmaine's
sudden disappearance, she would simply reply that the young
girl had gone to live with her birth mother. However, the
Wests knew differently.

Shortly after her father's release from prison in 1971,
Frederick West's nine-year-old daughter, Anne Marie, fell
victim to the unremitting sexual and physical abuse that had
become a staple of the West household. Anne Marie's horror
lasted until the age of fifteen, when she became pregnant by
her father, suffered a miscarriage, and finally decided to leave
home. Anne Marie, who later testified at her stepmother's
trial for murder, claimed that she was never aware that she
had suffered such significant abuse; she had been convinced
by the Wests that whatever they did to her was invariably for
her own good.[8]

In early 1972, the Wests moved to 25 Cromwell Street,

Gloucester, and began renting rooms to lodgers in order to earn money. It was behind the doors of this aging flat with cheap rooms, well out of the sight of neighbors, that drugs and sex became the centerpieces of the Wests' life of perversity.[9] The Wests would regularly lure young men and women from the local area to Cromwell Street for a night of sexual violence. To Rosemary West, the gender, age, or number of her sexual partners made no difference; and by any reasonable standards of morality, Frederick West was even less discriminating.

In 1973, twenty-year-old Lynda Gough angrily left her home after an argument with her mother. Gough had previously been a guest at the Wests' residence, where she had visited with one of the couple's male lodgers. Furious with her mother and unsure where to go, Gough decided to temporarily stay with the Wests on Cromwell Street. After she arrived at the lodgings, Gough calmed herself and notified her mother where she was staying. However, this would be the last time that Mrs. Gough would hear from her daughter, for that evening, Gough was raped, brutalized, and murdered by Rosemary and Frederick West.

For many years there were incessant comings and goings at 25 Cromwell Street. Rosemary West prostituted for her husband and endlessly catered to his insatiable appetite for voyeurism. The couple even had a secret room set up at Cromwell Street, complete with a peep hole, that had been especially outfitted to accommodate Frederick West's favorite pastime—the pair referred to it as "Rosie's room." The Wests also collected an enormous cache of sex toys, which they used on each other as well as on their willing, and unwilling, guests. Rosemary was known to be especially fond of games of bondage and had a collection of implements to complete any scene her troubled mind could muster.

Over the next ten years West was pregnant more often than not and bore children fathered by a number of different men, including her husband. In 1983, her eighth, and last, child was born. Not to be outdone by his sexually active wife, Frederick once boasted of fathering forty-two illegitimate children, most of whom were born to women he and his wife had lured to the home on Cromwell Street. It seems that this self-described Casanova, who in reality looked slightly simi-an to the casual observer, was merely keeping active while he waited for the day when his daughter (and the real target of his obsession), Heather, would become a teenager.[10] Ironi-cally, throughout these years, to the world beyond Cromwell Street the Wests seemed to be a loving family. Rosemary ap-peared to genuinely care for her children, and Frederick was often seen digging aimlessly in his garden. However, to those who experienced the horror of Cromwell Street from the in-side, the Wests personified debauchery and evil in a way that defied comparison.

In 1985, when Heather West turned fourteen, Fred began to use her as his primary sex partner. However, to his growing as-tonishment and anger, she proved to be far less compliant than her stepsister, Anne Marie. In 1987, Heather West abruptly announced that she was leaving home—forever. Apparently afraid that his daughter would tell the authorities about her or-deals, West responded to her claim of independence by stran-gling her. He then removed her head and legs with an ice saw so that the remains would fit into a garbage bag. West would later claim that his wife was out shopping when the murder and dismemberment took place. According to his later statements, Rosemary West first learned of her daughter's disappearance when she returned home from her shopping trip and was told that Heather had suddenly run off with a lesbian lover. How-ever, investigators later determined that Rosemary West was probably present at the murder and dismemberment of her daughter. Heather West was only sixteen years old on the day she was murdered.

Heather was not the last West child to be subjected to her parents' incredible reign of abuse. However, it took four more years before the crimes of Rosemary and Frederick West

came to light. In August 1991, Frederick West was charged
with sexual abuse against his thirteen-year-old daughter. Because of her age and in order to protect her identity, the victim's name remained anonymous and she was shielded from
any media attention. However, because of her intense fear,
the West's daughter eventually refused to testify against her
father, and in 1992, the charges against Frederick West were
formally dropped. In one of the few pleasurable events of her
young life, the teenage victim was befriended by Detective
Constable Hazel Savage of the Gloucester Police during the
investigation into her father's abuse. This friendship would
prove to be a turning point in the lives of Rosemary and Frederick West.

Detective Savage believed that there was every reason to
fear for her young friend's life, based on the teenager's insurmountable reluctance to testify against her father. Savage was
preoccupied with the inconsistencies in the various stories
provided by Rosemary and Frederick West and the strange
behavior of their daughter. Because of her growing suspicions, Savage worked incessantly to get her young friend to
tell her more about her older sister, Heather. Eventually, in a
startling admission, the teenager told Savage, "If I say anything [to you], my Dad says I'd end up in the back garden like
my sister Heather."[11] Savage was stunned; however, the implications of the admission were clear.

Because of her persistence, caring, and two years of solid
police work, Detective Constable Savage was able to convince her superior, Detective Superintendent John Bennett,
to obtain a search warrant for the West residence at 25
Cromwell Street. On February 24, 1994, the unsuspecting
Wests allowed undercover policemen (claiming to be council
workmen) into the backyard of 25 Cromwell Street. The following day, Rosemary and Frederick West were brought to
police headquarters for questioning under suspicion of murder. That night, Frederick West confessed to murdering his
daughter, Heather, and told police where her body could be
located.

Two days later, on February 26, 1994, a human skull was uncovered in a corner of the West's garden. Digging deeper in the shallow grave, the remainder of a dismembered body was discovered, which was later identified by a comparison of dental records. The results of the investigation soon made it apparent that Heather West had never gone to a remote holiday camp as she had discussed with friends shortly before her disappearance. Working on a hunch, the police constables searched the entire yard. Over the next few days, eight more bodies were discovered, including that of Lynda Gough, who had been missing since 1973. Gough's dismembered remains were located under the bathroom area of 25 Cromwell Street.

Another dismembered and badly decomposed body was later found not far from Heather's last resting place. She was identified as Shirley Robinson, an eighteen-year-old resident of 25 Cromwell Street and one of Frederick West's many live-in lovers. She had been eight months pregnant with West's child when she disappeared in May 1978. The remains of her aborted fetus were discovered a few feet away from her corpse.

Alison Chambers was identified soon after her dismembered body was discovered under the patio of the West's home. Her body was naked, bound, and gagged, with a belt tightly fastened around the skull. Chambers was last known to be alive in September 1979, when she wrote to her mother on her seventeenth birthday.

Five more bodies had been buried in the basement, including that of Lucy Partington, the twenty-one-year-old niece of author Kingsley Amis; a twenty-one-year-old Swiss national, Therese Siegenthaler, who had disappeared while hitchhiking in 1974; eighteen-year-old Juanita Mott, who was last seen in April 1974 after moving into the Cromwell Street residence; Shirley Hubbard, a fifteen-year-old who was last seen leaving her place of employment at about the same time that Therese Siegenthaler disappeared; and Carole Anne Cooper, another fifteen-year-old, who had spent the afternoon with her aging grandmother before vanishing in April 1973.

The gruesome discoveries at Cromwell Street led to charges of nine counts of murder against Frederick West. However, Rosemary West was sent home on bail pending further investigation. While Frederick West waited in prison for his trial, he confessed to his son, Stephen, that he had killed a woman named Anne McFall in 1967. According to West, McFall had been living with him as his lover and was seven months pregnant at the time of her murder. West continued his confessions by admitting he had murdered his first wife, Rena, on New Year's Day in 1969 and at least twenty other women throughout the 1960s. He claimed to have buried the bodies of his victims in a field near his childhood home of Much Marcle, Herefordshire. However, despite his detailed confession, only the remains of Anne McFall and Rena Costello West were ever located.

When law enforcement personnel discovered the body of West's first wife, they were immediately suspicious about the fate of his daughter, Charmaine. If she had not left home to live with her mother in 1971, as Rosemary West had claimed, where was she? Police began searching the area around West's previous residence at 25 Midland Road. In April 1994, Charmaine West's decomposed body was found beneath the kitchen floor.

In 1994, Rosemary Pauline West was formally charged with ten counts of murder, including that of her daughter, Heather, and stepdaughter, Charmaine. The West's trial was scheduled to begin in late 1995; however, Frederick West escaped his ordeal, leaving Rosemary to face justice alone. On New Year's Day 1995, Frederick West committed suicide inside his prison cell.

At the time of her arrest and then throughout her trial, Rosemary West maintained that she was innocent of any crimes. In support of her story, Frederick West had persistently told police he was responsible for all ten murders with which they were jointly charged and that his wife was completely innocent.[12] Initially, it seemed the Crown's case against Rosemary West was tenuous and highly circumstantial. No one had witnessed any of the murders, and there was no useful forensic or fingerprint evidence that could prove useful.

The prosecution of Rosemary West, led by Brian Leveson, QC (Queen's Counsel), required a way to conclusively tie West to the killings. Leveson found the break he desperately needed when Justice Mantell, the presiding judge, allowed the admission of testimony from three survivors of sexual attacks perpetrated against them by both Rosemary and Frederick West. It was on the basis of this *similar fact evidence* that the West case turned in favor of the Crown. The witnesses had confirmed that Rosemary West was clearly capable of extreme sexual violence.[13]

Given the testimony of witnesses and the predatory sexual history of Rosemary West, the Crown Prosecution Service believed it highly unlikely that she was ignorant of what her husband had done. The nine victims found at 25 Cromwell Street had each been dismembered and all but one was missing a different bone from the remains. All the victims had been sexually abused in some way. The effort needed to inflict such injuries, dispose of the body parts, and then clean up the crime scene would be difficult to hide from an intimate partner like a wife.

At the trial summation, Leveson asked the jury to consider the evidence against Rosemary West in a familiar context: "Like three brass monkeys, she saw nothing, heard nothing and said nothing."[14] It was a convincing argument. On November 20, 1995, after twenty-eight days of testimony, the jury retired to their hotel to deliberate the issue. On November 22, 1995, Rosemary Pauline West received their decision—she was found guilty on all counts and sentenced to ten life terms of imprisonment.

If the statements of Frederick West are to be believed, he raped and killed more than twenty women in his lifetime. That this brutal sexual predator acted alone, without the knowledge and complicity of his wife, seems as inconceivable to us today as it did to the jury that convicted Rosemary West.

"I Had Fun Out of It"

In 1984, while Frederick and Rosemary West were still at the height of their murderous escapades in England, an extraordinarily brutal sexual serial-killing team was rampaging through several states in the American Midwest. Unlike the particularly long lethal career of the Wests, the team of Alton Coleman and Debra Denise Brown was criminally active for only two months. However, in that short time they brutally murdered at least eight individuals, who ranged in age from only seven years old to adult (see Table 7.6).

Debra Denise Brown was born to a family of eleven children, which perpetually struggled against poverty. A high school dropout, Brown was engaged to marry a local man by 1984 when, at the age of twenty-one, she met Alton Coleman for the first time. Passive and easily manipulated, Brown was overwhelmed by Coleman, whose personality could fluctuate from easygoing and persuasive to domineering and extraordinarily violent within moments. Despite his volatility, Brown had never met as imposing a character as Coleman and quickly broke off her engagement in order to be with him. Shortly after moving in with Coleman, however, Brown discovered his unbridled propensity for violent sex and physical abuse as she became the target of his unpredictable bouts of rage.

At the age of twenty-eight, when Coleman met Brown, he was already a hardened and experienced career criminal and a sexual sadist with a long history of violence that started in his childhood. He was the son of a prostitute who died when Coleman was still a young teenager. Sent to live with his grandmother, Coleman exhibited a significant history of psychological and behavioral problems. By puberty, he had gained the nickname of "Pissy" from his schoolmates because of his propensity to wet his pants. By the time he met Debra Brown, Coleman had already served over three years in prison for a variety of offenses, including robbery, assault, and sexual molestation. While in prison, he quickly gained a reputation as a man who was driven to aggressive homosexual behavior and physical violence.

Table 7.6: Debra Denise Brown

Classification	Team Killer (with Alton Coleman).
Birth Information	Born in 1963.
Active Period	1984. Active at the age of twenty-one.
Victim Information	Murdered at least eight individuals who ranged in age from seven years to adult. All of the murders were sexual homicides.
Method	Their victims were bludgeoned, shot, tortured, and sexually molested.
Motive	Sexual homicides undertaken by Alton Coleman with Debra Brown as partner.
Disposition	Brown and Coleman were arrested in 1984 after a two-month crime spree of murder, rape, and kidnapping. They were subsequently found guilty at trial, and both received multiple death sentences.

During the summer of 1984, shortly after the pair met, Coleman and Brown began a rampage of assault, robbery, rape, and murder that extended through several Midwestern states and lasted for nearly two months. Although Coleman primarily led this murderous rampage, Brown was an active participant in each crime and was probably personally responsible for at least two murders. This serial-killing team was not discriminate in their attacks, raping and murdering both children and adults with a variety of weapons and methods.

Coleman and Brown's first victim was nine-year-old Vernita Wheat, whom they abducted from a friend's home and then beat, raped, and strangled. However, Wheat was not the youngest victim claimed by this murderous couple. Three weeks after the murder of Wheat, Coleman and Brown abducted two young girls aged seven and nine years. Both the girls were beaten, raped, and strangled. Although the seven-year-old died, her older companion managed to survive the assault and was later able to identify her attackers.

As Coleman and Brown rampaged their way through Indiana, Ohio, Illinois, and Michigan, the body count began to rise. Each of the pair's victims was brutally attacked—often by both partners—and repeatedly raped or sexually molested. Careless and disorganized throughout the weeks of robbery, assault, and murder, Alton Coleman was soon placed on the Federal Bureau of Investigation (FBI) Most Wanted list in July 1984. Less than two months after their heinous crime spree began, it ended with the couple's arrest in Evanston, Illinois.

The outrageous nature of their crimes was reflected by the bail set against Coleman and Brown—$25 and $20 million, respectively. Tried in different jurisdictions for several counts of murder, both Alton Coleman and Debra Denise Brown received two death sentences. However, Governor Richard Celeste of Ohio commuted one of Brown's death sentences to life imprisonment in 1991, as he left office. If there was any question about whether Brown was an active conspirator in the eight-week murder spree, it was answered by one of her own statements made at her trial. Speaking of one of the couple's victims, Brown told the court: "I killed the bitch and I don't give a damn. I had fun out of it."[15]

THE KILLING YEAR

In 1980, law enforcement personnel were confronted with three notorious male/female serial-killing teams operating concurrently across six American states. In California, Oregon, and Nevada, the *Sex Slave Murderers* had claimed their tenth victim. In Alabama, Tennessee, and Georgia, the *Night Rider* and *Lady Sundance* began their criminal careers, which eventually claimed at least fifteen victims, while in southern California, the *Sunset Slayer* and his partner had committed an undetermined number of murders, which may have run into the dozens. Together, these three teams murdered at least thirty-one, and possibly more than fifty, individuals between 1978 and 1982. Virtually all these crimes were classic sexual homicides.

The Sex Slave Murderers, Gerald and Charlene Gallego, were active from 1978 to 1980 and accounted for at least ten brutal homicides. As their moniker implied, this serial-killing team was obsessed with the idea of collecting sex slaves to serve the perverse pleasures of the primary partner and murderer, Gerald Gallego (see Table 7.7).

Gerald and Charlene Gallego seemed an unlikely pair, at least based on their respective backgrounds. Gerald was born in 1946, while his father was incarcerated in San Quentin prison on a felony conviction. Nine years later, when the senior Gallego was executed in Mississippi for the murder of two law enforcement officers, Gerald's mother explained this fact away by telling the young boy that his father had been killed in an automobile accident. Despite his mother's attempts to shield Gerald from any knowledge of his father's exploits, the boy seemed destined from an early age to repeat the senior Gallego's mistakes. By the age of thirteen, Gerald had been arrested for sexually molesting a six-year-old girl in his neighborhood, and by his early thirties, he had been married seven times, was a known bigamist, and was fleeing from charges of assault, incest, and a variety of sex crimes.

In stark contrast to Gerald Gallego was his last wife, Charlene, who had been a quiet, apparently well-adjusted child who attended school and church regularly. Charlene had no criminal record and no history of violence or abuse in her background. Nonetheless, she proved to be the perfect partner for Gerald Gallego, and was always willing to follow his perverse lead in whatever criminal activity suited him at the moment.

Table 7.7: Charlene Gallego

Classification	Team Killer (with Gerald Gallego, her husband).
Birth Information	Born in 1956 as Charlene Williams.
Active Period	1978 to 1980. Active from age twenty-two to age twenty-four.
Victim Information	Murdered ten individuals in three states (California, Nevada, and Oregon). The crimes were sexual homicides of a brutal nature. The Gallegos were known in the media as the Sex Slave Murderers.
Method	Bludgeoning, shooting, torture, and sexual molestation.
Motive	Gerald Gallego desired to collect "sex slaves." Charlene Gallego would lure young women on his behalf and help to hold them hostage while they were brutalized and eventually murdered.
Disposition	Both perpetrators were arrested in 1980. In 1982, Charlene Gallego confessed to her participation in ten murders and became a witness against her husband. In 1983, Charlene Gallego received a sentence of sixteen years in prison; Gerald Gallego received two death sentences at two separate trials.

Gerald Gallego's insatiable drive for domination and violence evolved into an obsession with the concept of sex slaves. He wanted nothing less than a collection of young virgins who would perform sexual favors for him, on demand, in the most perverse manner possible. In order to fulfill this obsession, Gerald enlisted the aid of his wife to help with the abduction, control, and eventual murder of his victims. His explanation to Charlene was that the only way he could cure his impotence was by this bizarre and gruesome plan. Incredibly, Charlene apparently accepted this outrageous excuse and willingly agreed to become the instrument of sexual perversion and serial murder for her husband. It became Charlene's role to help lure the victims into the Gallego car and ensure that they were under control while Gerald had his way with them.

The Sex Slave Murderers claimed their first known victims on September 11, 1978. On that day, a sixteen-year-old (Kippi Vaught) and a seventeen-year-old (Rhonda Scheffler) were abducted from the vicinity of a shopping center in Sacramento, California. Both teenagers were repeatedly sexually molested, severely beaten, and finally murdered with a single shot through the head. The following year, in June, another pair of teenagers disappeared from a fairground in Reno, Nevada. Brenda Judd, fourteen years old, and Sandra Colley, thirteen, were abducted in the same manner as Vaught and Scheffler. For the next three years they were considered missing persons—until Charlene Gallego confessed that the two Nevada teenagers had met the same fate as Vaught and Scheffler. In April 1980, the couple again abducted a pair of teenagers from a shopping mall, this time in Reno. The bodies of Karen Chipman and Stacey Redican were discovered three months later. Each had been brutally beaten and sexually molested.

Breaking with their previous methods, the pair then abducted a single female, Linda Aguilar, who was twenty-one years old and pregnant. She was kidnapped off a public street in Oregon, in June 1980. Aguilar was bound, severely beaten, brutally raped, and buried alive, dying in an exceptionally gruesome manner.

A month after Aguilar's abduction and murder, a thirty-four-year-old woman, Virginia Mochel, was kidnapped from a parking lot in Sacramento, California. Her body was discovered three months later, the remains indicated that she had been strangled after repeated sexual molestation. In November, the Gallegos kidnapped a couple, Craig Miller and Beth

Sowers, who were both in their early twenties. Miller and Sowers had been to a local fraternity dance and were last seen by friends sitting in the Gallego vehicle, apparently in a heated argument with its occupants. One of Miller's concerned friends copied down the license plate of the Gallego car but did not immediately contact the police.

The following day, police found Miller's body; he had been shot through the head. What law enforcement personnel did not yet know was that Beth Sowers had also been shot through the head after being raped by Gerald Gallego. When Miller's friend heard of his death, he immediately contacted the police with a description of the Gallego car and its license plate number, spawning an intensive manhunt for the serial killers. For the next two weeks, the Gallegos were able to stay a step ahead of pursuing authorities by traveling to the Midwest. However, their luck had finally run its course.

On November 17, 1980, federal agents arrested the Gallegos in Omaha, Nebraska, after tracing their location by monitoring panicked telephone calls made by Charlene to her parents. For the next eighteen months, a variety of delays and legal maneuvers kept the pair from going to trial for murder. However, in 1982, with a trial date fast approaching, Charlene Gallego agreed to testify against Gerald in exchange for a reduced sentence on the outstanding charges of murder.

Gerald Gallego was charged with two counts of murder (Miller and Sowers); he went to trial and was quickly found guilty. In April 1983, he received the death sentence. Shortly thereafter he went on trial again, this time for the kidnappings and murders in Nevada (Chipman and Redican). Once again, Gallego received the death sentence. However, because of her cooperation with authorities, Charlene Gallego received a sentence of sixteen years in prison for her role in the murders, finally closing the case file on the Sex Slave Murderers.

Active from 1980 to 1982, Alvin Neelley and his wife, Judith, liked to refer to themselves as the *Night Rider* and *Lady Sundance*.[16] This murderous couple, who delighted in the association of their heinous exploits with those of Butch Cassidy and the Sundance Kid, killed at least fifteen women in a reign of terror that ranged across three southern states (see Table 7.8).

Table 7.8: Judith Ann Neelley

Classification	Team Killer (with Alvin Neelley, her husband).
Birth Information	Born in 1963.
Active Period	1982. Active at age nineteen. Some murders may have been committed as early as 1980.
Victim Information	Participated in the murder of approximately fifteen women in three states (Alabama, Tennessee, and Georgia).
Method	The murders perpetrated by the Neelleys were sexual homicides. Most of the victims were shot; many were tortured and beaten.
Motive	Sexual homicides and robbery during an extended crime spree.
Disposition	Alvin Neelley confessed, pled guilty to murder, and received two life sentences. Judith Neelley went to trial, was found guilty of murder, and was sentenced to death.

Much like Gerald Gallego, Alvin Neelley was a man with a long history of violence that was particularly directed at women. He had been imprisoned while still in his early twenties for shooting and critically injuring his first wife. Neelley's second wife, Judith, was a decade his junior and under twenty years old when the pair was arrested on charges of murder. Whether Judith Neelley was a battered victim of her husband's insatiable compulsion for violence or, as he stated, the true organizer of their rampage of murder remains uncertain. However, Judith had a criminal history in her own right,

having committed her first armed robbery with her husband
while still a teenager and being known to have shot a man
shortly before her arrest for murder.

While briefly incarcerated for the armed robbery, Judith
Neelley gave birth to twins and anxiously awaited her husband's release from prison. By 1982, both Neelleys had
gained their freedom and began roaming throughout the
South, committing a string of minor offenses, swindles, and
robbery. However, within a few months the couple had escalated their crimes to a series of murders that claimed more
than a dozen victims.

On September 25, 1982, the Neelleys abducted thirteen-
year-old Lisa Millican from a shopping center in Rome,
Georgia. The couple then took Millican to a motel room and
continuously molested her for several days in the presence of
their young children. When they had finally finished with the
teenager, Judith Neelley repeatedly injected the victim with
drain cleaner in an effort to kill her. Despite this horrific
torture, Millican somehow survived. Frustrated and angry
with their young victim, the pair drove her to a rural area
in Alabama, shot her to death, and dumped the girl's body
near a river. Although Lisa Millican became the first confirmed murder committed by the Neelleys, it is likely they
had claimed other victims in the months before September
1982, and they may have claimed their first victims as early as
1980. However, it was Judith Neelley's behavior after the
Millican murder that proved instrumental in the capture of
this serial-killing team.

Shortly after the Millican murder, Judith Neelley inexplicably made a series of telephone calls to law enforcement
authorities, which directed them to where the couple had
dumped the victim's body. The police recorded each of these
calls, although they were unable to identify the caller at the
time. Within days of these telephone calls, the Neelleys
struck again. Judith Neelley introduced herself to a young
couple in Rome, Georgia, and convinced them to join her for

an afternoon party. John Hancock, twenty-six years old, and his girlfriend, Janice Chatman, who was twenty-three, were driven by Judith Neelley to a rural area outside Rome. When they arrived, Alvin Neelley joined the trio. Judith Neelley then immediately shot Hancock in the back and, believing him dead, joined her husband in the rape and murder of Chatman. The Neelleys then fled the crime scene, assuming they had left no witnesses behind. However, Hancock survived his wounds and was able to provide a description of the suspects. An astute Georgia detective had Hancock listen to the tape-recorded calls that Judith Neelley had placed to police days earlier, and Hancock immediately identified the voice of the woman who had shot him and participated in the murder of Janice Chatman. The police now had a description of the murderers and the vehicle that they used to transport Hancock and Chatman to the crime scene.

The Neelleys were apprehended when they were recognized while trying to cash a bad check in Tennessee. John Hancock was able to positively identify the couple as his attackers and the Neelleys were held on charges of murder. Once in custody, the couple confessed to a dozen homicides and provided a variety of details about each crime. However, Judith Neelley persistently claimed that she was the battered, victimized wife of a sex maniac and had no option but to follow his demands. On the other hand, Alvin Neelley claimed that his wife had organized and carried out most, if not all, the murders. Despite these conflicting claims, their one surviving victim, John Hancock, was adamant that Judith Neelley had been the perpetrator who shot him in the back and left him for dead. Prosecutors and law enforcement officials close to the investigation generally agreed that Judith Neelley had been an active participant in many or all of the murders that were perpetrated by the couple.

In a deal with prosecutors to save his life, Alvin Neelley pled guilty to two counts of murder in Georgia and received two sentences of life imprisonment. Judith Neelley went to trial for murder in Alabama (for the Millican homicide) and was found guilty by a jury. Despite the jury recommendation that she be given life imprisonment for her crimes, the presiding judge overruled the recommendation and sentenced Judith Neelley to death.

The last of the three notorious serial-killing teams that were active in 1980 was comprised of the infamous lovers Douglas Clark and Carol Bundy, who accounted for at least six sexual homicides in and around the Hollywood area of southern California. However, law enforcement personnel involved in the case generally believe that Clark and Bundy were responsible for many more than the six murders for which Clark was eventually convicted. Some officials have stated that the actual number of victims claimed by the Sunset Slayer and his partner may have been fifty or more (see Table 7.9).

Much like the case of Alvin and Judith Neelley, Douglas Clark and Carol Bundy each blamed the other for a series of brutal sexual homicides that held southern California in terror in 1980. Clark, who came to be variously known as the *Sunset Strip Slayer,* the *Hollywood Slasher,* and the *Sunset Slayer,* has persistently maintained that Carol Bundy committed the murders with which he was charged because she believed herself to be the secret wife of the infamous serial killer Theodore (Ted) Bundy (to whom she was, in truth, not related). Clark went on to claim that Carol Bundy's real partner in murder was her former boyfriend, whom she admitted stabbing to death and decapitating in 1980. For her part, Bundy confessed to the murder and mutilation of two individuals, including her former boyfriend, but claimed that all the other slayings were Clark's work—that her role in these brutal acts was minimal. In reality, the truth about the relationship between Douglas Clark and Carol Bundy will probably never be known, except for the fact that they were partners in a series of sexual homicides that probably claimed an extraordinary number of victims.

Table 7.9: Carol Mary Bundy

Classification	Team Killer (with Douglas D. Clark).
Birth Information	Born in 1942.
Active Period	1980. Active at age thirty-eight.
Victim Information	The team of Clark and Bundy murdered at least six female victims and are believed to have murdered as many as fifty. The murders were classic sexual homicides. Clark was known in the media as the Sunset Slayer.
Method	Various methods, including shooting, stabbing, and strangulation. Many of the victims were shot in the head during oral sex acts with Clark. Several of the victims were severely mutilated after death, including decapitation.
Motive	Sexual homicides perpetrated against young women.
Disposition	Clark was found guilty of multiple counts of homicide in 1983 and subsequently sentenced to death. Bundy received multiple consecutive prison terms ranging from twenty-five years to life imprisonment (with the possibility of parole).

Carol Bundy, a nurse, first met Douglas Clark in Burbank, California. Lonely and plain, Bundy was immediately enthralled by Clark, who was decisive, dominant, and apparently also attracted to her. Clark was soon able to move in with Bundy, and the two began a torrid sexual relationship. However, Clark was apparently insatiable in his drive for sexual domination over women. Often referring to himself as the "King of the One-Night Stands," it was not long before Clark was prowling the streets once again. Despite his behavior, Bundy continued to try to please her new lover in any way possible, including attempts to understand his incredibly perverse and hostile attitude toward women.

According to Bundy, Clark soon began to seek out young prostitutes on Hollywood's Sunset Boulevard for violent sex and, in short order, murder. He also discussed a plethora of sexual fantasies with Bundy, which included an obsession for necrophilia with girls and young women. As Clark's fantasies and obsessions became overwhelming, he was able to convince Bundy to act as his willing accomplice in abduction and murder. Clark would select the victims (who were typically young women and, frequently, prostitutes), and Bundy was assigned the task of helping lure them into Clark's control. She would then watch (and sometimes photograph) the incredible behavior that would follow, also helping him in carrying out acts of necrophilia.

Clark's favorite method of perversion was to force his victims to perform oral sex while he held a gun to their head. At the moment that he reached orgasm, he would shoot the victim through the head at point-blank range. Although many of his victims were prostitutes, Clark was generally indiscriminate in selecting the women to be murdered, taking advantage of any individual who could be lured away or abducted in relative safety and who met his criteria of youth. In some cases, Clark would dismember the body of his victim, removing the head and preserving it in Carol Bundy's refrigerator as a trophy and sex object. Bundy would later freshen the severed head with makeup, groom the hair, and provide it to Clark for his sexual pleasure.

According to Bundy's statements, Douglas Clark was solely responsible for the selection of the team's victims, their sexual abuse, and murder. However, Clark told a very different story. He claimed that the real serial-killing team was comprised of Bundy and her former boyfriend. According to Clark, Bundy was the true organizer of the 1980 serial-killing spree. The crimes, Clark said, were carried out by Bundy and her lover, using Clark as a convenient patsy when the team's activities became sensational. Bundy, by her own admission, is known to have murdered two individuals. One of the victims was her former boyfriend, who Bundy targeted because she had discussed her role in the serial killings with him in a moment of weakness. Afraid that her former lover would go to the police, Bundy lured him to a secluded location on the pretext of reinstating their relationship. After having sex with her victim, Bundy stabbed him to death, mutilated his torso, and removed his head in a slaying reminiscent of many that had claimed the lives of young women in the Hollywood area. After killing her former boyfriend, Bundy inexplicably began discussing the serial murders with others. Before long, she also confessed to police and named Douglas Clark as the infamous Sunset Slayer who had been terrorizing the southern California area throughout 1980.

Douglas Clark went to trial in 1983, charged with multiple counts of murder. The case against him rested primarily with Carol Bundy, who became the chief witness for the prosecution. Based largely on Bundy's testimony, Clark was found guilty of six counts of homicide and given a sentence of death. Bundy received two sentences, of twenty-five years to life and twenty-seven years to life in prison. Today, each member of this killing team continues to point to the other as the chief perpetrator in dozens of brutal sex slayings.

The gruesome serial murders carried out by Clark and Bundy, the Neelleys, and the Gallegos raise interesting and troubling questions about the role of the female partner in a serial-killing team. It is extraordinarily rare for a woman to commit crimes of the brutality attributed to these team killers when she is acting alone. Judges and juries generally accept the concept that the female member of a serial-killing team is typically less violent than her male counterpart. From a common perspective, when there is conflicting evidence in the case, the female team member is often relegated to the role of a willing accomplice to murder. For many male/female serial-killing teams, this scenario may be accurate. Because the crime of serial killing is covert and rarely committed in the presence of surviving witnesses, judges and juries are typically faced with controversial evidence that is difficult or impossible to assess. To compound this situation, it is not uncommon for the team members to turn against each other in an effort to minimize their roles in the crimes. This often leaves juries with little to assess except the credibility of two suspected perpetrators of murder.

However, there is no question that female members of a serial-killing team are capable of committing brutal and heinous crimes in the context of the partnership. The synergy of the killing team and the intense relationship that typically exists between its partners impels the team to acts of violence and aggression that often surpass those that would be committed by a lone serial killer—especially a woman. The crimes of Judith Neelley and the confessions of Carol Bundy make it clear that a woman who is teamed with a male serial killer can murder in ways that are incredibly callous and brutal, without regard to her individual propensity for violence.

FEMALE TEAM KILLERS

A serial-killing team comprised exclusively of women is an exceptional phenomenon, even by the rare standards of the female serial killer in general. Similar to serial murder cases that involve a male/female criminal partnership, the female killing team is typically comprised of a dominant member who orchestrates the murderous activities of the group and one or more submissive, easily manipulated partners. In the team scenario, the dominant member may be the most active murderer in the group or she may take on the role of the primary organizer of the crimes without personally committing murder. In some instances, there is a strong sexual relationship between or among members of the team or, alternatively, the members may join together for a more prosaic purpose.

These teams can come together for a variety of complex reasons, which may encompass several motivational categories, such as Profit or Crime and Angel of Death. In at least one case involving a female serial-killing team (Graham and Wood), the purpose of the murders was, in part, to enhance the sexual relationship of the partners, in addition to the more common motivation of domination and control over their victims. Regardless of the motivations for their actions, these team murderers are surprisingly prolific and cruel in acting out their aggressions against others, often favoring victims who are very young, elderly, frail, or incapacitated.

The earliest recorded case of a female serial-killing team operating in the twentieth century occurred in England just after 1900 and involved murders that were committed solely for profit (see Table 7.10). Amelia Sach and Annie Walters were both English-born women who came together to establish a private residence for unwed mothers in London. Sach and Walters specialized in offering lodging and adoption services for single mothers who wished to give birth in a confidential setting that would preserve their anonymity. In many cases, these young women were attracted to the Sach and Walters operation in order to relinquish their newborns for immediate adoption without any publicity or record keeping.

The two murderous proprietors regularly advertised their confidential services in London newspapers and soon found themselves with a steady stream of clients. Sach and Walters provided a popular, full-service operation, which, for a reasonable fee, included lodging, birthing services, and confidential adoption arrangements. What was unknown to the unfortunate women who used these services was that their newborn children were murdered rather than placed for adoption.

Greedy and unwilling to bear the expense of caring for a growing number of infants while they awaited adoption, Amelia Sach would turn the newborns over to Annie Walters immediately after birth. Sach would provide a terse explanation to her clients to the effect that the confidential adoption process forbade her from discussing the details of any transaction. Walters, who was said to be profoundly feeble-minded, had no capacity to deal with the complex arrangements that would be needed to successfully carry out an adoption. However, she was more than willing to follow the simple instructions of her dominant partner by murdering the infants using chlorodyne and disposing their bodies in the Thames river or a local garbage dump. The unsuspecting mother would then be told that her baby had been successfully adopted and asked to pay a small additional fee to cover extra expenses.

Table 7.10: Amelia Sach and Annie Walters

Classification	Team Killers.
Birth Information	Amelia Sach was born in 1873, in England. Annie Walters was born in England.
Active Period	For several years at the turn of the twentieth century.
Victim Information	The team killers murdered infants who were temporarily in their care for adoption. The number of victims has never been determined; however, it probably ranges into the dozens.
Method	Poison (often used chlorodyne).
Motive	Profit derived from "baby farming." The infants were to be helped with adoption services offered by Sach and Walters. However, they were murdered by Walters and the proceeds of adoption fees were kept by the two women.
Disposition	Sach and Walters were arrested in 1902. They were subsequently convicted of their crimes and sentenced to death. Both women were executed in 1903.

The gruesome baby farming operation went on for several years before Walters eventually disobeyed the instructions of her dominant partner and brought one of the new-borns home to her London flat. Walters's landlord, who was also a policeman, became immediately suspicious of her con-voluted story about how the baby had come to live with her. The landlord's suspicions grew even more profound when the infant inexplicably died just a few days after Walters brought him home and, within two months, she then produced another infant along with a tale more unbelievable than the first. Again, this infant mysteriously died within a few days of his arrival. Walters's landlord was now convinced that something was very wrong with his tenant and reported the bizarre inci-dents to his law enforcement colleagues. Because of the land-lord's persistent suspicions, an investigation was begun that soon led to the discovery of the murderous business that Sach and Walters had been operating for years.

Both women were quickly arrested, tried for multiple counts of murder, found guilty, and sentenced to death. The actual number of their victims was never determined because no records were kept and the perpetrator's clients were under-standably reluctant to discuss their use of Sach and Walters's services. However, it is likely that several dozen infants were slain during the years the murderous partners operated their home for unwed mothers. When Sach and Walters were fi-nally hung for their crimes, Mr. Pierrepoint, the hangman, made the following notation in his diary: "These two women were baby farmers of the worst kind and were both repulsive in type. They had literally to be carried to the scaffold and protested to the end against their sentences."[17]

A decade after the execution of Sach and Walters, another female serial-killing team was active on the European conti-nent. This team was comprised of several Black Widow serial murderers who operated in Nagyrev, Hungary. Between 1914 and 1929, this killing team specialized in the elimination of unwanted husbands by using poison, which was typi-cally served to the victims in a glass of strong red wine. The group was organized and headed by Mrs. Julius Fuzekos and

included, among others, Susi Olah, Juliane Lipka, and Mrs.
Ladislaus Szabo (see Table 7.11).

Table 7.11: Mrs. Julius Fuzekos, Susi Olah, and Others

Classification	Team Killers.
Birth Information	Fuzekos was born in 1865, in Hungary. Olah was born in 1869, in Hungary.
Active Period	1914 to 1929. Fuzekos was active from age forty-nine to age sixty-four and Olah from age forty-five to age sixty.
Victim Information	At least seven men (and probably dozens more) were murdered by a team of Black Widow slayers in Hungary.
Method	Poison.
Motive	Team killers who wished to rid themselves and others of their husbands in order to make way for younger lovers.
Disposition	Seven women were tried and convicted of poisoning male victims. Fuzekos, the team leader, committed suicide rather than be arrested. The other members of the killing team were hanged.

On July 1, 1929, the murderous group was finally discovered when one of the husbands who had been targeted for death managed to survive the poison wine that he had been offered by Mrs. Szabo, a woman with whom he had only a passing acquaintance. The bizarre story that he related to police about his encounter with Szabo resulted in an investigation of several women in the town. One of the women who was questioned, Juliane Lipka, confessed to poisoning seven victims at the direction of the group leader, Fuzekos. Based on Lipka's confession, the authorities immediately went to Fuzekos's house to arrest her on suspicion of murder. However, as they tried to enter her home, Fuzekos committed suicide.

Pursuing the investigation, the authorities eventually learned that Fuzekos had recruited seven other members of her murderous team. For fifteen years, these women had specialized in poisoning dozens of husbands for profit. At the end of the investigation, all seven of the remaining perpetrators were found guilty of murder and publicly hanged.

In recent decades, two cases of serial murder committed by female teams became notorious in the media because of their extreme viciousness and cruelty. Both cases occurred in the 1980s and involved the murder of patients in a medical facility—specifically, a large general hospital and a nursing home. In the murders committed at the Alpine Manor nursing home in the United States, at least ten elderly patients were brutally attacked by a pair of serial murderers whose sexual relationship was a fundamental component of their aggressive motivations. Five of these elderly and frail patients died.

The most devastating case of serial murder committed by a female team of killers occurred at the Lainz General Hospital in Vienna, Austria. This case involved four perpetrators who acted under the dominant leadership of a vengeful and determined serial murderer. It is uncertain how many victims were claimed by this murderous team; however, some estimates put the number as high as 300.

In both the Lainz hospital and Alpine Manor cases, the female serial-killing teams were controlled by a single member who directed the activities of the group and made life-or-death decisions about the patients under their care. The need for domination and control over their victims was apparent in both cases. The perpetrators who were active at the Lainz hospital did not engage in any apparent mutual sexual relationship; however, the case of the Alpine Manor nursing home murders involved two women, Gwendolyn Graham and Catherine May Wood, who were deeply involved in a torrid sexual relationship that culminated in repetitive acts of murder (see Table 7.12).

Table 7.12: Gwendolyn Graham and Catherine May Wood

Classification	Team Killers.
Birth Information	Graham was born in 1963, in California. Wood was born in 1962.
Active Period	1987. Graham was twenty-four and Wood was twenty-five at the time of the murders.
Victim Information	Graham murdered at least five elderly female patients and attempted to murder at least five others. Wood acted as lookout during the attacks.
Method	Suffocation.
Motive	Graham and Wood were lesbian lovers whose relationship was founded, in part, on the sexual thrill of murder.
Disposition	Both women went to trial in 1989. Wood testified against Graham and was given a prison sentence of twenty to forty years. Graham was convicted on five counts of first-degree murder and given multiple life sentences.

In 1986, Catherine May Wood was the supervisor of nurse's aides at the Alpine Manor nursing home in Walker, Michigan, a suburb of Grand Rapids. That year, Wood celebrated her twenty-fourth birthday and her first year at the nursing home. An unhappy and unassertive woman, Wood weighed approximately 450 pounds and had just experienced the traumatic disintegration of her seven-year marriage. This was also the year that she met Gwendolyn Graham.

Graham was born the year after Wood, in 1963, in California. She was raised in Tyler, Texas, by a family whose members claimed that her childhood had been a normal and happy one. In 1986, Graham moved to Michigan and was able to find work as a nurse's aide at the Alpine Manor nursing home. There she met her new supervisor, Catherine Wood, and apparently fell deeply in love.

The lonely and passive Wood fell immediately under the spell of Graham—a staunch and demanding woman who had many experiences to share with her new lover. Appreciated once again, Wood immediately began to diet and pay strict attention to her appearance. The two women also began a torrid sexual affair and an active social life, which sometimes included casual sex with other women, whom they would meet at gay bars and parties. Graham, in particular, had a sexual appetite that ran to the extreme and would often seek out new and innovative ways to enhance her pleasures. Wood, who was intent upon pleasing her lover, proved compliant and needy for the attention Graham could provide.

In October 1986, Graham first approached Wood with the thought of committing a murder in order to enhance their sexual encounters. Their sexual relationship had involved rough play and choking for some time, and Graham now wanted to experience the real thing. According to her later testimony, Wood did not take Graham's conversations about murder seriously and instead dismissed them as mere talk—at first. However, within three months of the first conversation, the lovers would mutually participate in murder.

In January 1987, Graham attacked and murdered her first victim. In a macabre plan, Graham had decided that she would murder six victims whose last names would spell out the word "murder." However, that plan proved to be too elaborate and, moreover, the tenacity of some of Graham's early victims surprised her. The women reconsidered their plan and decided to only attack the most vulnerable victims they could find.

Between January and mid-April, Graham and Wood attacked at least ten patients at Alpine Manor and were able to murder five of them. The course of each attack was the same: Wood acted as the lookout while Graham would attack the victims by smothering them with a dampened washcloth pressed over their mouth and nose. In some cases, immediately after the murder, Wood and Graham would make love in a vacant area of the nursing home, thus reliving the perverse thrill they had just experienced at the expense of their victims. Each victim was elderly and frail, ranging in age from sixty to ninety-five; most of them suffered from Alzheimer's disease.[1] In each murder, the duo left no physical evidence behind and there were no witnesses to their activities.

By the middle of April 1987, the murderous rampage came to an abrupt end when Wood and Graham argued over Wood's failure to participate directly in any of the killings. At the same time, Graham had been attracted to another lover and soon quit her job at Alpine Manor to move to Texas. By this time, Wood was emotionally devastated, guilt ridden, and alone once again.

For the next several months the former lovers kept in sporadic contact by telephone. However, Graham had moved on to a new life and job, giving little thought to Wood's deteriorating emotional state. In August 1987, Wood could no longer live with the guilt and loneliness, which had become an enormous burden. In a tearful conversation with her ex-husband, Wood admitted to the murders that had been committed at Alpine Manor. However, Kenneth Wood inexplicably waited for well over a year before he finally communicated that conversation to authorities.

Finally, in the fall of 1988, Kenneth Wood approached police with what he knew of the Alpine Manor murders, including his wife's involvement. Checking his startling story, the police investigated each death that occurred at the nursing home in early 1987 and concluded that eight of them

---

1. The victims and their ages were: Marguerite Chambers, sixty; Edith Cole, eighty-nine; Myrtle Luce, ninety-five; Mae Mason, seventy-nine; and Belle Burkhard, seventy-four.

were possible homicides while another five were definitely so. In early December, warrants were sworn out for Catherine Wood and Gwendolyn Graham and both women were arrested.

Graham was apprehended at her job in Tyler, Texas, where she worked as a nurse's aide at the Mother Frances Hospital. She was held against a bail of $1 million as a flight risk. An immediate investigation of recent deaths at the Mother Frances hospital was undertaken to determine if Graham had continued on with her murderous ways after leaving Michigan; however, it was soon decided that she had not attacked any patients during her months on the job.

On June 5, 1988, a preliminary hearing was held to determine if a murder trial should proceed against the two former lovers. The case for the prosecution would rely primarily on Wood's statements to her husband and the testimony of several coworkers at Alpine Manor who had overheard conversations between the lethal couple that detailed several of the murders. In addition to this testimony, Graham and Wood had kept various souvenirs from several of their victims and prominently displayed the items in the house they had shared as lovers. Several employees at Alpine Manor vividly remembered these souvenirs. Despite the fact that the prosecutors lacked hard physical evidence of murder, they felt that their circumstantial case was a strong one. The prosecutors were soon proven correct when Wood and Graham were bound over for trial on five counts of first-degree murder each.

In a surprise maneuver to avoid life imprisonment (or worse), Catherine Wood pleaded guilty to second-degree murder on September 8, 1989, just days before her trial was scheduled to begin. Wood confessed her role in the Alpine Manor murders and agreed to testify for the prosecution against Graham. With the added weight of Wood's confession and testimony, the case against Graham became irrefutable.

Graham's trial proved to be a short one. It ended on September 20, 1989, after five hours of jury deliberation, when she was found guilty on all five counts of murder and a single count of conspiracy to commit murder. Without question, the testimony of Catherine Wood weighed heavily in the jury's decision. Weeping during a particularly emotional part of her testimony, Wood described why she had finally admitted to the murders:

When she [Graham] was killing people at Alpine and I didn't do anything, that was bad enough. But when she would call me [from Texas] and say how she wanted to smash a baby, I had to stop her somehow. I knew she was working in a hospital there. She said she wanted to take one of the babies and smash it up against a window. I had to do something. I didn't care about myself anymore.[18]

Less than a month later, on October 11, 1989, Wood appeared before Kent County Circuit Judge Robert Benson for sentencing and received twenty to forty years in prison. In passing sentence, the judge noted Wood's cooperation and her unhealthy relationship with Graham: "Without you, I'm sure this matter would never have been cleared up. I'm convinced that you truly show remorse. I'm also convinced that you are in fact a follower and not a leader."[19] However, matters did not go as well for Gwendolyn Graham when she was sentenced on November 2, 1989. Graham received six life terms in prison without the possibility of parole.

In 1987, the year Catherine Wood and Gwendolyn Graham carried out their three-month reign of terror at the Alpine Manor nursing home, Stephanija Mayer emigrated from Yugoslavia to Vienna, Austria, to start a new life. Mayer was a recently divorced grandmother in search of a job when she called at the Lainz General Hospital and was offered a position as nurse's aide on the night shift. The Lainz hospital, built in 1839, was one of the largest and most respected medical institutions in Vienna, with a staff of some 2,000 employees. Mayer was elated to be employed at the hospital and anxious to make a good impression on her new coworkers.

When Mayer arrived at Lainz for her first night's work, she was introduced to Waltraud Wagner, the chief nurse's aide for Pavilion Five and her new supervisor. Wagner was the senior nurse's aide on the busy ward and had worked at the hospital since 1983. She was considered by her supervisors to be an efficient, reliable worker. Her colleagues considered Wagner to be highly experienced but also manipulative, sometimes aggressive, and often domineering. On that first night Mayer also met two other nurse's aides who worked with Wagner on the same shift: Maria Gruber and Irene Leidolf. Wagner, Gruber, and Leidolf were all in their twenties and had worked together on Pavilion Five for some time before Mayer's arrival. By comparison, Mayer was twenty years their senior and had little practical experience as a nurse's aid. However, despite the differences in age and background, Wagner and her colleagues were quick to welcome Mayer into their ranks—and quick to indoctrinate her into the ways of team murder on the hospital night shift (see Table 7.13).

Table 7.13: Lainz General Hospital

Classification	Team Killers.
Birth Information	Waltraud Wagner was born in 1959, in Austria. Maria Gruber was born in 1964, in Austria. Irene Leidolf was born in 1962, in Austria. Stephanija Mayer was born in 1939, in Austria.
Active Period	1983 to 1989. Wagner was active from age twenty-four to age thirty, Gruber from age nineteen to age twenty-five, Leidolf from age twenty-one to age twenty-seven, and Mayer from age forty-four to age fifty.
Victim Information	Murdered at least 49 patients in their

	care. Estimates of the total number of murders range up to 300.
Method	Use of lethal injections or drowning of the patients by pouring water down their throats.
Motive	Angels of Death who murdered from a sense of power and control over their victims.
Disposition	The four women were arrested in 1989 and went to trial in 1991. Wagner, the head of the team, was found guilty of multiple murders and sentenced to life imprisonment. Leidolf was also sentenced to life imprisonment. Mayer and Gruber each received sentences of fifteen years imprisonment.

Several years before Mayer's arrival at the hospital, Waltraud Wagner had committed her first murder at the age of twenty-four. In 1983, Wagner had been caring for a seventy-seven-year-old woman who had been admitted to Pavilion Five with little hope for survival. The elderly woman had pleaded incessantly with Wagner to help end her pain and suffering and, eventually, the nurse's aid agreed to help her die. Wagner carefully planned her attack and injected the woman with a fatal dosage of morphine. To Wagner's surprise and relief, the murder went completely undetected on the busy ward. The ease of the crime and the immense sense of power that Wagner derived from the ability to determine life and death led her to a career of serial murder that would last for another six years and involve three accomplices.

Over the next few years, Wagner recruited three members into her killing team: Maria Gruber, an Austrian who was five years her junior; Irene Leidolf, another Austrian three years her junior; and Stephanija Mayer, a Yugoslavian who was twenty years Wagner's senior. Each of the team members was employed as a nurse's aide on the night shift, and each was easily dominated and controlled by the woman whom prosecutors would later describe as a sadistic Svengali.[20] By 1987, with the arrival of Stephanija Mayer, Wagner was able to dramatically increase her lethal activities on Pavilion Five, using the members of her killing team to carry out her orders for execution.

Under Waltraud Wagner's direction and strict control, the killing team would attack their victims by use of either a lethal injection or what Wagner described as the "water cure"—a gruesome tactic of killing the victim by forcing water down his or her throat and into the lungs. Each victim was personally selected by Wagner, who based her lethal decisions on whether or not the patient had presented a problem to the Pavilion Five caretakers. Patients who proved to be demanding (or who even lodged a minor complaint) were quickly targeted for death by Wagner, with the sentence carried out by herself or by one or more of the team members. By 1988, the year after Stephanija Mayer joined the team, Pavilion Five was under siege by the four murderous caretakers and the unusual number of deaths had become a topic of conversation among the hospital staff. By then, Pavilion Five had become known to hospital employees as the "pavilion of death."

As is often the case with team killers, the members of Wagner's murderous gang could not resist the temptation to discuss and reexperience their heinous exploits. In February 1989, the four women were sharing drinks and tales of murder at a local tavern when their careless conversation was overheard by one of the Lainz hospital physicians. Aware of the rampant rumors that had surrounded Pavilion Five for over a year, the physician immediately relayed his concerns to local police and convinced them an investigation was needed. Law enforcement officials approached the physician in charge of Pavilion Five, Xavier Pesendorfer, to seek his help in carrying out their inquires; however, Pesendorfer refused to cooperate with the investigation.

Frustrated by Pesendorfer's lack of assistance and determined to understand what had happened at the hospital, the police independently moved ahead with their inquiries. Within two months, on April 9, 1989, investigators had established sufficient evidence to arrest all four perpetrators. On that same day, senior investigator Franz Priessnitz held a press conference to outline the details of his investigation, shocking the media and the public with the incredible story of murder that he had uncovered. Three days later, in response to the unprecedented public outcry generated by the arrest of Wagner and her accomplices, Pesendorfer was suspended from his position at the Lainz hospital for failing to cooperate with the police investigation.

On the day Pesendorfer was suspended, Waltraud Wagner confessed to thirty-nine murders that she had personally committed, while the other perpetrators confessed to an additional ten. The details of these multiple confessions prompted police to order the exhumation of several bodies in a search for supporting forensic evidence upon which to build their case. This decision proved to be vital to the prosecution because, on April 14, 1989, Wagner recanted most of her earlier confession. The case against Wagner now appeared to rest with forensic evidence and the confessions of her coconspirators.

A long process of legal bickering and forensic examinations followed, with prosecutors attempting to learn the actual number of victims claimed by the Lainz hospital team killers. By the end of 1989, Wagner's colleagues had told police that she had been personally responsible for over 200 deaths on Pavilion Five. However, the time that had passed since the murders and the vague details provided by the perpetrators resulted in an investigation of monumental proportions for prosecutors. Although the inquiries continued for over a year after the perpetrators were arrested, prosecutors eventually built a case against Wagner and her cohorts that was both horrifying and compelling.

On February 28, 1991, the four women went to trial on

combined charges of forty-two murders and multiple accounts of attempted murder. Shortly after the trial began, Waltraud Wagner was called to the stand to provide the details of her role in the crimes. The first of the team to testify, Wagner quickly admitted to murdering her patients by using lethal injections of morphine and her now-infamous "water cure." A week into the trial, Irene Leidolf also confessed to murdering patients with lethal injections of morphine under the direction of Wagner. With the confessions from the murderers now on record and the results of the forensic investigation as supporting evidence, the outcome of Vienna's most infamous trial in modern history was no longer in doubt.

On March 29, 1991, the four perpetrators learned their fate. Found guilty on all counts, they received sentences that reflected the public outrage at their incredible crimes. Wagner and Leidolf were each sentenced to life in prison without the possibility of parole—the maximum penalty possible in Austria. Mayer and Gruber each received a minimum of fifteen years in prison for attempted murder. However, despite the long investigation and public trial of the Lainz hospital team killers, officials were never able to learn the true extent of their crimes. It was frequently reported in Vienna newspapers that several of the officials who worked on the case believed that the four perpetrators may have murdered as many as 300 patients between 1983 and 1987. If these estimates were even remotely accurate, Wagner and her cohorts would easily rank as the most prolific female serial-killing team in Austria's history.

FAMILY TEAM KILLERS

Occasionally, serial-killing teams are comprised of individuals who form a family-like unit and whose members are primarily drawn together by their compulsion for mayhem and murder. These family killing teams typically engage in a variety of felonies other than murder—felonies that are often part of an extended crime spree. For example, in the 1930s, the notorious Karpis-Barker gang, headed by Ma Barker and including some of her family members, specialized in extortion, theft, and armed robbery. For this team of criminals, profit was the primary consideration, not murder. However, the history of female serial killers in this country provides a few cases in which women were members of a family killing team that was clearly committed to serial murder in the course of its other felonious activities.

It is important to broaden the common understanding of *family* in the context of this categorization of serial murderers. Members of a family serial-killing team may or may not be biologically related. In fact, it is more appropriate to consider this category of serial murderers as akin to an extended family whose structure remains intact because of their common compulsion to kill. Therefore, we define a family serial-killing team as *three or more individuals who share a mutual commitment to serial murder and view themselves as a family*. The members of this team may or may not be biologically related; however, they typically will reside in the same dwelling place. The team members will span more than a single generation and will pursue their crimes in a coordinated manner. Finally, to be considered a family unit, this association of serial killers must be comprised of members of both sexes.

As in the case of any serial-killing team, family team killers are controlled and managed by a figurehead who is a committed serial murderer in his or her own right, even if he or she does not directly partake in any homicidal activities.[1] The family is held together in its lethal activities by this individual, who acts as the head of the group and to whom the members commit their loyalty. Although the family

---

I. This situation can occur when the head of a serial-killing team plans and coordinates multiple homicides but does not directly involve him or herself in the actual execution of the crimes. Charles Manson and the members of his serial killing family are an example of this unique situation.

serial-killing team is comprised of both sexes, it is typical for its members to be dominated by an aggressive or lethal male.

Because of the narrowness of its definition, family serial-killing teams are quite rare. However, there are at least two notorious examples in this category: the McCrary family and the Manson family. Strictly speaking, the Manson family stretches the definition of a family serial-killing team because there was not a clear separation of generations among its members. Nonetheless, the head of this infamous family, Charles Manson, was approximately a generation senior to most of the family members and, moreover, the individuals in the group clearly related to each other as family members. Both of these serial-killing families specialized in gruesome sexual homicides that were carried out in conjunction with a variety of other felonies. In other instances, male and female family members alike were clearly involved in multiple murders.

However, the motives of the McCrary and Manson families were wildly disparate. The McCrary family crime spree was motivated primarily by profit and exacerbated by the male family member's compulsion for rape and murder. On the other hand, the Manson family, in addition to their other crimes, murdered for bizarre and twisted philosophical motives. Often exacerbated by prolonged drug use, the Manson family crimes were carried out at the direction of the head of the family, Charles Manson, in a credo of hatred that has remained beyond comprehension for most Americans.

The McCrary and Manson families also differed from each other in another important aspect. The female members of the McCrary family generally supported and aided the male members in their acts of serial killing, while rarely committing murder themselves. However, several female members of the Manson family were active serial murderers in their own right, albeit at the direction, and under the influence, of Charles Manson.

Fortunately, the active period of family serial-killing

teams tends to be short. Because this group of criminals typically engages in a variety of offenses that are often poorly planned and organized, the family members may come to the attention of law enforcement authorities before much time has passed. However, as the cases of the McCrary and Manson family will show, these killing teams can be shockingly lethal in their impact, often committing crimes of the most heinous nature.

The McCrary family was a classic organization of relatives by birth and marriage that engaged in a crime spree reminiscent of many of the infamous American gangs of the 1920s and 1930s. However, this felonious family separated themselves from all previous gangs by their incredible obsession with serial murder. From August 1971 until February 1972, the McCrary family was responsible for at least twenty-two abductions and murders, dozens of robberies, and countless other offenses, constituting a crime spree that ranks among the most intense and lethal in the history of American criminology (see Table 7.14).

Headed by the husband-and-wife team of Carolyn and Sherman McCrary, this lethal family also included the McCrarys' daughter, Ginger Taylor, their son-in-law, Raymond Carl Taylor, and their son, Daniel. Beginning in late 1971, the five McCrary family members rampaged across several states in a crime spree that involved burglary, robbery, extortion, kidnapping, and relentless murder.

The McCrary crime saga began as a series of armed robberies committed by Sherman McCrary and Raymond Taylor prior to 1971. According to later court testimony, Sherman McCrary perpetrated his first felony in Texas while suffering an extended period of unemployment. With Robert Taylor as his accomplice, McCrary committed armed robbery in what he claimed was a desperate effort to provide income for his family. However, Taylor and McCrary were not successful in their early attempts at a life of crime and instead were promptly arrested for their efforts. Court records indicate that Sherman McCrary's claim to a sudden life of crime may have been less than the full truth; both McCrary and Taylor had also served time in prison for a variety of other offenses, including burglary and forgery, in the Athens, Texas, area.

Table 7.14: The McCrary Family

Classification	Team Killers.
Birth Information	Various.
Active Period	1971 to 1972.
Victim Information	Linked to at least twenty-two kidnappings and murders.
Method	Most victims were shot with a small-caliber handgun; most were female and many were raped or otherwise sexually molested.
Motive	The murders were committed during a nationwide crime spree. Robbery and extortion comprised the primary motivation.
Disposition	In 1972, the McCrary family members were arrested and charged with a variety of crimes. Various family members received prison sentences that ranged from five years to life imprisonment.

By August 1971, Sherman McCrary and Raymond Taylor had gained their freedom and the McCrary family was together once again. The McCrarys quickly settled on a new course of criminal activity that they viewed as potentially more prosperous than their former careers—kidnapping and extortion. On August 17, 1971, the family, led by Sherman McCrary, Daniel McCrary, and Raymond Taylor, held up a Salt Lake City bakery at gunpoint, collecting the cash on hand and abducting a seventeen-year-old female employee named Sheri Martin. The McCrary family transported their teenage hostage to Nevada by car, raping her repeatedly along the way. Martin was then shot and her body was dumped by the side of a road near Wendover, Nevada, becoming the first known victim of the McCrary family. Her abduction and murder established a method of operation that the murderous family would use almost exclusively for the next six months.

Three days later, on August 20, 1971, the family was in Denver, Colorado. There they robbed another store and abducted an employee, Leeora Looney. Once again, the McCrary family raped and murdered their captive, using the same weapon that had killed Sheri Martin—a .32-caliber revolver. For the next several months, the McCrarys continued this pattern of robbery, abduction, and murder, ranging from Florida to California. Each of their victims was sexually assaulted and murdered with the same small-caliber weapon. In addition to the rampage of serial murders, the McCrarys committed a variety of other felonies, often netting a very small reward for the incredible mayhem they created. Throughout the crime spree, Carolyn McCrary and Ginger Taylor provided support to the primary perpetrators, Sherman McCrary, Daniel McCrary, and Raymond Taylor. However, it is uncertain if they directly participated in any of the murders, whose vicious nature became the McCrary family trademark.

The McCrary murder and crime spree came to an abrupt end near Santa Barbara, California, in June 1972. While attempting to rob a supermarket at gunpoint, the McCrary men and Raymond Taylor were interrupted by the unexpected arrival of a law enforcement officer. The responding officer was wounded in a shoot-out in front of the supermarket as the robbers tried to flee the crime scene. Even though the McCrarys and Taylor managed to escape, witnesses to the robbery were able to provide a description of the vehicle and its license plate number.

Police quickly located the McCrary family in Goleta, California, and arrested all five members. Taylor and the McCrary men immediately pled guilty to several robberies in an attempt to deflect attention from their dozens of murders.

Carolyn McCrary and her daughter were charged with harboring fugitives and several other minor offenses. Although they were convicted on charges of armed robbery and imprisoned, the McCrary men and Raymond Taylor were unable to avoid their murderous history for long.

The Federal Bureau of Investigation (FBI) was able to link Sherman McCrary, Daniel McCrary, and Raymond Taylor to the murder of Leeora Looney and at least ten other women in several states. FBI investigators also believed that the McCrary family had been involved in as many as a dozen other unsolved murders between August 1971 and February 1972. Carolyn McCrary and Ginger Taylor, who had already been imprisoned for earlier charges in connection with several robberies, were believed to be accomplices in several murders, although it proved impossible to produce sufficient evidence to indict them on charges of homicide. By the end of 1972, all five members of the McCrary family serial-killing team had received prison sentences ranging from five years to life in prison.

Helter Skelter—The Manson Family

Although the McCrarys stand alone as potentially the most lethal family serial-killing team in American history, their notoriety pales in comparison to that of the Manson family. In fact, the murders committed by the Manson family remain unparalleled in American criminology for a variety of reasons that are both factual, because of the public trial that followed, and visceral, because of their exceptionally brutal nature (see Table 7.15).

In August 1969, within a period of forty-eight hours, a series of homicides in Los Angeles captured national headlines and stunned the American public in a deeply personal way. Known as the Tate-LaBianca murders these crimes spawned a fury of outrage in the press and caused one of the most intensive manhunts and public trials in U.S. history. The brutal killing of seven prominent individuals was so extreme and

senseless in its execution that the crimes and its perpetrators
have become dark legends in the history of American criminology, even though most of the murderers were not much
more than teenagers when the crimes were committed. However, despite their sensational nature, the Tate-LaBianca murders did not represent the full extent of the Manson family's
lethal activities. Although it has been generally overlooked in
the media, this cult may have been responsible for as many as
twenty serial killings in all (see Table 7.16).

Table 7.15: The Manson Family

Classification	Team Killers (with Charles Manson).
Birth Information	Several female members of the "Manson family" were involved in a variety of murders. Most notable were: Susan Atkins, born in 1948. Patricia Krenwinkel, born in 1948. Leslie Van Houten, born in 1950. Mary Brunner, born in 1944. Linda Kesabian, born in 1950.
Active Period	1968 to 1969. Atkins was active from age twenty to age twenty-one, Krenwinkel from age twenty to age twenty-one, Van Houten from age eighteen to age nineteen, Brunner from age twenty-four to age twenty-five, and Kesabian from age eighteen to age nineteen.
Victim Information	Various family members murdered at least nine individuals. As many as twenty murders may be linked to the Manson family.
Method	Various methods, often of a ritualistic nature, including shooting, bludgeoning, and stabbing.

Motive	Murders ordered by Charles Manson and carried out by various family members.
Disposition	All of the perpetrators were arrested in 1969 and came to trial in 1970 and 1971. Death sentences were imposed on several of the perpetrators; however, the sentences were commuted to life imprisonment when the Supreme Court later overturned the death penalty.

Shortly before midnight, on August 8, 1969, Charles Manson informed several of the members of his cult—a group that was self-styled as the Manson family—that the time had arrived for "helter skelter" to begin. This bizarre cult dogma embodied the belief that a war between the races in America was inevitable and that it was the obligation of the Manson family to ensure its eruption. The twisted outcome of such a race war was to be the eventual recognition of the Manson family members as leaders of a post-revolutionary society. On that night, Manson directed several members of the cult, including three young women (Linda Kesabian, Susan Atkins, and Patricia Krenwinkel) and one young man (Charles Watson), to initiate the era of helter skelter, prompting his well-indoctrinated followers with the simple command, "You know what I mean."[21]

The residence selected as ground zero for the planned race war was the home of actress Sharon Tate and her husband, Roman Polanski. The Manson family scheme was both lethal and simple: the residents of the home would be murdered in as brutal a fashion possible, and evidence would later be planted in other areas of Los Angeles that would implicate members of the African-American community. Manson and his followers assumed that the outrage generated by such a heinous crime would ignite an unstoppable race war, which would eventually result in the Manson family's triumphant rise to restore order to a chaotic society.

When the Manson cult members arrived at the Tate/Polanski home to begin their well-planned onslaught, the results were incomprehensible. At the residence that night were five prominent individuals, including Sharon Tate, who was eight months pregnant. Her husband, Roman Polanski, was not at home when the Manson family members burst into the residence.

One of Tate's guests, Steven Parent, was attacked in his automobile in front of the Tate/Polanski residence as the perpetrators arrived to begin their siege. (Parent was shot four times and then stabbed.) Two other visitors, Abigail Folger and Voytek Frykowski, attempted to flee from the intruders before they were caught in the backyard of the home. Folger was stabbed twenty-eight times, while Frykowski was struck over the head thirteen times with a heavy object and then shot twice. Sharon Tate and Jay Sebring were murdered inside the residence. Both were tied and hung by their necks over a ceiling rafter. Tate had been stabbed sixteen times in the chest and back, Sebring had been stabbed seven times and shot once. Before leaving the home, the cult members further desecrated the crime scene by using their victim's blood to write words and phrases on the walls and doors of the residence.

Less than forty-eight hours later, on August 10, 1969, members of the Manson family invaded the home of Leno and Rosemary LaBianca. Unlike the method used in the Tate murders, Manson himself entered the LaBianca home and bound the two victims, telling them they would not be harmed. Manson then left the residence, turning the victims over to Charles Watson, Patricia Krenwinkel, and Leslie Van Houten. What happened next was another crime of unspeakable brutality and senselessness. Rosemary LaBianca died from forty-one stab wounds. Her husband had also been stabbed dozens of times and was left by the perpetrators with a knife and fork protruding from his body. Once again, the victims' blood was used to mark the crime scene.

Table 7.16: Murders Linked to the Manson Family

Date of Crime Crime Location	Details of Crime
October 13, 1968 Northern California (two victims)	Nancy Warren and Clida Delaney are found beaten and strangled to death in a ritualistic, dual homicide. Several members of the Manson family were in the area at the time of the slayings. Two of these individuals were later convicted of other homicides.
December 30, 1968 Southern California (one victim)	Marina Habe is abducted from her home and murdered by multiple stab wounds to the chest and neck. The victim was a close associate of several members of the Manson family.
May 27, 1969 Kentucky (one victim)	Manson's uncle, Darwin Scott, is hacked to death in his home at a time when Manson failed to contact his parole officer. At the time of Scott's death, citizens in the area report that an "LSD preacher" and several female followers from California are in the area.
July 17, 1969 Southern California (one victim)	Mark Walts is abducted while hitchhiking. He is subsequently beaten, shot multiple times, and run over by an automobile. Walts was a familiar figure at the Spahn ranch, where the Manson family lived.
July 1969 Southern California (one victim)	A murdered woman's body is found near the Spahn ranch. She is tentatively identified as Susan Scott, a Manson family member who inexplicably disappeared and was never located.

August 8–9, 1969 Southern California. (five victims)	Sharon Tate, Abigail Folger, Jay Sebring, Voytek Frykowski, and Steven Parent are brutally murdered and their bodies mutilated at Tate's home.
August 10, 1969 Southern California (two victims)	Leno and Rosemary LaBianca are murdered in their home in the same ritualistic manner as the Tate murders.
August 26, 1969 Southern California (one victim)	Donald "Shorty" Shea is murdered at the direction of Charles Manson. Shea was believed to have talked to individuals outside of the Manson family about their felonies.
November 5, 1969 Southern California (one victim)	John Haught, a member of the Manson family, is shot to death, allegedly while playing Russian roulette.
November 16, 1969 Southern California (one victim)	The body of Manson family member Sherry Cooper is discovered. She appears to have died at the same time and in the same manner as Marina Habe.
November 21, 1969 Southern California (two victims)	James Sharp and Doreen Gaul, both friends of various members of the Manson family, are each murdered with multiple stab wounds to the chest and neck.
December 1, 1969 England (one victim)	Joel Pugh, the husband of Manson family member Sandra Good, is found dead in a hotel room. His murder is ritualistic in nature, and his blood has been used to inscribe words at the crime scene.
November 27, 1970 Southern California (one victim)	Manson defense attorney Ronald Hughes disappears at the end of the Manson trial. He was apparently

	abducted by two Manson family members and then murdered. Hughes's remains are discovered approximately six months later.

Two months later, in what proved a fortunate turn of events, Charles Manson and several members of his cult were arrested for destroying a piece of construction equipment located near where the members lived (a communal setting in southern California). Among those arrested was Susan Atkins, who had been present at the Tate/Polanski residence on the evening of August 8–9, 1969. Incredibly, while in custody, Atkins began discussing the Tate murders with her cellmates. Her braggadocio led to indictments for murder against Manson and several other cult members. It also led to the public disclosure of one of the most bizarre and gruesome chapters in American criminology—the saga of a cult of serial murderers led by a man who had been a career criminal since his earliest years.

Charles Manson was born in Kentucky in 1934, to a sixteen-year-old prostitute. When he was five years old, Manson's mother was imprisoned for robbery. The boy was left with various relatives and subsequently shuffled off to a series of different institutions, none of which was able to hold him for long. Manson committed his first major felony—armed robbery—at the age of thirteen. By 1960, he was serving a ten-year prison sentence for pimping, grand theft, and fraud.

On March 21, 1967, Manson was paroled from the McNeil Island Prison and traveled to the Haight-Ashbury district of San Francisco. At the age of thirty-three, he was a hardened criminal who had spent more than half his life in prison. However, he was also an intelligent (IQ in excess of 120), articulate, and manipulative individual who held easy sway over the countless young transients who had gathered in San Francisco to participate in what came to be known as the "Summer of Love." An accomplished musician who mixed

easily with the youngsters in the Haight-Ashbury district,
Manson soon found himself the head of a loose-knit group of
wayward teenagers and young adults, primarily women, who
delighted in his company and hung on his every word. Manson began to refer to his growing cult as a family and blessed
most of the members with monikers that granted them special status in the association (see Table 7.17).

The Manson family was a migratory association that engaged in marathon sessions of unrestricted sex and drug use.
At its height, the family may have supported as many as fifty
members, who earned their money from a variety of illegal
activities and by living as simply as possible. For the next few
years, the Manson family traveled throughout California,
eventually settling at an abandoned film studio ranch in
southern California.

Table 7.17: Manson Family Monikers

Given Name	Manson Family Name
Charles Milles Manson	Jesus Christ
Charles Watson	Tex
Susan Denise Atkins	Sadie Mae Glutz
Leslie Van Houten	LuLu
Patricia Krenwinkel	Katie
Robert Beausoleil	Cupid
Mary Theresa Brunner	
Steve Grogan	Clem
John Haught	Zero
Bruce McGregor Davis	
Lynette Fromme	Squeaky
Sandra Good	Sandy
Ruth Ann Moorhouse	Ouisch
Catherine Gilles	Capistrano
Nancy Pitman	Brenda McCann
Catherine Share	Gypsy

Charles Manson completely dominated the members of
his cult, wooing them with his gift of conversation, relative

maturity, and sharp intellect. Over time, the philosophy that he imparted to his followers became increasingly dark and aggressive, perhaps even being linked to a variety of satanic cults that were already established in California. However, to the young and impressionable members of his cult, Charles Manson had already become the incarnation of Jesus Christ. So overwhelming was his control of the family that any perverse wish Manson might express was quickly put into action by his followers—including murder. Although unproved, it is believed that the Manson family may have slain its first victim as early as October 1968. In all, it is possible that the cult members accounted for some twenty murders between 1968 and 1970, including the notorious Tate-LaBianca killings.

In June 1970, after a long and intensive investigation, Manson was charged with the seven Tate-LaBianca murders. Also charged with homicide were Susan Atkins, Patricia Krenwinkel, and Leslie Van Houten. The trial proved to be as bizarre as the Manson cult itself. Manson, as head of the family, exhibited a plethora of disdainful behavior throughout the proceedings, always followed in lock step by his co-defendants and members of the family who had not been arrested. The persistently defiant and disdainful attitude of the defendants certainly did not help their case. In fact, it supported the contention of the prosecution that even though Manson did not take a personal hand in any of the murders, the crimes were committed at his sole direction, thereby making him fully culpable in the eyes of the law. With the help of a family member who testified against the cult and a strong case presented by chief prosecutor Vincent Bugliosi, the outcome of the trial was never in doubt.

At the end of the proceedings, all defendants were found guilty of murder and sentenced to death. However, their sentences were later commuted to life imprisonment when the U.S. Supreme Court outlawed the death penalty. The following year, in 1971, Charles Watson was also brought to trial on charges of murder for his role in the Tate-LaBianca killings. He, too, was found guilty and received the death penalty.

In August 1971, six other members of the Manson family, including Mary Brunner, were arrested after exchanging gunfire with police. They had attempted to steal weapons from a southern California gun shop in order to organize a prison break for Manson and the other family members. All six perpetrators were captured, charged, found guilty, and given prison sentences. In addition, Brunner was subsequently tried and convicted in a separate murder case.

Even as the Manson family seemed to disintegrate by virtue of its heinous crimes, the mayhem it had wrought on society continued. At the end of Manson's trial, in November 1970, defense attorney Ronald Hughes suddenly disappeared after being last seen in the presence of two Manson family members. Nearly six months later, his remains were found in an isolated area near Sespe Hot Springs, California, where he had been murdered.

Since 1970, nearly one hundred books have been written about Charles Manson and his infamous cult. The crimes perpetrated by this family serial-killing team have proved to be among the most gruesome and bizarre in our national history. The organization of the Manson family and the incredible hold its founder held over the members has proven to be a crucible of frightening information for those who ponder the extremism that is so often associated with cult activities. Finally, there is Charles Manson himself—an individual who remains enigmatic, beyond comprehension, and incredibly frightening, even from the quiet isolation of his prison cell.

NOTES

1. Harold Schechter and David Everitt, *The A to Z Encyclopedia of Serial Killers* (New York: Pocket Books, 1996), 152.

2. "Hunting Humans—James Marlow and Cynthia Coffman," in Kozel Multimedia, *Mind of a Killer,* CD-ROM (Chatsworth, CA: Cambrix, 1995), Section: "Hunting Humans."

3. David Millward, "Free Me, Begs Sorrowful Myra

Hindley," (London) *Electronic Telegraph* (Internet edition), 8 December 1994.

4. "Hunting Humans—Ian Duncan Brady and Myra Hindley" in Kozel Multimedia, *Mind of a Killer,* CD-ROM (Chatsworth, CA: Cambrix, 1995), Section: "Hunting Humans."

5. Schechter and Everitt, *A to Z Encyclopedia of Serial Killers,* 182.

6. Helen Gibson, "The Banality of an Evil Woman," *Time Magazine,* 146, no. 23 (Internet edition, 4 December 1995).

7. Colin Wilson and Damon Wilson, *The Killers among Us* (New York: Time Warner, 1996), 336.

8. Paul Stokes and Wendy Holden, "I Told My Dad I Would Marry Him," (London) *Daily Telegraph* (Internet edition), 21 October 1995.

9. "Lodgers Remember Drugs and Casual Sex at Cromwell Street," *Electronic Telegraph* (Internet edition), 13 October 1995.

10. Wilson and Wilson, *Killers among Us,* 353.

11. Ibid.

12. Neil Darbyshire, "Legal Oddities Clinched the Case against West," *The Electronic Telegraph* (Internet edition), 23 November 1995.

13. Ibid.

14. Neil Darbyshire and Paul Stokes, "The Rosemary West Trial: Common Sense Says That West Must Be Guilty," *Electronic Telegraph* (Internet edition), 15 November 1995.

15. Eric W. Hickey, *Serial Murderers and Their Victims* (Belmont, CA.: Wadsworth, 1991), 180.

16. "Hunting Humans—Alvin and Judith Ann Neelley," in Kozel Multimedia, *Mind of a Killer,* CD-ROM (Chatsworth, CA.: Cambrix, 1995), Section: "Hunting Humans."

17. "Hunting Humans—Amelia Sach and Annie Walters," in Kozel Multimedia, *Mind of a Killer,* CD-ROM (Chatsworth, CA.: Cambrix, 1995), Section: "Hunting Humans."

18. "Hunting Humans—Catherine May Wood and

Gwendolyn Graham," in Kozel Multimedia, *Mind of a Killer,* CD-ROM, (Chatsworth, CA.: Cambrix, 1995), Section: "Hunting Humans."

19. "Ex-Nursing Home Aide Sentenced in Killings," *Charlotte* (North Carolina) *Observer* (Internet edition), 12 October 1989.

20. "Hunting Humans—Angels of Death" in Kozel Multimedia, *Mind of a Killer,* CD-ROM (Chatsworth, CA.: Cambrix, 1995), Section: "Hunting Humans."

21. "Parole Hearing Minutes: Charles Manson (1992)," *State of California Board of Prison Terms* (Internet edition), 22 April 1992.

8

THE QUESTION OF SANITY

> I doubt if a single individual could be found from the whole
> of mankind free from some form of insanity. The only differ-
> ence is one of degree.
>
> —Desiderius Erasmus
> *Praise of Folly,* chapter 38

On January 20, 1843, Daniel McNaughton shot and killed
the private secretary to the prime minister of England. At
the time of the murder, McNaughton suffered from a significant psychological disorder and had been experiencing
bizarre delusions for some time. Contemporary behavioral
scientists would probably deduce that he had been suffering
from a condition known as paranoid schizophrenia at the
time that he murdered the private secretary. When Mc-
Naughton was tried for his crimes, he was found not guilty by
reason of insanity—a benchmark decision that has influ-
enced the Western practice of law since it was handed down.
By the standards of the day, the defendant was judged to be
incapable of understanding the nature and impact of his
actions—he could not discern right from wrong. Today, the
McNaughton test is the most commonly applied standard by
which the legal culpability of a defendant is adjudicated. In
part, it reads:

To establish a defense on the ground of insanity, it must be
clearly proved that, at the time of the committing of the act, the
party was laboring under such a defect of reason, from disease of

the mind, as to not know the nature and quality of the act he was doing, or, if he did know it, that he did not know he was doing what was wrong.[1]

This tenet of law has become the fundamental benchmark against which the question of sanity is measured in a court of law by judges and juries in America, the United Kingdom, and several other Western nations. The implication of the McNaughton test is clear: in the context of culpability at trial, insanity is a legal concept, not a medical one.

If the standard by which we judge the sanity of serial killers is the McNaughton test, the great majority of these perpetrators are sane and, therefore, fully culpable of their crimes. Although many medical practitioners may take issue with the question of sanity as defined by the McNaughton test, it has remained steadfast as a crucial point of law in the most heinous of crimes for more than a century. Today it is a fundamental standard by which juries in many English-speaking cultures measure responsibility and determine appropriate punishment.

In America, an insanity defense in response to a capital crime is rarely successful. This is particularly true when the crimes with which the defendant is charged are as calculating and egregious as serial murder. However, from time to time judges and juries conclude that a serial murderer was incapable of controlling his or her actions or, in a legal sense, was unaware of the impact of his or her crimes. When the McNaughton test is successful as a defense tactic in a case of serial murder, the evidence of insanity must generally be overwhelming and irrefutable. Because the crime of serial murder is so disturbing and inherently unforgivable to Western juries, the burden of meeting such a test is strenuous. This understandable encumbrance is equally onerous regardless of the sex of the accused serial murderer, although it is generally accepted that most juries are prone to mete out a more stringent punishment to a male perpetrator than a female.

The question of sanity is relatively clear in most cases of

serial murder that have been properly adjudicated. Although medical professionals and those who practice law may disagree on the question of sanity as it is applied to any given criminal case, the McNaughton test has withstood the rigors of time and proven to be a workable standard. Since the great majority of serial killers are legally sane, and given the heinous nature of the crime itself, the question of sanity should be answered by a standard appropriate to the egregious nature of the felony. In this sense, the McNaughton test has proven worthy for over a century.

However, from another viewpoint, the question of sanity is a much more difficult issue. For example, is a female serial murderer who suffers from Munchausen syndrome by proxy insane? In a legal sense, generally she is not, because in most cases the victim of this disorder is judged to be fully aware of the nature and impact of her actions, despite the fact that her compulsion to kill may have been psychologically irresistible. However, the uncertainty about the effect of significant psychological disorders persists in our courts of law. In some instances, a severe psychological disorder is viewed by juries to be of such magnitude that the question of sanity is foremost in any consideration of guilt; however, in many other cases the same psychological disorder may be quickly dismissed as an unacceptable defense. In the final analysis, the legal question of sanity must always be reconsidered (and, at least somewhat, redefined) each time it is brought forth as an issue in the courts.

Most crimes of serial murder are committed by obviously sane individuals, even though the question of sanity may ultimately be used as a defense strategy at trial. However, there are a few cases in which the crimes of the serial murderer were obviously committed by an individual who was incapable of understanding the meaning or impact of her actions. The majority of these cases involve an Angel of Death serial murderer who attacked victims dependent on her for care. Female serial killers who murder for profit, revenge, or as a member of a killing team are rarely judged incapable of understanding the nature of their actions. In fact, most female serial killers who have been classified in the categories of Black Widows, Profit or Crime, or Revenge are viewed as calculating murderers who have carefully scripted and carried out their crimes; in these cases, the question of sanity is rarely given more than passing consideration. However, at least in America, juries seem more prone to accept an insanity defense in cases that involve an Angel of Death typology. Since the Angel of Death tends to suffer a relatively high incidence of significant psychological disorders, like Munchausen syndrome by proxy, the openness to a question of sanity may be understandable. However, even for the Angel of Death, the burden of arguing for an inability to understand right from wrong is great.

In the final analysis, the line that divides sanity from insanity is not only fine, it is mutable, constantly changing, and subjective. At one extreme of belief, any individual who commits to a course of serial murder must be insane by the societal standards in which he or she operates; at the other, however, punishment for such a heinous crime must obviate any compassion that could be engendered by a tenet of law like the McNaughton test. Between these extremes we find the judges and juries, who must reinterpret culpability and responsibility with each new case. It can be seen that such decisions are not easily made and will inevitably change with time and differing cultural backgrounds. Therefore, there can be no final or absolute answer to the question of sanity. The judgment of legal culpability is an exercise in hitting a moving target, which is only somewhat slowed by the presence of tried and trusted tenets of law. However, at least in the U.S. system of justice, such a shortcoming is balanced by the principle of judgment by one's peers who, in the end, set and reset the moving target that we define as sanity.

MADAME MOULINET

Jeanne Weber was born in 1875 in a small fishing village
in northern France. At the age of fourteen, Weber left the village and moved to Paris, where she earned a meager living by
working at a series of menial jobs. In 1893, at the age of eighteen, Weber married an alcoholic Parisian and settled into a
rundown tenement in the seedier part of Paris. Over the next
twelve years, she also became a heavy drinker and eventually
gave birth to three children, two of whom died in their early
infancy. However, the death of her children proved to be only
the first of many tragedies that would surround Weber for the
remainder of her life (see Table 8.1).

Table 8.1: Jeanne Weber

Classification	Question of Sanity.
Birth Information	Born in 1875, in France.
Active Period	1905 to 1908. Active from age thirty to age thirty-three.
Victim Information	Murdered at least ten children, including three of her own. Injured many others.
Method	Strangulation.
Motive	Weber was declared insane in 1908.
Disposition	Weber first went to trial for murder in 1906 and was acquitted of the charges. She subsequently resumed her murderous ways and was again held for trial in 1908. In October of that year, she was declared insane and institutionalized. Weber committed suicide in 1910, while in custody, by strangling herself.

On March 2, 1905, while baby-sitting her sister-in-law's
two children, Weber's eighteen-month-old niece, Georgette,

suddenly became ill and died. Although there were obvious and unexplained bruises on the infant's neck, an examining physician ignored the possibilities of foul play and failed to order an autopsy. Nine days later, Weber was welcomed back into the bereaved and unsuspecting household to baby-sit Georgette's surviving sister, two-year-old Suzanne. Sadly, the little girl was dead before her mother had returned home from shopping. Once again, the attending physician determined that the child's death was due to natural causes.

Incredibly, two weeks after the death of her two nieces, Weber was asked to care for her brother's seven-year-old daughter, Germaine, while he was at work. When he returned home, Germaine's father discovered his daughter gasping for breath, with obvious red marks across her throat. Fortunately, the young girl survived the attack because of her father's early return. For whatever reason, however, no one in the household suspected that Weber had assaulted the child. On the following day, March 26, 1905, Weber was again able to attack the child and, this time, finish her brutal task. The doctor who attended Germaine attributed her death to diphtheria—an epidemic disease known to affect the throat and air passage. No explanation was provided for the welts on the victim's neck. Less than a week later, on March 30, 1905, the bereaved father's only surviving child, seven-year-old Marcel, suddenly died with no preceding illness. The bruises on Marcel's neck were again ignored, and no autopsy was performed when the young boy's death was determined to be an accidental choking.

Six days later, Weber's ten-year-old nephew, Maurice, narrowly escaped death. The youngster's mother, who had been out shopping, unexpectedly arrived home to witness a horrifying scene: her son was sitting up in his bed desperately gasping for air, as Jeanne Weber stood over him with a crazed look on her face. Maurice's stunned mother immediately called the police and had Weber arrested for assault.

During the course of their investigation into the tragedies that followed in Weber's wake, police soon discovered that

two children who were neighbors of the serial murderer—
Lucie Aleandre and Marcel Payatos—had also died while in
her care. With what authorities believed to be irrefutable evidence of her guilt, Weber was bound over for trial on eight
counts of homicide.

On January 29, 1906, the proceedings against Jeanne Weber began. However, the stunned prosecutors quickly realized
that their case was no match against a persuasive, and apparently deeply grieving, woman. Weber proved to be an extraordinarily sympathetic defendant whose ultimate credibility
with the jury had not been anticipated by the prosecutors. On
February 6, 1906, Weber was acquitted of all charges.

Nothing more was heard of Jeanne Weber until April 7,
1907, when a country doctor from the small town of Villediu,
France, met a woman who introduced herself as Madame
Moulinet. The doctor had been hastily summoned to the
Bavouzet residence by Moulinet, who was the baby-sitter for
nine-year-old Auguste Bavouzet. Greeted at the door by
Madame Moulinet, the physician was brought to the bed
where the young boy lay dead. Although the physician noticed the bruising on Auguste's neck, the possibility of foul
play was summarily ruled out, and spontaneous convulsions
were recorded as the cause of death.

The unexpected demise of Auguste Bavouzet prompted a
barrage of gossip throughout the small village. Popular
among the circulating rumors was the belief that Madame
Moulinet was really the notorious Parisian murderer, Jeanne
Weber, who had descended on the village to wreak mayhem
among the children. When this rumor reached Bavouzet's
physician, he promptly reconsidered the condition of Auguste Bavouzet's body and contacted the police.

Madame Moulinet was arrested and soon found to indeed
be Jeanne Weber. The local police decided to hold their suspect in custody while an autopsy was performed on Auguste
Bavouzet's body. However, in December 1907, Weber was set
free: the medical examiner who performed the Bavouzet

autopsy determined that typhoid fever had been the cause of death.

Spending the next few months working at various odd jobs, Weber (now using her own name again) finally accepted a position at the Children's Home, in Orgeville. After less than a week in her new job, however, Weber was discovered choking a child who had been entrusted to her care. However, with her considerable powers of persuasion, she was able to convince the home's owner that she was innocent of any wrongdoing. In an amazing example of naiveté (or, perhaps fear of involvement), the owners quietly covered up the incident and dismissed their lethal employee, without ever informing the police.

Now jobless and without funds, Weber returned to Paris, where she drifted into a life of prostitution. With the little money that she earned on the street, Weber rented a cheap room at an inn run by the Poirot family. From time to time, Weber would supplement her meager income by baby-sitting for the innkeeper's children. In May 1908, Poirot happened upon Weber just as she was in the process of strangling his ten-year-old son, Marcel, with a bloody handkerchief. Weber had been so obsessed with her heinous activities that Poirot had to strike her repeatedly before she finally released the lifeless youth.

Once again the police were summoned to arrest Weber; and once again she was charged with murder. Now, however, her long and lethal career quickly came to an unpredictable end. On October 25, 1908, having been credited with a least ten murders, Weber was declared insane and sent to an asylum in Mareville. In 1910, she was found strangled in her prison cell—by her own hand.

GRAVEYARD SHIFT

Born in Woodlawn, Illinois, in 1955, a nursing career seemed natural for Bobbie Sue Terrell because of the illnesses that had been so much a part of her formative years.

Her family consisted of seven siblings and included four brothers who had been stricken with muscular dystrophy, a chronic degenerative disease of the musculature system. Bobbie Sue herself suffered from myopia and chronic obesity. However, despite her own physical challenges, Bobbie Sue was generally healthier than most of her siblings and found herself thrust into the role of caretaker from early age—a part that she seemed to take on with quiet acceptance.

After graduating from high school in 1973, Bobbie Sue entered a nursing program, as those who knew her expected she would. Always an above average student, Bobbie Sue was able to complete her studies and obtain her license as a registered nurse in three years. In 1976, with her credentials in hand, Bobbie Sue embarked on a career that would forever change her life, as well as those of the hapless victims she would later encounter (see Table 8.2).

Shortly after beginning her nursing career, Bobbie Sue met and married Daniel Dudley, a local man. Although, at first, the marriage promised to be a happy one, Bobbie Sue and her new husband were devastated when they learned that she was unable to bear children. Bobbie Sue in particular reacted to the shocking news with a combination of anger and depression that seemed insurmountable. However, as the Dudleys desperately wanted a child, they decided to adopt an infant boy. Following the adoption, Bobbie Sue's spirits seemed to lift for a brief period; however, this was not to last.

Shortly after adopting her son, Bobbie Sue again experienced unremitting bouts of depression and anger that could no longer be ignored. Forced to seek professional help, Bobbie Sue was diagnosed as suffering from schizophrenia and started on a regimen of powerful tranquilizers. However, the medication seemed to only worsen the young woman's emotional turmoil and created significant problems with her husband. Confused, depressed, and unable to deal with her deteriorating condition, Bobbie Sue inexplicably fed a near-lethal dose of the prescription tranquilizers to her young son, resulting in his hospitalization. For Daniel Dudley, the attack

on his son signaled the finale to a marriage that had already
been severely strained by Bobbie Sue's deteriorating psychological state. He quickly filed for divorce and won custody of
their son.

Table 8.2: Bobbie Sue Terrell

Classification	Question of Sanity.
Birth Information	Born in 1955, in Illinois.
Active Period	1984. Active at the age of twenty-nine.
Victim Information	Believed to have murdered twelve elderly patients in thirteen days. The victims were reliant on her for medical care in a nursing home.
Method	Lethal injections.
Motive	Angel of Death motivation that targeted elderly patients. However, Terrell's crimes were also complicated by Munchausen syndrome.
Disposition	Terrell was taken into custody in 1985. Her trial was delayed for several years due to legal complications and her psychiatric condition. In 1988, Terrell pled guilty to second-degree murder charges and was sentenced to sixty-five years in prison.

Over the next few years, Bobbie Sue remained alone and
severely depressed, resulting in a series of hospitalizations
for a variety of physical and psychological problems. Eventually, the ailing woman admitted herself to a state mental
hospital for intensive treatment of her schizophrenia and remained institutionalized for over a year. During her year of
institutionalization, Bobbie Sue seemed to improve signifi-

cantly and was finally able to cope with her illness to the satisfaction of hospital personnel.

On her release from the psychiatric facility, Bobbie Sue was able to secure a nursing position at the Hillview Manor rest home, in Greenville, Illinois, as part of her continuing recovery program. However, it soon became apparent that Bobbie Sue remained unable to control her emotions—or her behavior. After a short time at Hillview Manor, Bobbie Sue's coworkers began to notice increasingly strange behavior, which was both frightening and self-destructive in nature. Her career came to an abrupt end when Bobbie Sue was rushed to nearby Barnes Hospital after she had severely mutilated herself with a pair of scissors, claiming to shocked staff that she had done so because she was infertile.

In July 1984, Bobbie Sue moved to St. Petersburg, Florida, in an effort to start a new life where she could benefit from complete anonymity. The following month, she obtained a Florida State nursing license and began working short-term, temporary nursing assignments throughout the Tampa Bay area. However, many of her assignments placed her in the stressful and chaotic surroundings of hospital emergency facilities. As a result, Bobbie Sue's emotional condition worsened considerably and she began to desperately look for more permanent, less stressful employment.

In October 1984, St. Petersburg's North Horizon Health Center hired Bobbie Sue as a shift supervisor, temporarily relieving the stress of her previous assignments. For a brief time, Bobbie Sue's condition seemed to improve, and she appeared comfortable with the more routine duties of her permanent position. However, a month later, on November 13, 1984, the death of a patient, ninety-seven-year-old Aggie Marsh, signaled an abrupt change in Bobbie Sue's outlook and behavior that remains unexplained to this day. Marsh became the first known victim of a very disturbed woman who suddenly and inexplicably turned to serial murder.

On November 18, 1984, ninety-four-year-old Anna Larson was found near death and was only saved because of extraordinary intervention measures by hospital personnel. The aging woman had been injected with a near fatal dose of insulin, despite the fact that she was not diabetic and had no need for the medication. Equally troubling to hospital administrators was the fact that the insulin had been kept in a locked cupboard, to which Bobbie Sue maintained the key during her work shift. This combination of suspicious circumstances, along with the unexpected death of Aggie Marsh, prompted hospital administrators to begin an internal investigation into procedures on Bobbie Sue's ward.

Within days of Anna Larson's mysterious brush with death, eighty-five-year-old Leathy McKnight unexpectedly died. The attending physician once again diagnosed insulin poisoning as the cause of death. Two nights later, in the midst of the internal investigation, two more elderly patients died without warning. The following day, November 26, 1984, stunned hospital administrators learned that five additional unexplained deaths had occurred within the preceding two weeks.

On November 27, 1984, local police received an anonymous telephone call claiming that a serial killer was operating on the hospital staff. When investigators arrived at St. Petersburg's to begin their investigation, they discovered Bobbie Sue suffering from a severe knife wound to her side, which had allegedly been inflicted by a prowler on the hospital premises. However, investigators could find no other staff who had witnessed the attack or, for that matter, who had noticed anything unusual that day—except for Bobbie Sue's behavior, which had become the focus of concern by several of her coworkers. Suspicious of Bobbie Sue's story and concerned about the possibility of a serial killer on the staff, police began an intensive investigation into the events of the prior month and the background of the shift supervisor. The early results of the police investigation proved inconclusive concerning Bobbie Sue's involvement in the recent hospital deaths; however, police did learn about her history of schizophrenia and another debilitating psychological disorder that she had avoided sharing with anyone—Munchausen syndrome. The hospital administrators had known none of this information when Bobbie Sue had been hired. However, when police investigators informed the hospital management of what they had learned, Bobbie Sue was immediately fired from her job.

Again out of work, desperate, and alone, Bobbie Sue's depression and bizarre physical maladies became rampant and, on January 31, 1985, she committed herself to the local county hospital for psychiatric treatment. Once again institutionalized, Bobbie Sue resumed the battle with her significant psychological problems. After several months of intensive treatment, she had once again progressed to the point where hospital personnel deemed her ready for outpatient care. However, during her months of hospitalization, the police had managed to piece together a significant body of evidence implicating Bobbie Sue in the St. Petersburg's hospital murders. Unfortunately, Bobbie Sue had been released from the psychiatric institution before investigators were able to arrest her.

Shortly after her release, Bobbie Sue met and married Ronald Terrell, a thirty-eight-year-old, unemployed plumber. However, the marriage was an abrupt affair between two lonely, nearly destitute individuals. Impoverished and unable to find any kind of employment, Bobbie Sue and her husband were forced to make their home in a roadside tent, with the barest of necessities for survival. It was in this makeshift home that police finally caught up to their suspect in the St. Petersburg murders, arresting Bobbie Sue and charging her with two counts of murder and one of attempted murder. Although investigators had determined Bobbie Sue was probably involved in a dozen or more murders at the St. Petersburg hospital, they were never able to develop sufficient evidence for additional indictments.

For the next few years, until February 1988, Bobbie Sue underwent persistent psychological testing and evaluation as prosecutors and defense attorneys tried to determine how to deal with the complex issue of her culpability. Both sides agreed that Bobbie Sue Terrell was a deeply disturbed, devastated individual who was often unable to control her behavior. However, neither the prosecutors nor the defense attorneys could easily agree on her ability to understand the nature of her heinous crimes. In the end, a compromise was reached that favored the defendant when Bobbie Sue was finally charged with a single count of second degree murder, found guilty, and sentenced to sixty-five years in prison.

IT RUNS IN THE FAMILY

Nearly a century before Bobbie Sue Terrell made headlines as a psychologically disturbed serial murderer, Jane Toppan claimed her own place in the history of criminology in a similar manner. Born Nora Kelly, in 1854, in Boston, Massachusetts, Toppan's familial background, in retrospect, may have foreshadowed her future life of madness and murder (see Table 8.3). Before the age of four, the young girl's mother had unexpectedly died and her father had been involuntarily committed to an insane asylum. Shortly after these early tragedies, Toppan and her four sisters were forced into an orphanage because their grandparents could no longer care for them. A few years later, one of Toppan's older sisters was committed to the same institution as their father.

In 1859, the Toppan family adopted Nora Kelly and legally changed her name to Jane Toppan. After her adoption, Toppan's life took an apparently traditional course, and the child seemed to thrive in her new family environment. Throughout her childhood and into her teenage years, Toppan excelled in school and developed strong social skills. To all outward appearances, she seemed to have overcome the crippling difficulties of her early years. However, her future would soon take an abrupt and bizarre course that could not have been anticipated by her adoptive family or friends.

During her twenties, Toppan suddenly began to develop odd and aggressive behavioral traits culminating in at least two suicide attempts. However, she temporarily rebounded from this traumatic period and regained sufficient stability to enroll in a nursing program at a hospital in Cambridge, Massachusetts. Much to her own satisfaction, Toppan excelled in the nursing program as she had earlier excelled in school and, for a time, appeared to be stable and happy. However, shortly after receiving her nursing license, two of Toppan's patients inexplicably died and she was summarily dismissed from her position for negligence. Toppan was furious about the treatment that she had received by hospital administrators and, blaming them for the harsh manner in which they oversaw the hospital and its staff, decided to pursue a career as a private nurse where she could be free from the constraints imposed by hospital bureaucrats. In the early 1880s, Toppan began her new, dual career as a private nurse and serial murderer—a

Table 8.3: Jane Toppan

Classification	Question of Sanity.
Birth Information	Born in 1854, in Massachusetts, as Nora Kelly.
Active Period	1880 to 1901. Active from age twenty-six to age forty-seven.
Victim Information	Confessed to thirty-one murders. It is believed that she murdered between seventy and one hundred individuals.
Method	Lethal injections of morphine.
Motive	A classic Angel of Death who was insane. Toppan explained her motive this way: "That is my ambition, to have killed more people—more helpless people—than any man or woman who has ever lived."[2]
Disposition	Toppan confessed to thirty-one murders in 1901. She was declared insane and institutionalized until her death in 1938.

role in which she thrived for the next twenty years. Remarkably, because Toppan specialized in the care and murder of
only elderly patients who had few surviving family members,
her killing career was not discovered until 1901.

The long, lethal career of this deeply disturbed caretaker
began to unwind on July 4, 1901, with the death of Mattie
Davis. An aging woman who had been under Toppan's care
for several years, Davis's death aroused little suspicion when
she succumbed to what physicians believed was natural
causes. At the time of Davis's death, Toppan reacted with
what family members believed to be genuine grief and offered to accompany the body of her charge to Cataumet,
Massachusetts, for burial. Throughout the days following
Davis's funeral, Toppan endeared herself to the patriarch of
the family, Alden Davis, and managed to settle in as the
family nurse. However, less than a month later, Davis's
daughter, Annie Gordon, suddenly died.

While the remaining Davis family was still recovering
from their dual loss, Alden Davis unexpectedly died of what
appeared to be a stroke. Reeling from the shock of yet another family funeral, none of the remaining family members
questioned Davis's death at the time. However, when Davis's
last surviving daughter, Mary Gibbs, died shortly thereafter
on August 19, 1901, the coincidences of the prior six weeks
proved too much for Gibbs's husband. The suspicious spouse
demanded that an autopsy be performed on his wife and that
the bodies of her sister and father be exhumed and examined.
The results of the three examinations shocked both the family
members and local authorities, for each body was found to
contain lethal amounts of morphine.

The police immediately suspected Jane Toppan in the
family deaths; however, before they could place her under arrest, Toppan fled to Amherst, New Hampshire, where, for
reasons that were never made clear, she murdered her stepsister, Edna Bannister. Shortly thereafter, on October 29,
1901, law enforcement officers caught up with Toppan and
arrested her on four counts of murder. However, the investi-

gators were further stunned when Toppan voluntarily admitted to thirty-one homicides that she had committed over a period of two decades. At first unwilling to believe Toppan's bizarre confession, the investigators were soon convinced of the truth of her story when she confidently named each victim and provided sufficient details for the police to verify her long career of serial murder.

Investigators and prosecutors also quickly realized that Jane Toppan was a significantly ill individual who had little conception of the heinous nature of her crimes. Because of her obvious mental illness, Toppan was never tried for her crimes. Rather, she was declared insane and confined to the Massachusetts state mental institution in Taunton, where, in August 1938, she died at the age of eighty-four after nearly four decades of institutionalization.

NOTES

1. Donald T. Lunde, *Murder and Madness,* (San Francisco: San Francisco Book Company, 1976), 114.

2. "Hunting Humans—Jane Toppan" in Kozel Multimedia, *Mind of a Killer,* CD-ROM (Chatsworth, CA: Cambrix, 1995), Section: "Hunting Humans."

9

THE UNEXPLAINED

So good and evil in the end become confounded.
—T. S. Eliot
The Hollow Men

Although the female serial murderer is often an elusive and challenging criminal, her motives generally become apparent once she has been apprehended and tried for her crimes. However, there are some cases of serial killing in which the motive for murder has never been satisfactorily discovered, despite the fact that the perpetrator was apprehended and even confessed her crimes. Obviously, such murders are especially troubling since they allow for no understanding of why they occurred. Particularly disturbing is the fact that many cases in which the motive for murder is never understood involve the deaths of children.

This chapter examines several incidents of serial murder in which the motive of the perpetrator has never been satisfactorily understood. We define the perpetrator whose crimes fit the category of Unexplained as: *a woman who systemically murders for reasons that are wholly inexplicable or for a motive that has not been made sufficiently clear for categorization.* As the following case histories will show, unexplained motives vary in their mystery and meaning. In some cases, the behavior of the murderer and the pattern of her crimes permit a reasonable assumption of motive. In other instances, it is impossible to even offer a somewhat reliable assumption. Ironically, in many of the cases categorized as Unexplained, even the serial killer was unable (or unwilling) to articulate an understandable motive for her crimes.

"I DON'T KNOW WHY I DONE WHAT I DONE"

By the time she began her murderous career at the age of seventeen, Christine Falling had already experienced a full life of illness, frustration, and misery which, in retrospect, seemed to irresistibly impel her to escalating violence. Falling (the name of her adoptive parents), was born Christine Laverne Slaughter on March 12, 1963, in Perry, Florida. Her mother, Ann, was only sixteen at the time of Falling's birth and had already given birth to an older sister. Her father, Thomas, was a sixty-five-year-old woodsman who was inattentive and violent by nature. Falling's early childhood years were marked by persistent poverty and illness. She was severely developmentally disabled, prone to obesity, epileptic, experienced bouts of aggressive behavior, and throughout her life was never able to surpass sixth grade vocabulary skills.[1] Within a few years after her birth, Christine and her older sister were adopted by the Falling family and given their surname. However, the two girls found themselves in constant conflict with their adoptive family and were eventually placed in a children's home near Orlando, Florida, when Christine was only nine years old.

By the time she entered the children's home, Falling already had a striking propensity for bizarre and violent behavior. One of her favorite pastimes was torturing and killing cats to determine whether they really had nine lives. Falling's caretakers at the children's home described her as a habitual liar, a compulsive thief, and "a child who would break rules to gain attention."[2] Her relationships with the other children in the refuge were horrific. Falling's obesity, poor social skills, and intellectual deficits were a constant source of cruel commentary from her peers.

At the age of twelve, Falling left the children's home to locate her birth mother, eventually finding her in Blountstown, Florida. There, at the age of fourteen, Falling met and married a local man a decade older than she. Within six weeks of the marriage, the relationship collapsed in a chaotic series of violent encounters and the couple permanently separated. The failure of this relationship triggered a new era of bizarre behavior for Falling and, over the next two years, she visited a local hospital more than fifty times with an endless series of strange medical conditions that could never be diagnosed. Although Falling was thoroughly examined by physicians, she would present herself with inexplicable and rapidly changing symptoms that invariably resulted in her being sent home without treatment or medication.

Now in her mid-teens, Falling earned money by baby-sitting for neighbors and friends in her mother's hometown. Despite her unsavory appearance and obvious mental difficulties, she somehow gained a reputation as a young woman who deeply cared for children and was reasonably reliable in her habits. However, at the age of seventeen, Falling began to covertly attack and murder the children who had been placed in her care (see Table 9.1).

On February 25, 1980, Cassidy Johnson, a two-year-old girl who had been in Falling's care was rushed to the local doctor, suffering from life-threatening symptoms that were assumed to be caused by encephalitis. However, when the child died three days later, an autopsy was ordered. The examination disclosed that Johnson had actually succumbed to blunt force trauma of the skull. The results of the autopsy spawned an immediate investigation, and Falling was quickly interviewed by police. She claimed that the child had toppled from her crib and fallen unconscious to the floor when Falling was out of the room. However, law enforcement personnel did not believe her story. Unfortunately, there was no evidence to contradict Falling's version of what had happened to the child, and the matter was not pursued further.

After the death of Cassidy Johnson, Falling moved to Lakeland, Florida, and again began baby-sitting to support herself. Within a few months of her arrival in Lakeland, a four-year-old boy who was in Falling's care suddenly stopped breathing without any prior signs of illness. The death of Jeffrey Davis was as suspicious as that of Cassidy Johnson, and an autopsy was again ordered. The examination disclosed that the boy had suffered from a condition that caused chronic heart inflammation; however, this was deemed insufficient to be the cause of his death. The medical examiner noted no other potential cause of death and the case was closed.

Table 9.1: Christine Falling

Classification	Unexplained.
Birth Information	Born in 1963, in Florida.
Active Period	1980 to 1982. Active from age seventeen to age nineteen.
Victim Information	Murdered at least five children and one elderly man. Injured several other children.
Method	Suffocation.
Motive	Unexplained. Falling was determined to be legally sane but had a history of violence and animal abuse that extended into her early childhood. Speaking of her crimes, Falling said, "I don't know why I done what I done."[3]
Disposition	In 1982, Falling confessed to three murders and was sentenced to life imprisonment. She will be eligible for parole in the year 2007.

Three days after the tragedy, the bereaved aunt and uncle of Jeffrey Davis asked Falling to baby-sit their two-year-old son, Joseph Spring, while they attended Davis's funeral. While his parents were at the services, Joseph inexplicably died while taking a nap. The local physician speculated that the young boy may have succumbed to a viral infection and that the same mysterious disease may have also accounted for the death of Jeffrey Davis. No investigation into the deaths of the two young boys was ever undertaken, and once again, Falling left the area, this time moving back to Perry, Florida.

In July 1981, Falling found a job as housekeeper to a seventy-seven-year-old invalid by the name of William Swindle. On the first day of Falling's new job, Swindle inexplicably died while in his kitchen, allegedly due to a heart attack. Because of his age and poor medical condition, local authorities did not investigate the elderly man's death.

Soon after Swindle's death, Falling accompanied her stepsister and eight-month-old niece, Jennifer Daniels, on some shopping errands. Daniel's mother left the baby in her car with Falling, to make a short stop at the local supermarket; however, when she returned, Daniels found her baby dead and Christine Falling in a panic. According to Falling, the girl had mysteriously stopped breathing. Once again, the death of Jennifer Daniels was determined to be of natural causes and no investigation ensued.

A year later, on July 2, 1982, a ten-week-old infant, Travis Coleman, also stopped breathing while in Falling's care. Coleman's parents cooperated with an autopsy request, and it was discovered that the infant had died from suffocation. Falling was immediately questioned by local law enforcement officials about the Coleman death and confessed to murdering three children by what she described as "smotheration." She claimed that she had heard voices ordering her to murder the children by placing a blanket over their faces.

Based on her confession, Christine Falling received a sentence of life imprisonment with the possibility of parole after twenty-five years. In speaking to law enforcement officials, Falling was never able to provide a motive for her heinous crimes, only saying: "I don't know why I done what I done. The way I done it, I seen it done on TV shows. I had my own way, though. Simple and easy. No one would hear them scream."[4]

Christine Falling will be eligible for parole in the year 2007.

MURDEROUS MOTHERS

Mothers who commit serial murder against their children are sometimes found to be suffering from Munchausen syndrome by proxy—a psychological disorder that is typically accompanied by a compulsive need to seek out the attention of medical personnel for emergency treatment of the induced ailments of their children. However, there are other, less common, motives for a mother to attack her own offspring, such as revenge against the father of her children (Revenge classification) or the profit derived from life insurance proceeds (Black Widow classification). Unfortunately, in some cases the motives of the murderous mother are simply not known to a certainty, although there may be strong indicators to help understand and explain her brutal behavior.

The following five cases of serial murder were each committed by mothers against their own children. In three of these cases (Williamson, Tuggle, and Tinning), the motives of the murderer remain mysterious and uncertain. In the other two (Turner and Green), it is possible that the killer suffered from Munchausen syndrome by proxy, even though there is no irrefutable evidence for this assumption. However, what is certain is that these five murderous mothers brutally attacked their own children and, in one case, children for whom the mother was an apparently trustworthy caretaker. Together, these women murdered twenty-one of their own children and injured several others.

The most bizarre and inexplicable case of a murderous mother is that of Stella Williamson (see Table 9.2). Williamson lived in the small town of Gallitzin, Pennsylvania, and was known to her neighbors as a lifelong spinster and recluse. Her few social contacts centered around her regular attendance at Sunday religious services and her church-related activities. She had no close friends, but did interact erratically with acquaintances near her home.

In 1975, at the age of seventy-five, Williamson had one of her legs amputated and, within a year, had died from the persistent complications of the surgery. Williamson died alone, without any known relatives and only a handful of acquaintances from Gallitzin to mourn at her funeral. However, after the services one of her acquaintances volunteered to put Williamson's affairs in order and began to review her personal effects. Among the documents that the old woman left behind was a sealed envelope bearing the instruction that it was only to be opened after her death. When the envelope was unsealed, it was found to contain handwritten instructions to locate and open a trunk that had been hidden in the attic of Williamson's house. Inside the trunk, the deceased woman's acquaintance made a gruesome and stunning discovery—the remains of five human infants.

Each of the infants had been carefully wrapped in newspaper and placed side-by-side in the old trunk. Williamson's letter, written in 1960, gave no explanation for the remains, and the only clues that could be discovered by local law enforcement personnel were from the newspapers that had been used to carefully wrap the tiny victims. All dated between 1923 and 1933, the newspapers had been published in the cities of Johnstown, Pittsburgh, and New York City. The local coroner determined that four of the infants were newborn at the time of their deaths and the fifth could have been as old as eight months when he met his fate, although the condition of the remains made a precise determination of age impossible.

Gallitzin town officials were at a complete loss to explain the remains found in Stella Williamson's attic. It was assumed that Williamson had given birth to the infants out of wedlock (while in her twenties and thirties), when she was living outside of Gallitzin. After giving birth, she must have murdered each infant and, for some inexplicable reason, preserved their remains. Although uncertain, it is possible that one of the children was allowed to live for several months before he met his fate at the hands of his murderous mother. Because of the condition of the bodies, the local coroner was unable to precisely determine the method of attack in any of the deaths. Certainly, no one was able to provide a clear motive for the murders and Williamson ultimately carried her covert reasons with her to the grave.

Table 9.2: Stella Williamson

Classification	Unexplained.
Birth Information	Born in 1900. Lived in New York and Pennsylvania.
Active Period	1923 to 1933. Active from age twenty-three to age thirty-three.
Victim Information	Murdered five infants. Four of the victims were newborns, while the fifth was approximately eight months old at the time of death.
Method	Unknown.
Motive	Uncertain. It was speculated that Williamson murdered her own illegitimate children shortly after they were born.
Disposition	Williamson died in 1976, leaving instructions that a sealed envelope be opened upon her death. The envelope contained a letter that had been written by her in 1960, directing investigators to a trunk that had been hidden in the attic of her home. The trunk contained the remains of five infants who had apparently been born to the lifelong spinster between 1923 and 1933.

Less mysterious but equally heinous were the crimes of Debra Tuggle (see Table 9.3). In 1974, Tuggle murdered two of her children by suffocation: Thomas Bates Tuggle, two and a half years old, and William Henry Tuggle, aged twenty-one months old. At the time of their deaths, medical personnel assumed that both children had succumbed to sudden infant death syndrome (SIDS); consequently, no autopsy was ordered and no formal investigation was undertaken. Two years later, in 1976, Tuggle's third son, Ronald Johnson Tuggle, died in the same manner as his two siblings. By this time, Tuggle was under suspicion for at least one murder; however, due to mistakes in the investigation and inefficiencies in the legal system, she was not arrested or charged with any crime.

Table 9.3: Debra Sue Tuggle

Classification	Unexplained.
Birth Information	Born in Arkansas.
Active Period	1974 to 1982.
Victim Information	Murdered three of her own children and the child of her fiancé.
Method	Three of the children were suffocated and one was intentionally drowned.
Motive	Unexplained. Tuggle was a former mental patient and may have been suffering from a significant psychological disorder.
Disposition	Tuggle was convicted of second-degree murder in 1984 and sentenced to ten years in prison. Multiple additional counts of murder were dismissed for lack of physical evidence.

In 1982, Tomekia Paxton, the daughter of Tuggle's fiancé, was deliberately drowned. Once again, Debra Tuggle was the primary suspect in the murder. Incredibly, she again managed to avoid the legal system for another two years due to a series of unfortunate legal blunders and poor handling of the case.

Finally, in March 1984, Tuggle was arrested and charged with four counts of murder. However, at her trial in September of that year, prosecutors were unable to provide a clear or convincing motive for any of the murders. At the end of the trial, Tuggle was found guilty of only a single count of second degree murder; all other charges against her were dropped for lack of evidence.

On February 4, 1986, Marybeth Tinning was arrested for the murder of her three-month-old daughter, Tami Lynne. Less than three months earlier, Tinning had claimed that she found the infant unconscious in her crib and rushed her to St. Clare's Hospital in Schenectady, New York. By the time Tinning arrived, the infant had already died. Although medical personnel recorded the official cause of Tami Lynne's death as sudden infant death syndrome (SIDS), they were suspicious of the circumstances surrounding the case and contacted police. Their concern was well founded, for Marybeth Tinning had lost nine of her children since 1972—and eight had died under inexplicable, and sometimes bizarre, circumstances (see Table 9.4).

Tinning's daughter, Jennifer, died on January 3, 1972, while under the care of doctors at St. Clare's Hospital. She was only eight days old when she succumbed to acute meningitis and had never been sufficiently healthy after her birth to leave the hospital. As law enforcement officials would later speculate, this was the only Tinning child who died from natural causes; all the others were probably murdered by their mother.

Less than a month after the death of Jennifer Tinning, two-year-old Joseph was rushed by his mother to the Ellis Hospital in Schenectady. The young boy had apparently suffered an inexplicable seizure and was dead on arrival at the hospital. Unlike Jennifer, Joseph Tinning had no history of illness prior to his death. Medical personnel believed that he had died from an undefined viral infection and felt that no autopsy was needed in the case. Three months later, in March

1972, Tinning's four-year-old daughter, Barbara, mysteriously died from the same symptoms as her younger brother. However, this time medical personnel considered the child's death suspicious and an autopsy was performed. The results of the examination proved inconclusive and the doctors eventually attributed her death to cardiac arrest. Even though the postmortem provided no significant information about Barbara's death, her attending physicians reported the case to police because of their suspicions. Law enforcement personnel conducted a brief investigation but soon decided that there was insufficient information to vigorously pursue the matter.

Table 9.4: Marybeth Tinning[I]

Classification	Unexplained.
Birth Information	Born in New York.
Active Period	1972 to 1985.
Victim Information	May have murdered eight of her own children.
Method	Suffocation.
Motive	Unexplained. Tinning began to murder her own children after she lost a newborn child due to natural causes in 1972.
Disposition	Arrested in 1986 for killing her last child, Tinning was subsequently tried and convicted of second degree murder in 1987.

By the end of 1975, Tinning had lost another two children under questionable circumstances: two-week-old Timothy, whose death was attributed to SIDS, and five-month-old

---

I. The surname of this perpetrator is sometimes spelled as *Twinning* when reference is being made to Marybeth Tinning. However, the majority of references use the proper surname of *Tinning*.

Nathan, who, doctors determined, had died of pulmonary edema. The diagnosis in the case of Nathan Tinning was further supported by an autopsy, which temporarily diverted any further suspicion from the boy's mother. However, both of the babies had died under unusual circumstances in the Tinning home. Nathan's death was especially troubling to medical personnel, who voiced some concern at the time of his postmortem examination; nonetheless, the autopsy seemed to substantiate Tinning's lack of involvement in the mysterious death.

On February 2, 1979, two-year-old Mary Tinning apparently died of SIDS; once again no autopsy was considered necessary in the case. A year later, on March 24, 1980, three-month-old Johnathan Tinning died of the same apparent affliction, although medical personnel were actually uncertain of the cause of death. Despite the unusual circumstances surrounding Johnathan's death, no autopsy or investigation was undertaken. Tinning then adopted a three-year-old boy, Michael, who immediately fell ill under mysterious circumstances after being placed in her care. On August 2, 1981, Tinning rushed the boy to St. Clare's Hospital in an unconscious condition. Physicians were unable to save the boy's life and concluded that he had succumbed to bronchial pneumonia. However, the medical personnel in attendance were once again suspicious of the circumstances and reported the incident to the police. When Tinning's last surviving child, Tami Lynne, was brought to the same hospital on December 20, 1985, law enforcement officials had already begun to suspect Tinning's involvement in the earlier deaths and immediately began an intensive investigation that led to her arrest three months later.

After her arrest, Tinning confessed to smothering Tami Lynne, Timothy, and Nathan. However, she denied any involvement in the deaths of her other children. During her confession, Tinning said to police, "I smothered them with a pillow because I'm not a good mother."[5] Despite her persistent denials, law enforcement personnel were convinced that

Marybeth Tinning had murdered eight of her children between 1972 and the date of her arrest. She was eventually charged with a single count of first-degree murder in the death of Tami Lynne Tinning.

More than a year after her arrest, Marybeth Tinning went to trial for her crime. However, she managed to evade the first-degree murder charge and was convicted of second-degree murder on July 17, 1987. Among the unsettling issues in the case that led to the jury's surprising verdict was the apparent lack of motive or evidence of planning in any of the mysterious deaths. In the final analysis, no one who was connected with the case was ever able to determine Tinning's true motives in the probable murder of eight of her children.

Although no motive was ever proven to a certainty, the crimes of Lise Turner seem to be linked to Munchausen syndrome by proxy (see Table 9.5). Turner, a native of New Zealand, presented her three-month-old daughter, Megan, to an emergency hospital in Christchurch on January 11, 1980. However, by the time they arrived at the hospital, the infant was already dead. According to Turner, the baby had simply stopped breathing for no apparent reason and with no prior history of illness. As is often the case in such situations, medical personnel attributed the baby's death to sudden infant death syndrome (SIDS).

On March 15, 1982, tragedy again struck the Turner family when two-month-old Cheney Louise Turner was discovered dead in her crib by a neighbor who had come to visit. As in the case of her older sister, medical personnel decided that the cause of death had been SIDS, and no investigation or autopsy was ordered. Turner was now childless—an apparently sorrowful and devastated woman. However, her murderous ways had not yet come to an end.

In October of the same year, Turner agreed to baby-sit the four-month-old daughter of a neighbor while she ran some errands. When Mrs. Parker returned from shopping, she found her daughter, Catherine, vomiting and bleeding from the mouth. She rushed the baby to the local hospital, and the quick intervention of medical personnel saved her life. Although the child recovered, Catherine Parker experienced a series of similar attacks over the next several months, each of which occurred when Lise Turner was visiting with the baby. Parker finally realized the connection and forbade Turner from ever again visiting her daughter; however, she never formally reported the matter to police and Turner was not investigated or charged with any crime.

Table 9.5: Lise Jane Turner

Classification	Unexplained.
Birth Information	Born in New Zealand.
Active Period	1980 to 1983.
Victim Information	Murdered three children and attempted to murder as many as six others.
Method	Smothering, asphyxiation.
Motive	Unexplained. Possibly linked to Munchausen syndrome by proxy.
Disposition	Turner was convicted of multiple counts of murder in 1984 and sentenced to life imprisonment.

After her attacks on Catherine Parker, Turner continued to seek out other young victims. While baby-sitting one-month-old Katrina Hall, the infant suddenly experienced the same frightening symptoms as Parker and was rushed to the emergency hospital. Fortunately, she survived the attack and was never again placed in the care of Lise Turner.

This murderous mother's last victim was eight-month-old Michael Tinnion, for whom she was the trusted baby-sitter. In 1983, while under Turner's care, the baby was inexplicably found dead in his crib, bleeding from the mouth. The circumstances of Tinnion's death were extremely suspicious, and law enforcement officials undertook an immediate investigation. Medical personnel determined that the boy had obviously died from asphyxiation. Based on this finding, Turner was arrested for murder.

By November 1984, the case against Lise Turner had been expanded and she was charged with three counts of murder and two counts of attempted murder. She was also the prime suspect in at least four other attacks on children, although no formal charges were brought against her in those cases. Even though no clear motive was articulated at her trial, the evidence against Lise Turner was overwhelming and she was found guilty on all counts. Turner was sentenced to life imprisonment for each count of murder and an additional five years' imprisonment for each count of attempted murder. Despite the fact that the issue of motive was apparently not critical to the prosecution of Turner's case, her pattern of criminality raised questions at the trial that may have linked her crimes to Munchausen syndrome by proxy.

Like Lise Turner, Ann Green was a murderous mother who probably suffered from Munchausen syndrome by proxy (see Table 9.6). She was also a hospital nurse who may have been involved in the suspicious deaths of children under her care in a pediatric ward, although this is uncertain. What is known about Green is that she attacked all three of her own children, murdering two of them. Both of the fatalities were attributed to natural causes (a malfunctioning heart and SIDS) at the time that they occurred.

However, after the birth of her third child in 1985, medical personnel recommended that the infant be kept in the hospital for observation and possible intervention should any indication of SIDS develop. After a two-week precautionary stay in the hospital without incident, the baby was released to Green to be brought home. The next day, according to Green, the infant suddenly stopped breathing and was rushed back to the hospital. Fortunately, medical intervention was successful and the baby was stabilized.

Table 9.6: Ann Green

Classification	Unexplained.
Birth Information	Born in 1946.
Active Period	1970 to 1985. Active from age twenty-four to age thirty-nine.
Victim Information	Murdered two of her children and attempted to murder a third. May have been responsible for Angel of Death murders at a hospital where she was employed for fifteen years.
Method	Uncertain, but probably suffocation.
Motive	Uncertain.
Disposition	Indicted for murder in 1986.

After the near-death of her last child, police became suspicious of Green's behavior and activities—sufficiently so to begin a formal investigation. She was subsequently indicted for murder in the deaths of her two children. Given her knowledge of medical procedures, her familiarity with hospital personnel, and the pattern of her crimes, it is likely that Ann Green suffered from Munchausen syndrome by proxy, even though law enforcement officials were unable to attribute a specific motive to her actions.

BEYOND THE CHILDREN

Not all unexplained serial murders committed by women involve only children as victims. The following two cases share the common characteristic that a range of victims was targeted for death by the perpetrator. Moreover, in both cases, a consistent motive for the murders was never positively determined.

Audrey Hilley was born in Alabama in 1933 and exhibited a normal childhood in every way. In 1951, at the age of eighteen, she married a local man, and by 1960, she had given birth to her second child, Carol. Although it was later learned that Hilley had a somewhat difficult relationship with her husband, nothing in her background indicated unusual or violent behavior.

By the mid-1970s, now in her early forties, Hilley began to exhibit bizarre and increasingly violent behavior that would culminate in a number of brutal murders (see Table 9.7). The first hint of Hilley's escalating violence began with a series of telephone calls to local police. In each case she would call to report prowlers in the neighborhood and threatening telephone calls. Although her requests for assistance were numerous and persistent, they seemed to be baseless and designed only to draw attention from local law enforcement personnel. Hilley would often show her appreciation to the responding police officers by brewing a fresh pot of coffee upon their arrival. In at least two documented instances, responding police officers became ill with stomach cramps and vomiting after drinking Hilley's coffee. Apparently, none of the officers were taken so seriously ill as to require hospitalization and, in fact, no connection was immediately made between Hilley's coffee and the sudden onset of their illnesses. That connection would only be realized years later.

Also during this period, several children in the neighborhood became suddenly afflicted with mysterious ailments that also involved nausea and stomach difficulties. Unfortunately, one of the children (an eleven-year-old girl) died of the mysterious disorder in 1975. All the children had been neighborhood playmates of Hilley's child, Carol.

That same year, Hilley's husband, Frank, died of what doctors assumed to be an undiagnosed and fatal form of cancer. Although his death was shocking and certainly unexpected, no autopsy was performed and the matter was not pursued. Two years later, in 1977, Hilley's mother, Lucille Frazier, died under similar circumstances, with strikingly similar symptoms. Once again, the death was assumed to be from natural causes. Incredibly, in 1979, Hilley's daughter began to exhibit the same frightening symptoms as her father and she became so ill that it was presumed she would soon die from the mysterious disease. During the long course of Carol's struggle for life (that went on throughout much of 1979), Hilley's mother-in-law, Carrie Hilley, also died—however, she had been ill for a number of years and her death was not completely unexpected.

Table 9.7: Audrey Marie Hilley

Classification	Unexplained.
Birth Information	Born in 1933, in Alabama.
Active Period	1975 to 1979. Active from age forty-two to age forty-six.
Victim Information	Murdered at least three family members, injured another, and was a suspect in a number of other violent incidents.
Method	Poison.
Motive	Uncertain. Hilley's motives were never determined, and she was unable to provide an explanation for her crimes.
Disposition	Hilley was indicted for murder in 1979 but was able to avoid apprehension until 1983. In that year she was convicted and sentenced to life imprisonment.

Remarkably, Carol Hilley did not succumb to the mysterious illness that had claimed at least two other members of her family. During the course of many tests to determine how to save the life of the young woman, medical personnel were shocked to discover that Carol Hilley had been administered near-lethal doses of arsenic. When doctors reported their findings to the local police, Audrey Hilley became the focus of an immediate investigation for attempted murder.

Concerned that Carol Hilley may not have been her mother's first victim, an exhumation and postmortem examination were ordered on the body of Frank Hilley. In the meantime, on October 25, 1979, Audrey Hilley was indicted on the charge of the attempted murder of her daughter and a preliminary hearing was set for the following month.

Within a few weeks, Audrey Hilley had fled the Anniston, Alabama, area, where her hearing had been scheduled. By January 1980, police had received the results of the postmortem examination on Frank Hilley and were not particularly surprised to learn that he, also, had been poisoned. On January 11, 1980, Hilley was indicted on a charge of first-degree murder; however, her whereabouts were unknown.

For the next three years, Audrey Hilley lived on the run from police. She adopted a series of aliases and, in 1981, married a man while living in New Hampshire. The marriage lasted for barely a month before Hilley again changed her name and suddenly moved on to Texas. In a series of bizarre encounters, Hilley pretended to be her own twin sister, made efforts to fake her own death on at least one occasion, attempted to reconcile with her ex-husband, and even visited him claiming to be the twin to his ex-wife. Finally, her strange behavior attracted the attention of local authorities. She was eventually identified as the missing Audrey Hilley and arrested in January 1983.

Four months later, Hilley stood trial and was convicted of one count of first-degree murder in the death of her husband and one count of attempted murder for her attack on Carol Hilley. Throughout the proceedings, Hilley claimed that she had not been involved in any violence against another individual. As a defense, she offered a strange story of intermittent periods of loss of consciousness and memory failures during which she was unaware of her actions. Not surprisingly, the jury found her defense unacceptable. Hilley was sentenced to life imprisonment for murder and an additional twenty years for attempted murder. However, her strange and violent odyssey had not yet come to an end.

Hilley was assigned to a prison at Wetumpka, Alabama, where she could eventually earn the privilege of a pass to the outside world with good behavior. After nearly four years in prison, Hilley was considered a model inmate and had earned the coveted privilege. On February 19, 1987, she received a three-day furlough from the prison, walked out of the gates, and never returned. A week later, on February 26, 1987, Hilley was found on the porch of a home in Anniston, the town in which she had been tried and convicted of her crimes. When she was discovered, Hilley was incoherent and suffering from hypothermia. She was immediately transported to a local hospital for treatment; however, by the time she arrived, Audrey Hilley had died from an unexpected and fatal heart attack.

More than two decades before Audrey Hilley committed her first murder, another women in Germany set out on a lethal course of killing that seemed somewhat predictable; however, her motives have been defined only by assumption and were never clearly stated by the perpetrator herself. Christa Lehman was the daughter of a woman who was institutionalized for severe mental illness and a father who was abusive, alcoholic, and disinterested in children. Her childhood was marked by a nearly complete lack of supervision, periods of unpredictably violent behavior, and indiscriminate sexual encounters that belied her young age. By the time she was twenty-two, Lehman had married a man much like her father, with a reputation as an unsavory, often drunk, and frequently violent individual. She had also gained her own widespread reputation for indiscriminate love affairs in the neighborhood and a hair-trigger temper. Acquaintances generally considered Lehman to be a woman whose behavior was frequently unpredictable and often unsavory (see Table 9.8).

By the age of thirty, Lehman had grown tired of the abusive relationship with her husband and unable to control the several affairs that were a constant source of conflict in her life. In September 1952, she poisoned her unsuspecting husband with a powerful pesticide known as E-605. Although

Karl Lehman's death was both sudden and unusually violent in its symptoms, local doctors attributed his demise to a ruptured stomach ulcer and closed the case. A year later, on October 14, 1953, Lehman's father-in-law died with the same symptoms as his son. Remarkably, local medical personnel did not recognize the similarities between these two unusual deaths and determined that no autopsy or investigation was required.

Table 9.8: Christa Lehman

Classification	Unexplained.
Birth Information	Born in 1922, in Germany.
Active Period	1952 to 1953. Active from the age of thirty to the age of thirty-one.
Victim Information	Murdered her husband, father-in-law, and at least two neighbors.
Method	Poison (a pesticide known as E-605).
Motive	Uncertain. Possibly a profit motive.
Disposition	Lehman was arrested and tried in 1953 on several counts of homicide. She was found guilty and sentenced to life imprisonment.

Now convinced that she could get away with murder, Lehman began to plot against her neighbors. On February 15, 1954, she offered chocolate truffles laced with the deadly poison to several women in the neighborhood. One of the unfortunate women suffered severe convulsions, lapsed into a coma, and died. Finally realizing that something was amiss with Christa Lehman, a police investigation was launched and she was arrested less than ten days after the death of her last victim. Once in custody, Lehman confessed to poisoning her neighbors and claimed it was an act of revenge for the gossip that had been spread about her various (and less than secret) relationships. However, the woman whom she had murdered was not one against whom Lehman had ever expressed animosity. Furthermore, Lehman never provided a consistent motive for the attacks against her husband or father-in-law. Nonetheless, a reasonable assumption could be made that she had tired of the criticism of her free-ranging lifestyle and wished to be released from the abusive relationship with her spouse.

On September 20, 1954, Christa Lehman was convicted on multiple charges of homicide and sentenced to life in prison. However, she never provided a definitive motive for her murderous actions.

NOTES

1. Eric W. Hickey, *Serial Murderers and Their Victims* (Belmont, CA: Wadsworth, 1991), 123.

2. Ibid.

3. "Hunting Humans—Christine Falling," in Kozel Multimedia, *Mind of a Killer,* CD-ROM (Chatsworth, CA: Cambrix, 1995), Profile 6-4.

4. Ibid.

5. Ibid.

10

THE UNSOLVED

Evil being the root of mystery, pain is the root of knowledge.
—Simone Weil
New York Notebook

Although most cases of serial murder are eventually solved, it is likely that many such crimes never come to the attention of law enforcement personnel because of a failure to recognize the very presence of a serial killer or because the murderer inexplicably ceases his or her lethal activities. In a few, highly notorious cases of serial murder, like that of the *Green River Killer* (who operated in Washington and California) or the *Zodiac Killer* (who operated in California), the crimes were never solved and the killings apparently ceased for reasons that remain unknown. In these baffling situations, it is possible that the perpetrator was apprehended and imprisoned for other felonies, died, or stopped murdering because of age, illness, infirmity, or complex psychological factors.

Other serial murders are considered unsolved because, even though the perpetrator was thought to have been irrefutably identified by law enforcement personnel and properly charged with the felonies, he or she was never convicted of the crimes. Because serial murder committed by a woman is often discreet, quiet, and carefully planned, the perpetrator is frequently a difficult adversary for law enforcement personnel. Even after she has been successfully apprehended and brought to trial, the female serial murderer presents unusual difficulties for those in the legal profession, judges, and juries. It is generally a difficult task to prove the guilt of a female serial murderer with anything less than overwhelming evidence. Because her crimes are usually subtle and secretive and because she rarely leaves viable survivors to her actions, it requires an extraordinary burden of proof for the female serial murderer to be convicted by most juries. It is simply not adequate to rely on circumstantial evidence to prove the guilt of such a perpetrator.

To compound this matter even further, Western culture is slow to perceive a woman as a brutal serial murderer unless she has been a partner with another, blatantly guilty individual. If the female serial killer is a member of a killing team, she is far more likely to be found guilty of her crimes than if she acted alone. Since the crimes of Team Killers tend to be egregious sexual homicides or similarly outrageous felonies, juries are understandably less reluctant to assign full guilt to a female partner of a team. However, this perception does not extend to the quiet, unnoticed serial murderer who acts alone.

It is obvious that we cannot know how many cases of serial murder go unsolved each year. It is clear that many crimes of this type are probably never recognized as such. However, when a case of serial murder is properly recognized and acknowledged, the outlook for solving the crime is good. Unfortunately, the outlook for convicting the perpetrator may not be as bright.

In this chapter, we examine three cases of serial murder that are classified as unsolved. However, they all share a remarkable characteristic—in each case, law enforcement officials were able to identify the perpetrators to their own satisfaction and, in one case, their hard work actually resulted in a conviction. However, in each case the perpetrators were eventually found not guilty of the crimes with which they were charged. Technically, these three cases of serial murder remain unsolved; however, none of the law enforcement personnel who worked on these cases would hold such an opinion.

DEATH IN A CASTLE

William Hodges Bingham and his family were employed as caretakers for the historical Lancaster castle in England for generations. In addition to William Bingham, several other family members lived on the castle grounds and held a variety of jobs related to the upkeep of the estate, including three of William's children: his son James, and his daughters Margaret and Edith Agnes.

After some thirty years as chief caretaker for Lancaster Castle, William Bingham suddenly died in January 1911. The Bingham children were devastated by the unexpected loss of their father, and James Bingham took on the responsibilities of chief caretaker for the estate. James's sister, Margaret, carried on as a housekeeper in the castle. However, within a few weeks of her father's death, Margaret also died unexpectedly, in the same manner as her father. Although both deaths were inexplicable, no autopsy was performed on either of the Binghams.

James Bingham was left with only his half-sister, Edith, to help with the endless chores on the estate and soon decided to recruit another housekeeper to supplement their depleted ranks. The new housekeeper was eventually located, and she agreed to report to Lancaster Castle on August 14, 1911. However, two days before her scheduled arrival, James Bingham mysteriously died despite excellent health. Like his father and sister before him, James had died rapidly and with ominous symptoms.

Local law enforcement officials were concerned about the three mysterious deaths that had struck the Bingham family in less than a year. At their insistence, an autopsy was performed on James Bingham and it was quickly discovered that he had died from arsenic poisoning. The medical examiner's findings led investigators to immediately order the exhumation

and examination of the bodies of William Bingham and his
daughter, Margaret. In both cases, a postmortem examination disclosed that father and daughter had died from arsenic
poisoning.

Once law enforcement officials received word of the results of the three medical examinations, they moved rapidly
to arrest Edith Agnes Bingham and charge her with three
counts of murder. Since Edith stood to inherit a small estate
from her deceased relatives, both police and prosecutors
were convinced that they had sufficient evidence and an understanding of motive to convict her on all three counts (see
Table 10.1).

Table 10.1: Bingham Family Murders

Classification	Unsolved (possibly the crimes of a Black Widow serial murderer).
Birth Information	The perpetrator is officially unknown. A family member, Edith Agnes Bingham, was accused of the crimes but subsequently acquitted.
Active Period	1911. All three murders occurred within a year.
Victim Information	Three members of the Bingham family, caretakers to the Lancaster castle in England.
Method	Poison (arsenic).
Motive	Assumed to be a profit motive (family inheritance).
Disposition	Edith Agnes Bingham, the chief suspect, was tried and acquitted of the crimes. No other suspect was considered and the case remains officially unsolved.

Edith Bingham went to trial for murder in 1912, with her
barrister arguing that there was no concrete evidence to indi-

cate his client had ever possessed or used arsenic in any way. He further argued that the case against his client was purely circumstantial and gave grave doubt to the Crown's legal arguments since there were no hard facts brought forward to indicate Edith Bingham's involvement in any of the deaths. Bingham's barrister further pointed out to the jury that the small inheritance that his client stood to receive was an inadequate motive to murder three members of her own family.

The jury obviously agreed with the defense argument in the case; it took them less than thirty minutes to find Edith Bingham not guilty of any of the charges brought against her. Since the police had no other suspects and no additional information to bring forward, the Bingham family murder case was abandoned and remains officially unsolved to this day. However, in the minds of most who have investigated this case, Edith Bingham remained the most likely suspect. If she was indeed responsible for the murder of her father, brother, and sister, this would make Bingham the first recorded Black Widow serial murderer in twentieth-century England.

UNSOLVED MURDERS BY CARETAKERS

The concept of a lethal caretaker, particularly if the perpetrator is a nurse or doctor, is both abhorrent and frightening to anyone who has even a passing familiarity with the Hippocratic Oath. Unfortunately, this type of serial killer has become more prolific in recent decades, as he or she strikes against the most vulnerable victims—the aged, young, and infirm. Murders committed by a lethal female caretaker who functions in a medical environment, such as a hospital or nursing home, are often difficult to recognize and even more difficult to comprehend. Because death is a relatively common event in these institutions, it is only after the discovery of a significant increase in the expected mortality rate that an investigation is typically begun. Even then, many hospital administrators are slow to seriously consider the possibilities of a murderous doctor or nurse among their staff.

It is impossible to estimate the number of victims who are claimed each year by a lethal caretaker. For those perpetrators who attack only a small number of victims, the possibilities of discovery and apprehension may be minimal. However, those lethal employees who claim a significant number of lives are usually apprehended successfully, even though they may be initially successful in their ability to murder several individuals over a relatively short period of time. Nonetheless, from time to time the lethal caretaker manages to avoid the best efforts of law enforcement personnel and prosecutors. In some cases, the perpetrator is successfully identified but eventually able to avoid punishment for his or her crimes because the evidence available at trial is inadequate or mistakes are made during the investigation phase that jeopardize the prosecution's case. Fortunately, the known number of such incidents is few, although they are quite disturbing.

Two notorious cases of lethal caretakers who managed to escape punishment for their crimes occurred a decade apart, in 1975 and 1985, in this country. Both these cases were extraordinarily frustrating for law enforcement because in the first, the perpetrator had actually confessed to her crimes yet ultimately managed to escape justice, and in the second, the perpetrators were properly convicted of their crimes but later had their convictions overturned. In the end, both cases remain officially unsolved.

The first incident occurred at the Veterans' Administration hospital in Ann Arbor, Michigan, in 1975. For a period of two months of that year (July and August), the hospital experienced an inexplicable and alarming increase in the number of patients who suffered sudden respiratory arrest that required emergency medical intervention in order to save their lives. In all, nearly thirty patients experienced severe bouts of respiratory arrest, some of them on multiple occasions. Nine of the patients died from these mysterious attacks—a number so extraordinary for the hospital that administrators launched an immediate investigation into the matter (see Table 10.2).

Table 10.2: Veterans' Administration Hospital Murders—Michigan

Classification	Unsolved (provisional classification: Angel of Death).
Birth Information	Two nurses (ages twenty-nine and thirty-one) were charged and convicted on five counts of murder. The convictions were later overturned and all charges were dismissed.
Active Period	1975.
Victim Information	At least five patients were murdered and another nine injured during their hospitalization. The actual number of victims who may have been murdered by the same means remains unknown but is believed to be between eleven and twenty-seven.
Method	Injection of a muscle relaxant (Pavulon).
Motive	Possible Angel of Death motivation.
Disposition	The primary suspects had their convictions overturned. No other suspects were named in the case.

The probe into these deaths disclosed that eighteen of the patients who had suffered severe respiratory arrest had been injected with a potent muscle relaxant known as Pavulon, a synthetic form of the lethal poison curare. Nine of their patients were never able to recover from the attack. The alarmed hospital administrators quickly requested the assistance of federal investigators in an effort to pinpoint the source of the lethal attacks on their patients. It was soon discovered that virtually all the inexplicable cases of respiratory arrest had occurred in the intensive care unit (ICU) during the afternoon work shift. Investigators also learned that the muscle relaxant had been injected into the bodies of the victims through their intravenous feeding tubes—a routine procedure that would be generally unsuspected by most patients and not closely monitored by hospital staff.

Investigators began to compare the work schedules of the hospital staff with the times and locations of the attacks and soon discovered that two nurses, thirty-one-year-old Leonora Perez and twenty-nine-year-old Filipina Narciso, had been in attendance with each of the victims. One of the surviving patients, a sixty-one-year-old male, was able to identify Perez as the nurse who had entered his room to attend to him and suddenly fled when he screamed for help during the onset of respiratory arrest.

Both nurses vehemently denied any involvement in the injuries or deaths of the patients in their care. However, law enforcement officials continued to build their case and both women were eventually charged with multiple counts of murder. In July 1977, Perez and Narciso were brought to trial and found guilty on all counts. However, less than six months later, all the charges against the pair were dropped for insufficient evidence and legal errors in their earlier trial. Following the dismissal of the charges, investigators were left with no other evidence and the unusual deaths at the Veterans' Administration hospital had long ceased.

A decade later, at Prince George's Hospital in Maryland, a remarkably similar series of unexplained deaths suddenly became apparent to hospital administrators. Like the case of Perez and Narciso, the mysterious deaths at Prince George's Hospital would also go unresolved (see Table 10.3).

Jane Bolding, an intensive care unit (ICU) nurse, was hired by the hospital in 1976 and, for most of her nine years on the job, was considered to be an efficient and trustworthy employee. However, between January 1984 and March 1985 the mortality rate in the ICU skyrocketed, and Bolding soon came under suspicion for murder. Nearly sixty patients had inexplicably died from cardiac arrest following surgery or other emergency procedures in a period of slightly more than a year.

Table 10.3: Prince George's Hospital Murders—Maryland

Classification	Unsolved (provisional classification: Angel of Death).
Birth Information	Uncertain.
Active Period	January 1984 to March 1985.
Victim Information	At least seventeen hospital patients were murdered and at least another seven injured while in the intensive care unit.
Method	Injections of potassium.
Motive	Possible Angel of Death motivation.
Disposition	A suspect (Jane Bolding) confessed to the murders after intense interrogation from law enforcement officials. The suspect was brought to trial in 1988 and her confession was declared to be inadmissible by the presiding judge. Based on the inadmissibility of the confession, the suspect was acquitted on all counts. No other suspects were charged in the case.

An investigation by the federal Centers for Disease Control (CDC) into the extraordinary number of unusual deaths at the hospital disclosed alarming results. The hospital employed over ninety nurses in various capacities, yet only two of these employees had lost more than four patients during the 1984–1985 year of unexplained deaths. A single nurse had witnessed the death of five of her patients, while Bolding had experienced an amazing fifty-seven deaths, virtually all from cardiac arrest while under her care. Of all the patients who had experienced any form of cardiac arrest during that year, 65 percent were in the ICU, directly under Bolding's care, at the time of the attack. The statistics against Bolding were so overwhelming as to make it immediately apparent that she was deeply involved in the dozens of mysterious deaths at Prince George's Hospital.

On March 9, 1985, Bolding was suspended from her duties while the investigation continued. Two weeks later, at the end of the probe, she was arrested and formally charged with first-degree murder in the case of an aging female patient who had succumbed to cardiac arrest on September 29, 1984.[1]

Law enforcement officials interrogated Jane Bolding for over thirty hours before she eventually confessed to injecting her patients with potassium, a chemical known to cause cardiac arrest. She claimed that her motive in attacking the patients was to save them from further pain and suffering. On March 26, 1985, Bolding was officially terminated from her position with the hospital while the final details of the state's case were being assembled.

On March 28, 1985, the state attorney for Prince George's County told the press that law enforcement officials had disobeyed his instructions in arresting Bolding because her confession, which was the only substantial evidence in the case, was insufficient to proceed with a successful prosecution. Two months later, all charges against Bolding were dropped. However, investigators soon reopened the probe into the deaths at Prince George's in a renewed effort to uncover additional evidence to again bring charges against Bolding, who they were now convinced had murdered at least seventeen patients.

By December of that year, prosecutors felt that they had sufficient evidence to present to the grand jury and again bring Bolding to trial. The grand jury agreed with the prosecutors, and the former nurse was charged with three counts of murder and seven counts of assault with the intent to commit murder. In May 1988, she was finally brought to trial for her crimes.

At the trial, Bolding waived her right to present her case to a jury and relied solely on the presiding judge in the case. Before the trial got underway in earnest, however, the judge ruled that Bolding's confession to murder was inadmissible as evidence because of the duration of her interrogation and a lack of proper representation. Without Bolding's confession as evidence, the prosecution's case against her was fatally weakened and she was subsequently acquitted of all charges. Like the murders committed at the Veteran's Hospital in Michigan a decade earlier, the Prince George's Hospital killings remain officially unsolved to this day, although none of the law enforcement personnel or prosecutors who worked on the case would agree with that designation.

NOTE

1. "Hunting Humans—Hospital Murders, Maryland," in Kozel Multimedia, *Mind of a Killer*, CD-ROM, (Chatsworth, CA: Cambrix, 1995), Section: "Hospital Murders."

APPENDIX 1:
STATISTICAL INFORMATION

Table A.1 shows the distribution of American female serial killers by classification. It includes both those perpetrators who operated alone and those who acted as a member of a team in committing their crimes. Only perpetrators who committed murders within American borders were considered. In addition, any suspected serial murders that took place prior to 1900 were excluded.

Table A.1: Female Serial Killers by Classification

Classification	Including Team Killers		Excluding Team Killers	
	Number	Percent	Number	Percent
Team Killer	14	28	—	—
Black Widow	13	26	13	36
Unexplained	6	12	6	17
Revenge	4	8	4	11
Question of Sanity	4	8	4	11
Profit or Crime	3	6	3	8
Angel of Death	3	6	3	8
Unsolved 2	4	2	6	
Sexual Predator	1	2	1	3
Totals	**50**	**100**	**36**	**100**

Table A.2 shows the primary weapons used by American female serial killers who operated either alone or as a member of a team. As in Table A.1, only perpetrators who committed murders within American borders were considered, and any suspected serial murders that took place prior to 1900 were excluded.

Table A.2: Primary Weapon of Female Serial Killers

Primary Weapon	Including Team Killers		Excluding Team Killers	
	Number	Percent	Number	Percent
Poison	19	38	19	53
Various	9	18	0	0
Suffocation	9	18	7	19
Lethal injection	6	12	6	17
Shooting	5	10	3	8
Strangulation	2	4	1	3
Totals	**50**	**100**	**36**	**100**

APPENDIX 2:
ALPHABETICAL LISTING OF FEMALE SERIAL KILLERS

This is an alphabetical listing of the female serial killers (or cases in which a female serial killer was suspected) used in researching this book:

Allitt, Beverley
Ambrose, Lyda C.
Atkins, Susan
Barfield, Margie Velma
Beck, Martha
Becker, Marie Alexander
Beier, Greta
Bell, Mary Flora
Besnard, Marie
Birnie, Catherine
Bombeek, Cecile
Brown, Debra Denise
Brunner, Mary
Buenoano, Judias Anna Lou
Bundy, Carol M.
Coffman, Cynthia
De Melker, Daisy Louisa C.
Doss, Nanny Hazel
Enriqueta, Marti
Etheridge, Ellen
Falling, Christine
Fugate, Caril
Fuzekos, Mrs. Julius

Gallego, Charlene
Gates, Ann
Gbrurek, Tillie
Gibbs, Janie Lou
Gilligan, Amy
Gonzales, Maria de Jesus
Graham, Gwendolyn
Green, Ann
Grills, Caroline
Gruber, Marie
Gunness, Belle
Hahn, Anna Marie
Hilley, Audrey Marie
Hindley, Myra
Holmolka, Karla
Hoyt, Waneta E.
Johnson, Martha Ann
Jones, Genene
Kesabian, Linda
Kinne, Sharon
Krenwinkel, Patricia
Lehman, Christa
Leidolf, Irene

Lumbrera, Diana
Lyles, Anjette
Martin, Rhonda Bell
Mayer, Stephanija
McCrary, Carolyn
McGinnis, Virginia
Mitchell, Alice
Moore, Blanche Taylor
Moore, Patricia
Neelley, Judith Ann
Olah, Susi
Pavlovich, Milka
Popova, Madame
Puente, Dorothea
Rachals, Terri
Renczi, Vera
Rendell, Martha
Sach, Amelia
Scieri, Antoinette
Tannenbaum, Gloria

Terrell, Bobbie Sue
Tinning, Marybeth
Toppan, Jane
Trueblood, Lydia
Tuggle, Debra Sue
Turner, Lise Jane
Van Houten, Leslie
Velten, Maria
Vermilyea, Louise
Waddingham, Dorthea
Wagner, Waltraud
Walters, Annie
Weber, Jeanne
West, Rosemary
Williamson, Stella
Wise, Martha Hasel
Wood, Catherine May
Woods, Martha
Wuornos, Carol Aileen
Young, Lila Gladys

APPENDIX 3:
MUNCHAUSEN SYNDROME
BY PROXY

In 1951, Richard Asher introduced the term *Munchausen syndrome* to describe an unusual psychological disorder that had been previously unrecognized by the medical profession. Victims of this disorder were characterized by behavior involving the fabrication of a variety of self-induced illnesses so that the individual could demand and receive extensive, intense attention from medical professionals. Asher noted that individuals who were afflicted with this disorder would typically falsely create elaborate medical histories, induce a variety of physical symptoms to validate the medical attention they desperately craved, and travel great distances to a large number of medical facilities in search of the desired interaction. Asher's recognition of Munchausen syndrome was a significant contribution to medical science; it explained a growing number of medical and psychiatric case histories that had been previously considered inexplicable or been severely misdiagnosed.

In 1977, an English pediatrician recognized a derivation of this complex psychological disorder and introduced the concept of *Munchausen syndrome by proxy* (MSBP) into the medical literature. Unlike Munchausen syndrome, in which the victim of the disorder inflicts injury to herself in order to gain medical attention, MSBP involves the fabrication of illnesses in a dependent individual, who is typically a child or ward of the adult affected by the disorder. With MSBP, the perpetrator indirectly assumes the role of patient (by proxy) by fabricating or inducing illnesses in another person. Both

Munchausen syndrome and MSBP are overwhelmingly diagnosed in females, although there exist case histories in which these disorders have been recognized in males.

The unfortunate victim of the adult who suffers from MSBP is most often a child under the age of six. However, on rare occasions the individual who suffers from MSBP will victimize another adult in order to induce or fabricate illnesses. In either case, the American Psychiatric Association (APA) has recognized MSBP as a disorder in which there is an intentional production of physical or psychological symptoms in a person who is under the care of a MSBP sufferer. Unfortunately, the ultimate victim of this disorder is frequently a very young child or an infant. When MSBP is considered in the context of a female serial killer, the victims are overwhelmingly young children in the direct care of the MSBP sufferer, who eventually succumb after years of intense and excruciating suffering. The case of Martha Woods exemplifies the impact of this order (see Table A.3).

MSBP is a complex psychological disorder that is often misdiagnosed, despite its well-documented history in the medical literature. Victims of MSBP will induce a wide range of illnesses in their dependent victims. At times, these illnesses are psychological; however, most often they are very real, and frequently they are life threatening. Mothers who suffer from MSBP will usually fabricate disorders in their children by such means as suffocation, induced seizures, induced bleeding, chronic poisoning with drugs such as ipecac (which leads to vomiting) or phenolphthalein (which induces diarrhea), or the injection of excrement in order to induce other severe physical symptoms.

MSBP sufferers who attack their children are often trying to communicate their own anxiety, depression, extreme need for attention, and inability to care for their children. They are crying out for help and may be attempting to compensate for traumatic losses in their own early life. It is not uncommon to learn that individuals who suffer from MSBP have experienced a childhood dominated by discord, domestic violence, and abuse. Unfortunately, these victims later become the

Table A.3: Martha Woods

Classification	Black Widow (Munchausen syndrome by proxy).
Active Period	1946 to 1969 in a variety of locations. Woods was the wife of a military officer and was often transferred to a variety of locations throughout the nation.
Victim Information	Murdered seven children. Three of the victims were her own children. Additional victims included her nephew, niece, the child of a neighbor, and an adopted child.
Method	Suffocation and smothering. The children were rushed to nearby hospitals with inexplicable attacks that caused respiratory failure. A total of nine children were attacked, resulting in twenty-seven incidents of respiratory attacks that required emergency intervention. Seven of the nine children died from these attacks.
Motive	Munchausen syndrome by proxy.
Disposition	Woods was eventually arrested in Baltimore after the death of her seven-month-old, adopted son. After extensive psychiatric analysis she was found to be suffering from Munchausen syndrome by proxy but legally sane and capable of standing trial. After a trial that lasted for five months, Woods was found guilty of first-degree murder and sentenced to life imprisonment.

perpetrators of violence against their own children—violence that is unremitting and often fatal. Mothers who suffer from MSBP will use their "ill" children to create complex relationships with medical professionals, which they can control. In so doing, MSBP sufferers will go to extraordinary lengths to fabricate illnesses in their children; they will usually construct elaborate stories to justify their continuing need for medical attention.

Since the typical victim of an MSBP sufferer is under six years of age and completely dependent on the adult perpetrator, it is often difficult for medical professionals to quickly recognize the presence of the illness. In most instances the individual who suffers from MSBP is pleasant, cooperative, and apparently deeply concerned about the welfare of her child. It is therefore difficult for many medical professionals to come to an early realization that the mother who has presented her child for medical treatment is the same individual who has induced the illness. Often, a prolonged period of testing and evaluation is undertaken in an effort to disclose the true nature of what appears to be an inexplicable, and often very serious, medical condition.

Despite the complexity of the disorder, there are behavioral clues that can lead a medical professional to suspect MSBP. The adult who presents her child for treatment may have a nursing or medical background of her own; she will be quite familiar with medical terminology and practices. In fact, she may seem to thrive in the medical environment and will insist on being intimately involved in even the most insignificant aspects of her child's treatment. Often, she will be unwilling to be separated from her child for any significant period of time, even during complex diagnostic procedures that would normally not involve the parent or guardian.

MSBP represents a grave danger for the child-victim. Significant physical harm to the child is frequent, and the death of the victim is not uncommon. Since the MSBP sufferer may induce any number of confusing illnesses in her child and since the symptoms presented to medical professionals are often convoluted and unclear, the young victim frequently suffers profoundly and for prolonged periods. To compound the effects of MSBP, it is a disorder that is rarely treated with any significant degree of success. Generally, the MSBP sufferer stubbornly maintains a strong denial of her illness and rarely tells the truth about any aspect of her life or that of her children. In fact, MSBP sufferers are renowned for their extremes of lying and fabrication in an effort to perpetuate their ability to manipulate others.

It is impossible to know the extent of this disorder or the number of young victims who are annually claimed by MSBP sufferers. Indeed, it is clear that many children die each year at the hands of individuals who are victims of MSBP. It is likely that many instances of sudden infant death syndrome (SIDS) and similar disorders may, in fact, result from the actions of an individual who suffers from MSBP. In the context of analyzing the motives and actions of the female serial killer, it is not uncommon to learn of the presence of MSBP in those perpetrators who murder their children, particularly among killers who have been classified as Black Widows or Angels of Death.

SELECTED BIBLIOGRAPHY

Abrahamsen, D. *The Murdering Mind.* New York: Harper Colophon, 1984.

Adler, F. *Sisters in Crime.* New York: McGraw-Hill, 1975.

American Psychiatric Association (APA), *Diagnostic and Statistical Manual of Mental Disorders* (DSM IV). 4th ed., Washington, DC: APA, 1994.

Bard, M., and Sangrey, D. *The Crime Victim's Book.* 2nd ed., New York: Brunner Mazel, 1986.

Brian, D. *Murderers Die.* New York: St. Martin's Press, 1986.

Brownmiller, S. *Against Our Will: Men, Women, and Rape.* New York: Simon and Schuster, 1975.

Bugliosi, V. *Helter Skelter: The True Story of the Manson Murders.* New York: Bantam, 1974.

Cameron, D., and Frazer, E. *The Lust to Kill.* New York: New York University Press, 1987.

Caputi, J. *The Age of Sex Crime.* Bowling Green, OH: Bowling Green State University Press, 1987.

Cullen, T. *The Mild Murderer.* Boston: Houghton Mifflin, 1977.

Daly, M., and Wilson, M. *Homicide.* New York: Aldine Degruyter, 1988.

Dickson, G. *Murder by Numbers.* London: Robert Hale Press, 1958.

Dietz, M. L. *Killing for Profit*. Chicago: Nelson-Hall, 1983.

Eitzen, D. S., and Timmer, D. A. *Criminology*. New York: Wiley, 1985.

Fox, J. A., and Levin, J. *Overkill: Mass Murder and Serial Killing Exposed*. New York: Plenum, 1994.

Gaute, J. H. *Murderers Who's Who*. New York: Methuen, 1979.

Godwin, J. *Murder USA*. New York: Random House, 1978.

Goldman, H. H., ed. *Review of General Psychiatry*. Norwalk, VA: Appleton and Lange, 1988.

Hickey, Eric W. *Serial Murderers and Their Victims*. Belmont, CA: Wadsworth, 1991.

Holmes, Ronald M. *Profiling Violent Crimes: An Investigative Tool*. Newbury Park, CA: Sage, 1990.

Holmes, Ronald M., and De Bruger, J. *Serial Murder*. Beverly Hills, CA: Sage, 1988.

Holmes, Ronald M., and Holmes, S. T. *Murder in America*. Thousand Oaks, CA: Sage, 1994.

James, E. *Catching Serial Killers*. Lansing, MI: International Forensic Services, 1991.

Jeffers, H. Paul. *Who Killed Precious?* New York: Pharos Books, 1991.

Kahaner, L. *Cults That Kill*. New York: Warner Books, 1988.

Karpman, B. *The Sexual Offender and His Offenses*. New York: Julian Press, 1954.

Keppel, R. D. *Serial Murder: Future Implications for Police Investigations*. Cincinnati, OH: Anderson, 1989.

Kozel Multimedia. *Mind of a Killer.* Chatsworth, CA: Cambrix, 1995. CD-ROM.

Langlois, J. L. *Belle Gunness.* Bloomington, IN: Indiana University Press, 1985.

Lester, David. *Questions and Answers about Murder.* Philadelphia: Charles Press, 1991.

Lester, David. *Serial Killers: The Insatiable Passion.* Philadelphia: Charles Press, 1995.

Lester, David, and Lester, G. *Crime of Passion.* Chicago: Nelson-Hall, 1975.

Leyton, E. *Compulsive Killers.* New York: New York University Press, 1986.

Leyton, E. *Hunting Humans.* London: Penguin, 1989.

Lunde, D. T. *Murder and Madness.* San Francisco: San Francisco Book Company, 1976.

Masters, R. E., and Lea, E. *Perverse Crimes in History.* New York: Julian Press, 1963.

McDonald, R. R. *Black Widow.* New York: St. Martin's Press, 1986.

Megargee, E. I., and Bohn, M. J. *Classifying Criminal Offenders.* Newbury Park, CA: Sage, 1979.

Microsoft. *Encarta 96 Encyclopedia.* MS-Windows 95. 1996 Edition. Redmond, WA: Microsoft, 1995. Computer software.

Microsoft. *Microsoft Bookshelf.* MS-Windows 95. 1995 Edition. Redmond, WA: Microsoft, 1995. Computer software.

Newton, M. *Hunting Humans.* Port Townsend, WA: Loompanics, 1990.

Norris, J. *Serial Killers.* New York: Anchor, 1989.

Ressler, Robert K., Burgess, Ann W., and Douglas, John E. *Sexual Homicide: Patterns and Motives.* New York: Lexington, 1988.

Samenow, S. E. *Inside the Criminal Mind.* New York: Time Books, 1984.

Schechter, Harold, and Everitt, David. *The A to Z Encyclopedia of Serial Killers.* New York: Pocket Books, 1996.

Segrave, K. *Women Serial and Mass Murderers.* Jefferson, NC: McFarland, 1992.

Sifakis, C. *The Encyclopedia of American Crime.* New York: Facts on File, 1982.

Sparrow, G. *Women Who Murder.* New York: Abelard-Chuman, 1970.

Terry, M. *The Ultimate Evil.* Garden City, NY: Doubleday, 1987.

Wilson, Colin, and Wilson, Damon. *The Killer Among Us.* New York: Time Warner, 1996.

Wolfgang, M., and Ferracuti, F. *The Subculture of Violence.* New York: Tavistock, 1969.

INDEX

A

Aguilar, Linda, 191
Aleandre, Lucie, 239
Allitt, Beverley,
    98–102, 287
Alpine Manor
    nursing home,
    205–207
Ambrose, Lyda C,
    286
Amis, Kingsley, 183
angel of death,
    definition of, 15
Antigny, Auguste, 39
Antonio, Walter,
    116–17
apnea, 78
apnea monitor, 81–83
Atkins, Susan,
    222–23, 227–29,
    287

B

Barfield, Jennings,
    64, 66
Barfield, Margie
    Velma, 62–67, 287
Barrow, Clyde, 156
Bartlett, Betty, 159
Bartlett, Velda, 159
Bavouzet, Auguste,
    239–40
Beausoleil, Robert,
    228
Beautiful Blonde
    Killer, 21
Beck, Martha, 287

Becker, Marie,
    57–59, 287
Beier, Greta, 287
Bell, Mary Flora, 287
Belle of Indiana, 21
Bennett, John, 182
Bennett, Keith, 174,
    177
Besnard, Leon, 39–42
Besnard, Lucie, 40
Besnard, Marie,
    38–43, 287
Bexar County
    Medical Center
    Hospital, 89–94
Beyer, Lambert, 58
Bingham, Edith
    Agnes, 275–77
Bingham, James, 275
Bingham, Margaret,
    275–76
Bingham, William
    Hodges, 275–76
Bingham poison case,
    275–77
Birnie, Catherine,
    287
black widow,
    definition of, 15
black widow
    murders, 27–30
Blahovec, Susan,
    112–13
Bolding, Jane,
    280–83
Bombeek, Cecile,
    287

Borgia of America,
    21
Borgia of Somerville,
    21
Boston Strangler, 21
Brady, Ian, 172–77
Braggs, Charles, 48
Braggs, Florine,
    48–49
Brinkamp, Frank, 53
Brinkamp, Frederick,
    52
Brown, Debra,
    186–88, 287
Brunner, Mary, 222,
    228, 230, 287
Budsberg, Ole, 36
Buenoano, Judias,
    30–31, 287
Bugliosi, Vincent,
    229
Bullard, Lillie, 64–66
Bundy, Carol,
    196–200, 287
Burgess, Ann W., 12
Burke, Thomas,
    62–64, 67
Burress, Eugene, 116
Butch Cassidy and
    the Sundance Kid,
    192–93

C

Cannibal, The, 21
Carskaddon, Charles,
    115

Centers for Disease Control, 281
Chambers, Alison, 183
Chatman, Janice, 195
Chipman, Karen, 191, 192
Cincinnati Strangler, 21
Clark, Douglas, 196–99
Clown Killer, ix, 21
Coed Killer, 21
Coffman, Cynthia, 162–66, 287
Coleman, Alton, 186–88
Coleman, Travis, 255
Colley, Sandra, 191
Collison, Merle, 161
Colvert, Robert, 159
cooling-off period, 7–8
Cooper, Carole Anne, 183
Cooper, Sherry, 226
Costello, Rena, 184
Cowle, Rhodes, 57
Crampton, Paul, 99–100

D

Dahmer, Jeffrey, ix
Daniels, Jennifer, 255
Dateline NBC, 119
Davaillaud, Marie, 38–40
Davis, Bruce McGregor, 228
Davis, Jeffrey, 254–55
De Melker, Daisy, 56–57, 287
Delaney, Clida, 225

Demon of the Belfry, 21
DeSalvo, Albert Henry, ix
Dooley, Robert, 45
Doss, Nanny Hazel, 47–50, 287
Doss, Samuel, 49–50
Douglas, John E., 12
Downey, Lesley Ann, 174–76

E

Edwards, Dollie, 65
Enriqueta, Marti, 106, 287
Etheridge, Ellen, 126–27, 287
Evans, Edward, 175–76

F

Falling, Christine, 252–56, 287
family teams, 151, 153–55
female serial killers, classification of, 15–16
female teams, 151–55
Fencl, Lillian, 160
Fitzpatrick, William, 78–80, 82, 84
Folger, Abigail, 224, 226
Freeway Killer, 21
Fromme, Lynette, 228
Frykowski, Voytek, 224
Fugate, Caril Ann, 156–63, 287
Fuzekos, Mrs. Julius, 203–205, 287

G

Gacy, John Wayne, ix–x
Gallego, Charlene, 189–92, 287
Gallego, Gerald, 189–92
Gates, Ann, 287
Gaul, Doreen, 226
Gbrurek, Tillie, 50–52, 287
Gibbs, Janie Lou, 55–56, 287
Giggling Grandma, 21, 47–50
Gilles, Catherine, 228
Gilligan, Amy, 44–45, 287
Gonzales, Maria de Jesus, 287
Good, Sandra, 228
Gough, Lynda, 180, 183
Graham, Gwendolyn, 205–10, 287
Grantham and Kesteven Hospital, 98–102
Green Man, The, 21
Green, Ann, 265–66, 287
Green, Cammie March, 113
Grese, Irma, 173
Grills, Caroline, 287
Grody, Lori, 112
Grogan, Steve, 228
Gruber, Maria, 211–15, 287
Gsellman, George, 138
Gunness, Belle, 31–38, 287
Gunness, Peter, 35
Gunness, Philip, 35
Gurhold, Eric, 36

Guszkowski, Joseph, 51

H

Habe, Marina, 225
Hahn, Anna, 136–38, 287
Hahn, Philip, 136–37
Haight-Ashbury, 227–28
Hall, Katrina, 264
Hancock, John, 195
Hardwick, Tim, 100
Harrelson, Frank, 49
Haught, John, 226, 228
Hay, Almetta, 38
helter skelter, 223
Hess, Myra, 173
Hilley, Audrey, 266–70, 287
Hindley, Myra, 171–77, 287
Hippocratic Oath, 277
Hitler, Adolph, 172–73
Holland, Kathleen, 90–92
Holmolka, Karla, 287
Hoyt, Waneta, 287
Hubbard, Shirley, 183
Hughes, Ronald, 226–27, 230
Humphreys, Richard, 116

I

I-5 Killer, x, 21
Ideal Maternity Home, 147–49
intensive care unit, 279–80

J

Jensen, Robert, 160
Johnson, Cassidy, 253–54
Johnson, Martha, 127–29, 287
Jones, Genene, xiii, 89–94, 287
Judd, Brenda, 191

K

Kasabian, Linda, 222, 223, 287
Kerr County clinic, 89–93
Kilbride, Danny, 171
Kilbride, John, 174, 176
Kilmek, Anton, 52
King, Carol, 160
Kinne, Sharon, 287
Kiser, Blanche, 70–71
Koch, Ernest, 137
Krenwinkel, Patricia, 222–24, 228, 229, 287
Kretsch, Sandra, 111
Kupczyk, Frank, 51

L

LaBianca, Rosemary, 221, 222, 224, 226, 229
Lady Bluebeard, 21
Lady Sundance, 188, 192
Lainz General Hospital, 205, 210–15
Lalleron, Pauline and Virginie, 41
Lamphere, Ray, 36–38

Lancaster castle, 275, 276
Lanning, Arlie, 49
Lee, John, 65–66
Lehman, Christa, 270–72, 287
Leidolf, Irene, 211–15, 287
Leopold and Loeb, 173
Letts, Rosemary ("Rose") Pauline, 177–78
Leveson, Brian, 185
Lewis, Harlan, 46–47
Lindblom, Olaf, 36
Lipka, Juliane, 204–208
Lonely Hearts Killer, 21, 166–70
Lumbrera, Diana, 59–62, 288
Lyles, Anjette, 288

M

Mad Biter, The, 21
Madame Moulinet, 239
male/female teams, 151–52, 155–56
Mallory, Richard, 114, 118–19
Manson, Charles, 216–18, 221–30
Mantell, Justice, 185
Marlow, James, 162–66
Marquis de Sade, 173
Martin, Rhonda Bell, 54–55, 288
Maryland Hospital Murders, 280–83
Mayer, Stephanija, 210–15, 288

McClellan, Chelsea, 90, 91, 93
McCrary, Carolyn, 217–21, 288
McFall, Anne, 184
McGinnis, Virginia, 288
McHaffie, William, 46
McNaughton test, 233–36
Mein Kampf, 172
Meyer, August, 160
Meyer, Edward, 47
Michigan Hospital Murders, 278–80
Miller, Craig, 191–92
Millican, Lisa, 194
Mitchell, Alice, 288
Mitkiewitz, John, 50–51
Mochel, Virginia, 191
Montoya, Bert, 142–43
Moo, John, 36
Moon Mania, The, 21
Moore, Blanche, 70–77, 288
Moore, Patricia, 288
Moore, Tyria, 112–13, 117–18
Moorhouse, Ruth Ann, 228
Moors Murderers, 171–77
Morton, Richard, 49
Mott, Juanita, 183
Mrs. Bluebeard, 21
Much Marcle, Herefordshire, 184
Munchausen syndrome by proxy, 80, 83, 99, 102, 256, 289–93
murder spree, 6

N

Nagyrev, Hungary, 203
Narciso, Filipina, 278–80
Nebraska Fiend, 21
Neelley, Alvin, 192–95
Neelley, Judith, 192–96, 200, 288
Night Rider, 188, 192
Night Stalker, x, 21
Norton, Linda, 78–80

O

Obendoerfer, George, 138
Olah, Susi, 203–204, 288
Old Shoebox Annie, 21
Olsen, Jennie, 34–36
Ordorica, Richard, 140–42
organized and disorganized serial murderers, 12–13

P

Parent, Steven, 224, 226
Parker, Albert, 138
Parker, Bonnie, 156
Parker, Catherine, 263–64
Partington, Lucy, 183
Pavilion Five, 211–14
Pavlovich, Milka, 288
Paxton, Tomekia, 259
Payatos, Marcel, 239
Peck, Clare, 101
Perez, Leonora, 278–80

Pesendorfer, Xavier, 213–14
Philips, Becky, 101
Phoebe Putney hospital, 95, 98
Pied Piper of Tucson, 21
Pitman, Nancy, 228
Pittman, Aileen Carol, 108
Pittman, Leo, 109
Polanski, Roman, 223, 224
Polish Borgia, 21
Popova, Madame, 146–47, 288
Pratt, Diane, 109–10
Priessnitz, Franz, 214
Prince George's Hospital, 280–83
profit or crime, definition of, 16
Puente, Dorothea, 141–45, 288
Pugh, Joel, 226

Q

Queen of Poisoners, 38–43
Queen Poisoner, 21
question of sanity murders, definition of, 16

R

Rachals, Terri, 94–98, 288
Reade, Pauline, 174
Red Demon, 21
Redican, Stacey, 191
Renczi, Vera, 67–70, 288
Rendell, Martha, 288

Ressler, Robert K., 12
revenge, definition of, 15–16
Ripper, The, 21
Robinson, Shirley, 183
Rossignol, Joseph, 139
Ruskowski, John, 51

S

Sach, Amelia, 201–203, 288
Saddleworth Moor, 174–77
Savage, Hazel, 182
Scheffler, Rhonda, 191
Scieri, Antoinette, 138–40, 288
Scott, Darwin, 225
Scott, Susan, 225
Sebring, Jay, 224, 226
Sex Beast, 21
Sex Slave Murderers, 188–92
sexual predator, definition of, 15
Share, Catherine, 228
Sharp, James, 226
Shea, Donald, 226
Siegenthaler, Therese, 183
Siems, Peter, 115–16, 118
Simpson, Robert, 79
Sister Amy, 21
Skid Row Slasher, 21
Slaughter, Christine Laverne, 252
Smith, David, 175–76
Son of Sam, x, 21
Sorenson, Alex, 34

Sorenson, Caroline, 34
Sorenson, Lucy, 34
Sorenson, Mads, 33–34
Sorenson, Myrtle, 34
Sowers, Beth, 191–92
Spahn Ranch, 225
Spears, David, 115
Spring, Joseph, 254–55
Starkweather, Charles, 156–62
Steinschneider, Alfred, 78
Stocking Strangler, 21
Storset, Bella, 33
Storset, Brynhild Paulsdatter, 32
Sudden Infant Death Syndrome, 78–84, 293
Suicide Sal, 21
Sunday Morning Slasher, 21
Sunset Slayer, 189, 196–200
Swindle, William, 255
Szabo, Mrs. Ladislaus, 204

T

Tacoma Ax Killer, 21
Tannenbaum, Gloria, 288
Tate, Sharon, 223, 224, 226
Tate-LaBianca murders, 221–30
Taylor, Liam, 100
Taylor, Stuart, 65, 66
team killer, definition of, 16

Terrell, Bobbie Sue, xiii, 240–46, 288
Thrill Killer, The, 21
Tinning, Barbara, 261
Tinning, Jennifer, 260
Tinning, Johnathan, 262
Tinning, Joseph, 260
Tinning, Mary, 262
Tinning, Marybeth, 260–63, 288
Tinning, Michael, 262
Tinning, Nathan, 262
Tinning, Tami Lynne, 260, 262–63
Tinning, Timothy, 261
Tinnion, Michael, 264–65
Toppan, Jane, xiii, 246–49, 288
Torture Doctor, 21
Trailside Killer, x, 21
Trueblood, Lydia, 45–47, 288
Tuggle, Debra Sue, 258–60, 288
Tuggle, Ronald Johnson, 259
Tuggle, Thomas Bates, 258–59
Tuggle, William Henry, 259
Turner, Cheney Louise, 263
Turner, Lise, 263–65, 288
Turner, Megan, 263

U

unexplained murders, definition of, 16
unsolved murders, definition of, 16

unsolved serial killings, 273–83

V

Van Houten, Leslie, 222, 224, 228, 229, 288
Vaught, Kippi, 191
Velten, Maria, 70, 71, 288
Vermilyea, Charles, 52–53
Vermilyea, Louise, 52–54, 288
Veteran's Administration hospital, 278–80

W

Waddingham, Dorthea, 288
Wagner, Jacob, 138
Wagner, Waltraud, 211–15, 288
Walters, Annie, 201–203, 288
Walts, Mark, 225
Want Ad Killer, 21
Ward, C. Lauer, 160–61
Warren, Nancy, 225
Watson, Charles, 223, 224, 228, 229
Weber, Jeanne, 237–40, 288
West, Anne Marie, 178, 179, 181
West, Charmaine, 178–79, 184
West, Frederick, 177–85
West, Heather, 179–81
West, Rosemary, 156, 177–85, 288
Wheat, Vernita, 187–88
Williamson, Stella, 256–58, 288
Wise, Martha, 124–26, 288
Wood, Catherine May, 206–10, 288
Wood, Kenneth, 208
Woods, Martha, 288, 290–91
Wuornos, Aileen, xii, 105–20, 288
Wuornos, Britta, 110
Wuornos, Keith, 110, 111

Y

Young, Lila Gladys, 147–49, 288
Young, William, 147–49

MICHAEL D. KELLEHER, who has written widely on the subject of violence, specializes in threat assessment, strategic management, and human resource management for organizations in the private and public sectors.

C. L. KELLEHER is a volunteer counselor and human rights advocate.